CHRIST
the
CONTROVERSIALIST

CHRIST the CONTROVERSIALIST

CHRISTIAN CLASSICS SERIES

The basics of belief

by
John Stott

Inter-Varsity Press

INTER-VARSITY PRESS
38 De Montfort Street, Leicester LE1 7GP, England

First published 1970
First published in Christian Classics, 1996

British Library Cataloguing in Publication Data
A catalogue record for this book is available from the British Library.

ISBN 0-85111-238-2

Printed and bound in Great Britain by Cox & Wyman Ltd, Reading,
Berkshire.

*Inter-Varsity Press is the book-publishing division of the Universities and
Colleges Christian Fellowship (formerly the Inter-Varsity Fellowship), a
student movement linking Christian Unions in universities and colleges
throughout the United Kingdom and the Republic of Ireland, and a member
movement of the International Fellowship of Evangelical Students. For
information about local and national activities write to UCCF, 38 De Montfort
Street, Leicester LE1 7GP.*

CONTENTS

PUBLISHER'S NOTE

As with most books in the Christian Classics series, this issue is a facsimile of the original edition. No revision or updating has therefore been possible.

Christ the controversialist was originally published in February 1970.

PREFACE

The title *Christ the Controversialist* is intended to indicate not that Jesus Christ was a controversial figure, but that He engaged in controversy. Many of His public discourses were debates with the contemporary Palestinian leaders of religion. They did not agree with Him, and He did not agree with them.

My objects in studying these controversies of Christ are to clarify the issues being debated, to demonstrate that they are live issues still, and to argue that the position which Christ adopted in each debate is the very position which 'evangelical' Christians have always sought to maintain. Why I believe this exercise to be necessary I have explained further in two introductory essays.

In the first I try to defend the task of theological definition. It is not a popular task today. The non-Christian world is imbued with the spirit of pragmatism and confesses itself sick of the church's unpractical theologizing. And in some parts of the contemporary church the same spirit prevails. Many have given up any hope of doctrinal certainty, let alone of doctrinal agreement. I try therefore to unearth the roots of this hostility to theological definition, and to argue that we must still pursue and not abandon the task.

In the second introductory essay I make a plea for 'evangelical' Christianity. That is, having urged the continuance of theological definition, I go on to urge that we must define Christianity 'evangelically'. A brief (and I think necessary) account is given of the historical origins and use of the term 'evangelical'. My concern is not with words and names, however, but with truth, and in particular with the doctrinal position held by so-called 'evangelical' Christians. What name we take or others give

us is a trifling question in comparison with the great doctrines
by which we seek to live, and whether they are true. The complex
of doctrines we hold is commonly known as 'the evangelical
faith'. Whether it is correct to style it thus is of little consequence.
What matters is the substance, not the style. And the substance,
we claim, is biblical, original, fundamental Christianity. We
believe (with conviction I know, with humility I hope) that
this faith is the true faith of Christ, as He taught it to His apostles
and especially as He defended it against its opponents and
detractors.

So the chapters which follow the introductory essays are
devoted to a consideration of Christ's controversies. I do not
attempt an exhaustive treatment of them, but concentrate on
those major topics of debate which (it seems to me) were dominant in His day and still are in ours. We shall consider, therefore,
such basic questions as the character of the Christian's God and
of the Christian religion, the authority and purpose of Scripture,
the way of salvation, the kind of morality and worship which are
acceptable to God, the nature of Christian responsibility and
of Christian ambition. On each of these matters Jesus Christ
disagreed with the teaching of either the Pharisees or the
Sadducees, and on each matter 'evangelical' Christians are in
disagreement with others in today's church. Indeed, so my
argument runs, when we put together the truths on which
Christ insisted in these controversies, the result is a fairly com-
prehensive exposition of what is meant by 'evangelical religion'.

I ask the indulgence of my readers that in some chapters,
especially those on Scripture and salvation, the supporting
illustrations are drawn largely from Anglicanism. This is partly
because I happen to be a member and minister of the Church
of England, but also because, according to its own formularies,
this Church is reformed and evangelical, and therefore the
illustrations appear to me to be apt.

My theme has lingered and matured in my mind over a
number of years. I took it for a series of sermons in All Souls
Church in 1962 and again, further developed, in 1968/9. I
also gave a series of popular lectures under the same title *Christ
the Controversialist* both in Edinburgh in November 1968 (for
the Edinburgh Evangelical Council) and in Auckland in May
1969 (for the New Zealand Evangelical Alliance). I am grateful

to these organizations for their invitation and hospitality.
I now send the book on its way with the earnest prayer that
God will forgive its imperfections, overruling what it contains
of error that it may bring harm to no-one and owning what it
contains of truth that it may bring blessing to some.

J.R.W.S.

CHIEF ABBREVIATIONS

Abbott	*The Documents of Vatican II* edited by Walter M. Abbott and J. Gallagher (Chapman, 1966).
AV	English Authorized Version (King James), 1611.
Carus	*Memoirs of the Life of the Rev. Charles Simeon* edited by William Carus (Hatchard, 1847).
Coulson	*Science and Christian Belief* by C. A. Coulson (OUP, 1955; Fontana, 1958).
Cranfield	*The Gospel according to St. Mark (Cambridge Greek Testament)*. Commentary by C. E. B. Cranfield (CUP, 1959).
Edersheim	*The Life and Times of Jesus the Messiah* by Alfred Edersheim. 2 vols. (Longmans, 1883).
Farrar	*The Life of Christ* by F. W. Farrar (Cassell, 1874).
JB	*Jerusalem Bible* (Darton, Longman and Todd, 1966).
JBP	*The New Testament in Modern English*. A translation by J. B. Phillips (Bles and Collins, 1958).
Josephus	*The Works of Flavius Josephus* incorporating both *The Wars of the Jews* (AD 77–78) and *The Antiquities of the Jews* (*c.* AD 94). Translated by William Whiston (1737).
Moulton and Milligan	*The Vocabulary of the Greek New Testament* by J. H. Moulton and G. Milligan (Hodder and Stoughton, 1930).
NEB	*The New English Bible: New Testament* (Oxford and Cambridge, 1961).
RSV	American Revised Standard Version, 1946–52.
Scott	Article 'Pharisees' by Hugh M. Scott in Hastings' *Dictionary of Christ and the Gospels* (Clark, vol. II, 1908, pp. 351–356).
Swete	*The Gospel according to St. Mark*. Commentary by H. B. Swete (Macmillan, 1898).

INTRODUCTORY ESSAYS

A   A DEFENCE OF THEOLOGICAL DEFINITION

The aim of this book can be simply stated. It is to argue that 'evangelical' Christianity is authentic Christianity, true, original and pure, and to demonstrate it from the teaching of Jesus Christ Himself.

To attempt in the latter half of the twentieth century to expound and to establish a particular brand of Christianity will be greeted by many with disapproval, by some with dismay, and by a few even with disgust. Let me therefore try at once to anticipate, and perhaps to disarm, some of my readers' possible criticisms.

Dislike of dogmatism

The first resistance to the theme of this book will be due to a dislike of dogmatism. The spirit of our age is very unfriendly towards dogmatic people. Folk whose opinions are clearly formulated and strongly held are not popular. A person of conviction, however intelligent, sincere and humble he may be, will be fortunate if he escapes the charge of being a bigot. Nowadays the really great mind is thought to be both broad and open – broad enough to absorb every fresh idea which is presented to it, and open enough to go on doing so *ad infinitum*.

What are we to say to this? We must reply that historic Christianity is essentially dogmatic, because it purports to be a revealed faith. If the Christian religion were just a collection of the philosophical and ethical ideas of men (like Hinduism), dogmatism would be entirely out of place. But if God has spoken (as Christians claim), both in olden days through the prophets and in these last days through His Son,[1] why should it be thought

[1] Heb. 1:1, 2.

'dogmatic' to believe His Word ourselves and to urge other people to believe it too? If there is a Word from God which may be read and received today, would it not rather be the height of folly and sin to disregard it?

Of course the fact that God has spoken, and that His revelation is recorded in a Book, does not mean that Christians know everything. I fear we may sometimes give the impression that we think we do, in which case we need the forgiveness of God for our cocksure pretensions to omniscience. But we do not know all things. The Authorized Version of 1 John 2 : 20 'ye know all things' is almost certainly wrong; the better manuscripts read 'you all know' (RSV) or 'you all have knowledge' (NEB). What John is asserting is that all Christians have some knowledge, not that some Christians have all knowledge. He himself confesses in the same Epistle that, with regard to the next life, 'we don't know what we shall become in the future'.[2] Similarly Moses, to whom God gave such unique revelations, exclaimed 'O Lord God, thou hast only begun to show thy servant thy greatness and thy mighty hand . . .'.[3] In the same vein the apostle Paul, whose profound teaching in his Epistles the church is still seeking to fathom, likened our present and partial knowledge to the ignorant patter of a child and the dim reflections of a mirror.[4] If then Moses in the Old Testament, and John and Paul in the New, thus humbly confess their ignorance of much truth, who are we to claim to be know-alls? We need to hear again the sobering word of Jesus: 'It is not for you to know . . .'[5] He was referring to the times and seasons, 'which the Father has fixed by his own authority'. But the same principle applies to other spheres of truth. The limits of our knowledge are set, not by what we want to know, but by what God has wanted to make known to us.

Perhaps the most balanced statement of this is given us towards the end of the book of Deuteronomy: 'The secret things belong to the Lord our God; but the things that are revealed belong to us and to our children for ever . . .'[6] Here the sum-total of truth is divided into two parts, 'the secret things' and 'the things that are revealed'. The secret things belong to God, we are told. And since they belong to Him and

[2] 1 Jn. 3:2, JBP.   [3] Dt. 3:24.   [4] 1 Cor. 13:9-12.
[5] Acts 1:7.   [6] Dt. 29:29.

He has not seen fit to give them to us, we should not attempt to wrest them from Him but be content to leave them with Him. The revealed things, on the other hand, 'belong to us and to our children for ever'. That is, since God has given them to us and they are ours, He means us to possess them ourselves and to hand them on to our posterity. God's purpose for us, therefore, is to enjoy what is ours (because He has revealed it), and not to covet what is His alone (because He has not revealed it). We are to be dogmatic about what has been plainly revealed and agnostic about what has not; and it is this Christian combination of dogmatism and agnosticism which we find it difficult to preserve. Our troubles begin when we allow our dogmatism to invade the realm of 'the secret things' or our agnosticism to obscure 'the things that are revealed'. We need 'the gift of true discrimination',[7] so that we may discern between these two realms of truth, the secret and the revealed. It is as much a sign of maturity to say 'I don't know' about one thing as it is to say 'I know' about another – provided that our admission of ignorance concerns something kept secret and our claim to knowledge something revealed.

So then Christian dogmatism has, or should have, a limited field. It is not tantamount to a claim to omniscience. Yet in those things which are clearly revealed in Scripture, Christians should not be doubtful or apologetic. The corridors of the New Testament reverberate with dogmatic affirmations beginning 'We know', 'We are sure', 'We are confident'. If you question this, read the First Epistle of John in which verbs meaning 'to know' occur about forty times. They strike a note of joyful assurance which is sadly missing from many parts of the church today and which needs to be recaptured. 'It is quite mistaken', Professor James Stewart has written, 'to suppose that humility excludes conviction. G. K. Chesterton once penned some wise words about what he called "the dislocation of humility" . . . "What we suffer from today is humility in the wrong place. Modesty has moved from the organ of ambition. Modesty has settled upon the organ of conviction, where it was never meant to be. A man was meant to be doubtful about himself, but undoubting about the truth; this has been exactly reversed. We are on the road to producing a race of men too

[7] Phil. 1:10, NEB.

mentally modest to believe in the multiplication table." Humble and self-forgetting we must be always,' Professor Stewart continues, 'but diffident and apologetic about the Gospel never.'[8] It is hardly fair of one dictionary to define dogma as an 'arrogant declaration of opinion'. To be dogmatic is not necessarily to be either proud or opinionated.

We are in a position now to say that a broad and open mind, so loudly applauded in our day, is by no means an unmixed blessing. To be sure, we must keep an open mind about matters on which Scripture seems to speak equivocally, and a receptive mind so that our understanding of God's revelation continues to deepen. We must also distinguish between a doctrine and our fallible interpretation or formulation of it. But when the biblical teaching is plain, the cult of an open mind is a sign not of maturity, but of immaturity. Those who cannot make up their minds what to believe, and are 'tossed to and fro and carried about with every wind of doctrine', Paul dubs 'babies'.[9] And the prevalence of people 'who will listen to anybody and can never arrive at a knowledge of the truth' is a characteristic of the 'times of stress' in which we are living.[1]

An interesting illustration of this is given by G. K. Chesterton in his *Autobiography*. He describes H. G. Wells as a man who 'reacted too swiftly to everything', was indeed 'a permanent reactionary' and never seemed able to reach firm or settled conclusions of his own. He goes on: 'I think he thought that the object of opening the mind is simply opening the mind. Whereas I am incurably convinced that the object of opening the mind, as of opening the mouth, is to shut it again on something solid.'[3] Samuel Butler held a similar view, although he thought of the mind rather as a room than as a mouth: 'an open mind is all very well in its way, but it ought not to be so open that there is no keeping anything in or out of it. It should be capable of shutting its doors sometimes, or it may be found a little draughty.'

Hatred of controversy
The second way in which the spirit of the age is unfriendly towards the theme of this book concerns the modern hatred

[8] *Heralds of God* by James S. Stewart (Hodder, 1946), p. 210.
[9] Eph. 4:14 (Gk. *nēpioi*).   [1] 2 Tim. 3:1, 7.
[3] *Autobiography* by G. K. Chesterton (Hutchinson, 1937), pp. 223, 224.

of controversy. That is to say, it is bad enough to be dogmatic, we are told. But 'if you must be dogmatic', our critics continue, 'do at least keep your dogmatism to yourself. Hold your own definite convictions (if you insist), but leave other people alone in theirs. Be tolerant. Mind your own business, and let the rest of the world mind theirs.'

Another way in which this point of view is expressed is to urge us to be always positive, if necessary dogmatically positive, but to eschew being negative. 'Speak up for what you believe,' we are urged, 'but don't speak against what other people believe.' Those who advocate this line have not remembered the double duty of the presbyter-bishop which is 'to give instruction in sound doctrine' and 'to confute those who contradict it'.[3] Nor have they heeded what C. S. Lewis wrote in a letter to Dom Bede Griffiths: 'Your Hindus certainly sound delightful. But what do they *deny*? That has always been my trouble with Indians – to find any proposition they would pronounce false. But truth must surely involve exclusions?'[4]

This second attitude (opposition to intolerance) arises naturally from the first. Indeed, the two usually go together. It is very easy to tolerate the opinions of others if we have no strong opinions of our own. But we should not acquiesce in this easy-going tolerance. We need to distinguish between the tolerant mind and the tolerant spirit. Tolerant in spirit a Christian should always be, loving, understanding, forgiving and forbearing others, making allowances for them, and giving them the benefit of the doubt, for true love 'bears all things, believes all things, hopes all things, endures all things'.[5] But how can we be tolerant in mind of what God has plainly revealed to be either evil or erroneous?

Certainly every right-minded person finds controversy distasteful, and we should studiously avoid argument for argument's sake. 'Have nothing to do with stupid, senseless controversies,' wrote the apostle Paul; 'you know that they breed quarrels.'[6] To relish controversy is to have 'a morbid craving', a form of spiritual sickness.[7] Rather should we shrink from it. We should

---

[3] Tit. 1:9; *cf.* 2 Tim. 3:16, 17, NEB: 'teaching the truth and refuting error'.
[4] *Letters of C. S. Lewis* edited by W. H. Lewis (Bles, 1966), p. 267.
[5] 1 Cor. 13:7.   [6] 2 Tim. 2:23.
[7] 1 Tim. 6:4 (Gk. *nosōn*, meaning 'ailing' or 'sick').

also eschew all bitterness, the *odium theologicum* which has be-
smirched the pages of church history, controversy conducted
in an acrimonious spirit which descends to personal insult and
abuse. But we cannot avoid controversy itself, for we are called
to 'the defence and confirmation of the gospel'.[8]

Perhaps the best way to insist that controversy is sometimes a
painful necessity is to remember that our Lord Jesus Christ
Himself was a controversialist. He was not 'broad-minded' in
the popular sense that He was prepared to countenance any
views on any subject. On the contrary, as we are to see in the
later chapters of this book, He engaged in continuous debate
with the religious leaders of His day, the scribes and Pharisees,
the Herodians and Sadducees. He said that He was the truth,
that He had come to bear witness to the truth, and that the
truth would set His followers free.[9] As a result of His loyalty
to the truth, He was not afraid to dissent publicly from official
doctrines (if He knew them to be wrong), to expose error, and
to warn His disciples of false teachers.[1] He was also extremely
outspoken in His language, calling them 'blind guides', 'wolves
in sheep's clothing', 'whitewashed tombs' and even a 'brood
of vipers'.[2]

The apostles also were controversialists, as is plain from the
New Testament Epistles, and they appealed to their readers
'to contend for the faith which was once for all delivered to the
saints'.[3] Like their Lord and Master they found it necessary to
warn the churches of false teachers and to urge them to stand
firm in the truth.

Nor did they regard this as being incompatible with love. For
example, John the apostle of love, to whose pen we owe the
sublime affirmation that God is love, and whose Epistles abound
in entreaties to mutual love, roundly declares that whoever
denies that Jesus is the Christ is a liar, a deceiver and antichrist.[4]
Similarly Paul, who gives us in 1 Corinthians 13 the great
hymn to love, and declares that love is the firstfruit of the
Spirit,[5] yet pronounces a solemn anathema upon anybody

---

[8] Phil. 1:7.   [9] Jn. 14:6; 18:37; 8:31, 32.
[1] *E.g.* Mt. 7:15–20; Mk. 13:5, 6, 21–23; Lk. 12:1.
[2] Mt. 15:14 and 23:16, 19, 24, 26; 7:15; 23:27 and Lk. 11:44; Mt. 12:34 and
23:33.
[3] Jude 3.   [4] 1 Jn. 2:22; 2 Jn. 7.   [5] Gal. 5:22.

(human or angelic) who presumes to distort the gospel of the grace of God.[6]

We seem in our generation to have moved a long way from this vehement zeal for the truth which Christ and His apostles displayed. But if we loved the glory of God more, and if we cared more for the eternal good of the souls of men, we would not refuse to engage in necessary controversy, when the truth of the gospel is at stake. The apostolic command is clear. We are to 'maintain the truth in love',[7] being neither truthless in our love, nor loveless in our truth, but holding the two in balance.

The call to close our ranks

A third argument against the attempt to define the Christian faith too clearly or too narrowly is based on the contemporary world situation. Christianity, we are reminded, is steadily losing ground.[8] Not only is the population explosion outstripping the conversion rate, but anti-Christian forces are rallying. Communism is on the march. In some areas Islam claims to be winning more converts than Christianity. The ancient religions of the East are waking from slumber, and their resurgence is in several countries allied to a passionate nationalism, which dismisses Christianity as the religion of unwanted foreigners. Then there is the strong current of secularism in the West, sucking individuals and societies into its powerful vortex. Surely, it is said, in face of this manifold menace to the Christian religion, we must close our ranks. We cannot afford the luxury of division any longer. We are fighting for our very survival. We must stand together, or perish.

An up-to-date example of this pressure comes from the (perhaps) unlikely pen of Professor Arnold Toynbee. Now an octogenarian and still calling himself agnostic, he has nevertheless expressed in his latest book his hope that the resurgence of the historic religions will check the dehumanizing process of modern

---

[6] Gal. 1:6–9.
[7] Eph. 4:15, literally 'truthing in love' (Gk. *alētheuontes en agapē*).
[8] This is true only in the western world, however. Other parts of the world, *e.g.* Indonesia and some areas of Central and South America, are today witnessing a remarkable work of the Holy Spirit in conversion and church growth.

technology. To this hope, however, he adds a fear: 'The evil genius of the higher religions . . . has been their inveterate factiousness and the unbridled rancour with which they have pursued their quarrels.' It is to this factiousness that he attributes western man's alienation 'from his ancestral religion'. But now, he says, 'the unlooked-for all-important change of heart' has taken place, and he gives the ecumenical movement and the *aggiornamento* of the Roman Catholic Church as evidence. He expresses the opinion that 'this change of heart has removed the age-old stumblingblock', and he continues: 'Is this change going to prove permanent or to prove ephemeral? All depends on its being permanent, and, at this early stage of the new era, we cannot be sure that the change will last.'[9]

This call to close our ranks is a moving plea, and we are not insensitive to it. Indeed, it contains much with which we whole-heartedly agree. Some of our divisions are not only unnecessary, but sinful and debilitating, an offence to God and a hindrance to the spread of the gospel. In my own conviction, the visible unity of the church (in each region or country) is both biblically right and practically desirable, and we should be actively seeking it. At the same time, we should ask ourselves a simple but searching question. If we are to meet the enemies of Christ with a united Christian front, with what kind of Christianity are we going to face them? The only weapon with which the opponents of the gospel can be overthrown is the gospel itself. It would be a tragedy if, in our desire for their overthrow, the only effective weapon in our armoury were to drop from our hands. United Christianity which is not true Christianity will not gain the victory over non-Christian forces, but will itself succumb to them.

The spirit of ecumenism

The fourth contemporary influence which is unfriendly towards the exercise of this book is the spirit of ecumenism. In saying this, I am far from wishing to make a sweeping condemnation of the whole ecumenical movement or of all the activities of the World Council of Churches to which it has led. On the contrary,

[9] Quotations from *Experiences* by A. Toynbee (OUP, 1969) published in *The Times* of 5 April 1969.

much that has been accomplished in mutual understanding and in such projects as Christian Aid is right and good. I am trying rather to describe what may fairly be called 'the ecumenical outlook'. According to this point of view, no individual or church has a monopoly of the truth. Instead, every Christian, whatever his opinions, has his own 'insights' into the truth and therefore his own 'contribution' to make to the common life of the church. Men of this outlook, therefore, look forward to the day when all Christians and churches will come together and pool their different contributions. The resulting *pot-pourri*, hard as it is to imagine, is regarded by many as the ultimately desirable goal. It is natural that to such ecumenical people the evangelical desire to define some truths in such a way as to exclude others is regarded as misguided and damaging.

I welcome the decision taken by the Third Assembly of the World Council of Churches at New Delhi in 1961 to amplify its basis of membership in order to include a reference (albeit indefinite) both to the Trinity and to the Scriptures.[1] This was certainly a step in the right direction. But the basis remains minimal. Indeed, when you compare it with the so-called 'catholic' creeds (the Apostles', the Nicene and the Athanasian), let alone the great confessions of the sixteenth-century Reformation, it is extremely thin. This 'lowest common denominator' approach gives the impression (although it has often been denied) of a regrettable indifference to revealed truth. It has also led sometimes to a love of the ambiguous statement which conceals deep and sincerely held differences and does no lasting good. It merely papers over the cracks. This looks nice and tidy for a while, for the cracks are temporarily hidden from view. They remain there beneath the surface, however, and will one day break into sight again, by that time probably wider and deeper than before. It is neither honest nor helpful to make out that divergent opinions are in reality different ways of saying the same thing.

This need for the frank recognition of disagreement is helpfully emphasized by a Jesuit writer, Francis Clark, in his *Eucharistic*

---

[1] The enlarged basis reads as follows: 'The World Council of Churches is a fellowship of Churches which confess the Lord Jesus Christ as God and Saviour according to the Scriptures and therefore seek to fulfil together their common calling to the glory of the one God, Father, Son and Holy Spirit.'

Sacrifice and the Reformation.[2] It is a careful, scholarly investigation of the Reformation conflict over the Mass, although I understand that it has been heavily criticized, especially on the Continent. His thesis is that what the Reformers were opposing was 'not merely practical abuses and popular superstition connected with the altar' (as Newman argued in Tract XC and as many have credulously believed ever since) 'but the authorized theology of the Mass as currently taught in the Roman Catholic Church'.[3] The sixteenth-century controversy was, in fact, he continues, 'a clash between two systems of thought derived from different and irreconcilable first principles'.[4] In conclusion he writes: 'There are books on ecumenism which charitably seek to draw a veil over the differences of belief that divide Christians; there is also need for books which charitably make clear why those differences arose and what they mean. In the long run the ecumenical cause will be better served by frank scrutiny of the roots of disagreement than by ignoring them. The clear-sighted candour of writers like Bishop Neill, who are able to recognize the incompatibility of two doctrinal positions and to point out the reason, is more useful than the well-meant but undiscerning eirenism of writers who treat contradictory doctrines as complementary insights, as different emphases of the same truth, as different colours in one spectrum of Christian witness.'[5]

The proper activity of professing Christians who disagree with one another is neither to ignore, nor to conceal, nor even to minimize their differences, but to debate them. Take the Church of Rome as an example. I find it distressing to see Protestants and Roman Catholics united in some common act of worship or witness. Why? Because it gives the onlooker the impression that their disagreements are now virtually over. 'See,' the unsophisticated spectator might say, 'they can now engage in prayer and proclamation together; what remains to divide them?'

But such a public display of unity is a game of let's pretend; it is not living in the real world. Certainly we can be very thankful for the signs of a loosening rigidity and of a greater biblical awareness in the Roman Church. In consequence,

[2] Darton, Longman and Todd, 1960.
[3] Clark, p. 509.   [4] Clark, p. 511.   [5] Clark, p. 522.

many individual Roman Catholics have come to embrace more biblical truth than they had previously grasped, and some for conscience' sake have left their church. Vatican II has so let Scripture loose in the church that no man can guess what the final result may be. We pray that under God it will prove to be a thoroughgoing biblical reformation. In some places, however, an alarming opposite tendency is appearing, a theological liberalism as radical as anything to be found in Protestant Christendom. The third possibility is that victory will go to the forces of reaction.

We have to recognize ruefully that, in keeping with Rome's proud boast that she is *semper eadem* (always the same), none of her defined dogmas has yet been officially redefined. This is a logical deduction from her claim to infallibility. Obviously if an utterance is infallible, it is also irreformable. At the very least we must say that what restatement or redefinition there has been contains as yet no explicit repudiation of any statement or definition of the past. There has been no public and penitent confession of past sins and errors although this, for a church as for an individual, is an indispensable condition of reconciliation. Instead, contemporary Roman pronouncements oscillate between the progressive and the conservative, expressing the painful inner tensions of the church. Occasionally a word of encouragement is spoken to the biblical scholars, which raises one's hopes that Rome is at last going to allow the Scriptures to judge and reform it. And then all at once this flickering hope is snuffed by a reactionary statement of the old order.

Perhaps the best recent example is the 'Credo of the People of God' composed by Pope Paul. Those who think that there is now no easily discernible difference between the Roman and the Reformed churches should weigh this carefully. It was the last day of June 1968. About 50,000 people had assembled in St Peter's Square in Rome for a mass which was to mark the end of 'the year of faith' which Pope Paul had proclaimed and the beginning of the sixth year of his 'reign'. It was also a few days before the opening in Uppsala of the Fourth Assembly of the World Council of Churches – a fact which some observers believe to have been significant. The Pope chose this occasion to make a profession of faith, which he likened to that made by the apostle Peter at Caesarea Philippi. He was making it, he said, because of 'the disquiet which agitates certain modern quarters with regard to the faith' and because he saw 'even Catholics allowing themselves to be seized by a kind of passion for change and novelty'. He began with an elaboration of the Nicene Creed, spelling out the whole church's historic belief in 'one only God, Father, Son and Holy Spirit'. Then followed a paragraph about Mary, the mother of Jesus, which stated in the clearest terms her perpetual virginity, immaculate conception and bodily assumption. Further, 'we believe that the Blessed Mother of God, the New Eve, Mother of the Church, continues in Heaven her maternal role with regard to Christ's members, co-operating with the birth and growth of divine life in the souls of the redeemed'. Later the Church of Heaven is described as 'the multitude of those gathered around Jesus and Mary in Paradise'.

The Credo also contained an uncompromising assertion of the infallibility of the Pope and the Bishops: 'We believe in the infallibility enjoyed by the Successor of Peter when he teaches *ex cathedra* as Pastor and Teacher of all the faithful, and which is assured also to the Episcopal Body when it exercises with him the supreme magisterium.' It is clear from this that the new concept of 'collegiality', embracing all the Bishops, has not abolished infallibility but extended it. Next comes a statement of the uniqueness of the Church of Rome: 'We entertain the hope that the Christians who are not yet in the full communion of the one only Church will one day be reunited in one Flock with the one only Shepherd.'

Towards the end of the Credo there are three paragraphs about the Mass, which unequivocally reaffirm the doctrines of both transubstantiation and eucharistic sacrifice: 'We believe that the Mass . . . is the Sacrifice of Calvary rendered sacramentally present on our altars. We believe that . . . the bread and wine consecrated by the priest are changed into the Body and Blood of Christ enthroned gloriously in Heaven, and We believe that the mysterious presence of the Lord, under what continues to appear to our senses as before, is a true, real and substantial presence. Christ cannot be thus present in this Sacrament except by the change into His body of the reality itself of the bread and the change into His blood of the reality itself of the wine, leaving unchanged only the properties of the

bread and wine which our senses perceive. This mysterious
change is very appropriately called by the Church *transubstantiation*. . . . In the reality itself, independently of our mind,
the bread and wine have ceased to exist after the Consecration
so that it is the adorable Body and Blood of the Lord Jesus
that from then on are really before us under the sacramental
species of bread and wine. . . . The unique and indivisible
existence of the Lord glorious in Heaven . . . remains present,
after the Sacrifice, in the Blessed Sacrament which is, in the
tabernacle, the living heart of each of our churches. And it is our
very sweet duty to honour and adore in the Blessed Host which
our eyes see, the Incarnate Word Whom they cannot see, and
Who, without leaving Heaven, is made present before us.'[6]

The reassertion of these entirely unbiblical traditions regarding
the Virgin Mary, the Pope and the Mass is distressing in the
extreme, especially as they appear alongside true biblical teaching
about the Trinity, as if the two sets of teaching were comparable
in truth, authority and importance.

In the light of these things, what is needed today between
Protestants and Roman Catholics is not a premature outward
show of unity, but a candid and serious 'dialogue'. Some Protestants regard such conversation with Roman Catholics as
compromising, but it need not be so. The Greek verb from which
it is derived is used in the Acts for reasoning with people out of the
Scriptures. Its purpose (for the Protestant) is twofold: first, that
by careful listening he may understand what the Roman Catholic
is saying, and thereby avoid mere shadow-boxing, and secondly,
that he may witness plainly and firmly to scriptural truth as
he has been given to see it.

Now in such dialogue theological definition is indispensable.
Two people cannot understand each other's convictions if they
have not first taken time and trouble to express their own
clearly. Much discussion is from the outset doomed to failure
because of this very lack of understanding. 'There are many
who prefer to fight their intellectual battles in what Dr Francis L.
Patton has aptly called a "condition of low visibility".'[7] What

---

[6] These quotations are taken from 'The "Credo" of the People of God' as
recorded in *The Tablet* of 6 July 1968, pp. 681-683.
[7] J. Gresham Machen in *Christianity and Liberalism* (Macmillan, 1923), Eerdmans edition (1960), p. 1, quoting from Dr Francis L. Patton's introduction

is needed is more defining of terms, not less. This is the only
way to clear the fog.

Dislike of dogmatism, hatred of controversy, love of tolerance,
the call to close our ranks, and the spirit of ecumenism – these
are some of the modern tendencies which are unfriendly to the
purpose of this book. But the Christian church, whether universal
or local, is intended by God to be a *confessional* church. The
church is 'the pillar and foundation of the truth'.[8] Revealed
truth is thus likened to a building, and the church's calling is
to be its 'foundation' (holding it firm so that it is not moved)
and its 'pillar' (holding it aloft so that all may see it). However
hostile the spirit of the age may be to an outspoken confession
of the truth, the church has no liberty to reject its God-given
task.

---

to William H. Johnson's *The Christian Faith Under Modern Searchlights* (1916).
[8] 1 Tim. 3:15, literally.

B A PLEA FOR EVANGELICAL CHRISTIANITY

I have tried to argue in the first introductory essay that it is not only legitimate to define what we mean by 'Christianity', but wise and indeed necessary.

Supposing this were to be granted, what justification is there for defining it in 'evangelical' terms? This is the second preliminary question which we must consider. In reply to it, I will make (and attempt to defend) four assertions about the word 'evangelical'.

Evangelical means theological

It is not unusual to hear people use the term 'evangelical' as if it were a synonym for 'evangelistic'. One of my colleagues recently received a letter of instructions about a speaking engagement he had soon to fulfil. His correspondent informed him that, because they were all Christians in their group, they did 'not want anything evangelical'! He meant, of course, that they were not asking for an evangelistic address. But the words 'evangelical' and 'evangelistic' should not be confused. The adjective 'evangelistic' describes an activity, that of spreading the gospel, so that we speak of evangelistic campaigns and evangelistic services. 'Evangelical', on the other hand, describes a theology, what the apostle Paul called 'the truth of the gospel'.[1] Ideally, of course, the two words belong to one another, because they both contain the 'evangel', the gospel. Since, strictly speaking, an 'evangelical' is a person who believes the doctrines of the gospel, and an 'evangelist' is a person who proclaims them, it sounds inconceivable that anybody could be one without the other. Yet the truth is that 'evangelism' and 'evan-

[1] Gal. 2:5, 14.

gelicalism' have often been divorced. Some claim to be keen
on 'evangelism' who do not subscribe to the distinctive doctrines
associated with 'evangelical' people, while not all 'evangelicals'
have been conspicuously zealous in 'evangelistic' enterprise. Be
that as it may, this book is concerned not with the practice of
'evangelism' (except to some degree in chapter 7) but with
'evangelicalism', the theological convictions of 'evangelical'
Christians.

Having emphasized that the word 'evangelical' denotes
primarily a theology, I may perhaps be allowed to illustrate
this from the Church of England. It is well known that in
Anglican circles since the Reformation there have been three
main traditions. The popular (and somewhat misleading)
names for these are 'High Church', 'Low Church' and 'Broad
Church'. Further, the difference between the first two is commonly supposed to be one of ceremonial. 'Low Church' people
are thought to like simplicity and even austerity in their services
and buildings, whereas 'High Church' people favour ornate
ritual and go in for such things as are called (with a touch of
innocent humour) 'bowing and scraping' or 'bells and smells'.
There is certainly some truth in this distinction between simplicity and pageantry, but it is not the main difference. If
we use the correct names and call 'High Church' people 'catholic'
and 'Low Church' people 'evangelical', the real divergence
begins to be apparent. The essence of 'catholicism' is not what
may appeal to the eye ('bowing and scraping'), the ear ('bells')
or the nose ('smells'), but what is presented to the mind, a
coherent theology. In the same way 'evangelicals' would wish
to be understood and judged not by an appeal (or lack of appeal)
to the senses, but by their doctrine.[2]

Moreover, it is important to add that evangelical doctrine
and those who hold it are found in nearly all the Protestant
churches. For example, there are evangelical Anglicans, evan-

[2] This identification of the terms 'Low Church' and 'evangelical' is true only
in a rough and ready popular sense, however. Historically, the point of contention between Low Church and High Church Anglicans concerned episcopacy, the latter asserting its divine institution, the former holding it to be
ancient and lawful, but not indispensable. The dispute later extended to the
question of ritual. But there have always been people with Low Church views
about episcopacy and ritual who are more liberal than evangelical in their
theology.

gelical Presbyterians and evangelical Methodists. Indeed, evangelical believers often experience deeper fellowship with each other across denominational frontiers, than with their non-evangelical fellow-churchmen. For this is true fellowship, the fellowship of the gospel,[3] a partnership in believing its truth, enjoying its benefits and making it known to others. It has resulted in the formation of such interdenominational bodies as the Evangelical Alliance in Britain (affiliated to the World Evangelical Fellowship) and the Inter-Varsity Fellowship of Evangelical Unions (affiliated to the International Fellowship of Evangelical Students). It means also, in the judgment of many, that the real cleavage in Christendom today, at least in Protestant Christendom, is not between Episcopalians and non-Episcopalians (whether Presbyterian or Independent), or between so-called State Churches and Free Churches, or between Baptists and Paedo-baptists, or between Arminians and Calvinists, but between evangelicals and the rest.

But I am moving ahead too fast, for I am assuming a theological meaning of the term 'evangelical' without having attempted to demonstrate it historically. The Latin adjective *evangelicus* was used quite early in the history of the church with reference to the gospel. Augustine, for example, declared that 'the blood of Christians is, as it were, the seed of the fruit of the gospel' (*semen fructuum evangelicorum*).[4]

It was with the Continental Reformation, however, that the word came into common use, whether in Latin or German, to describe the reforming party. At first they used expressions like *ecclesia reformata, emendata, repurgata*. But their favourite self-designation was *evangelici* (short for *evangelici viri*, 'evangelical men'), in German 'die Evangelischen'. Luther himself gave the word currency. The Papal Bull of 1521 which excommunicated him called his followers 'Lutherans'. This horrified him. 'Please do not use my name,' he wrote. 'Do not call yourselves Lutherans, but Christians. . . . The doctrine is not mine; I have not been crucified for anyone. . . . Why should I, a miserable bag of worms, give my meaningless name to Christ's children?'[5] Apart from 'Christians' (the Reformers came to call the unreformed

---

[3] *Cf.* Phil. 1:5.
[4] Quoted by Latimer, *Works*, Parker Society Edition (CUP, 1844-45), vol. I, p. 361.   [5] *Works* (St. Louis edition), X. 370.

Roman Catholics 'pseudo-Christians'), Luther adopted the title 'evangelicals'. In 1524 he wrote: 'A truly evangelical man would not run here and there, he will stick to truth to the end.'[6] And the following year he wrote: 'People are good evangelicals as long as they hope that the message of the gospel will pasture and enrich them.'[7]

In his lectures on the Epistle to the Galatians, delivered in 1531, he was already able to look back to 'the beginning of the reformation of the Gospel' (*causae evangelicae*).[8] He styles his fellow-believers 'those who boast themselves to be' either 'Gospellers' or 'professors of the Gospel' (*evangelicos*).[9] They are equivalent in his commentary to those who have been 'freed from the tyranny of the Pope' and have entered into the liberty of Christ.[1]

Another German word in common use was 'reformiert'. Indeed, not only were 'evangelisch' and 'reformiert' synonyms during most of the sixteenth century, but they were often used in combination. Even as late as 1690 the Dukes of Brunswick designated the whole German Protestant Church 'evangelisch-reformiert'. Towards the end of the sixteenth century, however, when the Lutherans and Calvinists were drifting further apart, 'evangelical' was already being applied more particularly to the former and 'reformed' to the latter. In 1602 Polycarp Leyser of Dresden distinguished what he termed three 'religions': 'the evangelicals, who are being called "Lutherans", the Calvinists who call themselves "Reformed" and the Papists who call themselves "Catholics".' But two centuries later 'evangelical' had become an umbrella term covering both Lutheran and Reformed. Thus the *Evangelische Kirche* in Prussia (1817) was a united church of Lutheran and Reformed, while the *Evangelische*

---

[6] *Works* (Weimar edition), 10.3, 354.4.

[7] *Works* (Weimar edition), 33.11.

[8] *A Commentary on St. Paul's Epistle to the Galatians*, based on lectures delivered by Martin Luther in 1531 and published in 1535 ('Middleton edition', 1575, revised, James Clarke, 1953), p. 395 (on Gal. 4:12).

[9] *Galatians*, pp. 217, 482.

[1] *Galatians*, p. 217 (on Gal. 3:5) and p. 482 (on Gal. 5:13). Erasmus also wrote of the title *evangelici*, adding in parenthesis *sic enim appellari gaudent*, 'for thus they are pleased to be called'. It is not surprising, therefore, that in 1535 the Elector of Saxony used 'evangelical' in contrast to 'Erasmian', to distinguish the true reformers from the Christian Humanists.

Kirche Deutschlands, founded in 1948, embraces all Germany's Protestant Churches – United, Lutheran and Reformed.

In England the Latin word *evangelicus* can be traced back at least as far as John Wyclif He was named *doctor evangelicus*, and at the time of his death, in 1384, he left an unfinished work entitled *Opus Evangelicum*, which with its emphasis on the sufficiency of Scripture had considerable influence on Hus in Bohemia. The first date for the English word which the Oxford English Dictionary gives is 1532, when Sir Thomas More referred to 'those euaungelicalles' in his *The Confutacyon of Tindale's Answere*.

We find Thomas Cranmer using it (though in Latin again) in a letter he wrote in 1537 to the Swiss scholar and reformer Joachim Vadian. The context is particularly interesting because at that time Cranmer was still in the twilight of the Reformation and not yet himself fully 'evangelical'. Vadian had sent him six books which sought to disprove the notion of Christ's corporal presence in the sacrament. In his reply Cranmer stoutly defended the 'catholic faith . . . respecting the real presence'.[2] His entreaty to Vadian was expressed in the following terms: 'to agree and unite in a Christian concord, to exert your whole strength in establishing it . . . so that we may, with united strength, extend as widely as possible one sound, pure, evangelical doctrine,[3] conformable to the discipline of the primitive church.'[4]

In the eighteenth century the word came to be applied to the Methodists and their successors both within and outside the Church of England, while the remarkable work of God associated with the names of Wesley and Whitefield became known as the 'Evangelical Revival'.

In the light of its history briefly sketched above, it is not surprising that nowadays the word 'evangelical' has various shades of meaning. In those countries of Europe and Latin America where the Church of Rome is strongly entrenched, 'evangelical' is virtually the equivalent of 'protestant'. The European 'evangelical' churches (*e.g.* in Germany and Scandinavia) are Lutheran, in contrast to the 'reformed' churches

---

[2] He did not repudiate it until 1546.

[3] *Evangelicam doctrinam unam, sanam, puram.*

[4] *Miscellaneous Writings and Letters of Thomas Cranmer*, Parker Society Edition (CUP, 1846), pp. 342–344.

(*e.g.* in France, Holland and Switzerland) which trace their
ancestry to Calvin.[5] In the United States some 'Calvinists'
prefer not to be called 'evangelical' because they use the word
of 'Arminians', whereas in the Protestant Episcopal Church
of America 'evangelical' often tends to mean little more than
'Low Church liberal'. These examples of current usage should
be regarded as deviations, however. The classic connotation of
'evangelical' is bound up with a theology of the gospel which
goes back to the Reformation, and indeed beyond the Reformation to the Bible itself. It is in this sense that the term is used
in this book.

Evangelical means biblical
If 'evangelical' describes a theology, that theology is biblical
theology. It is the contention of evangelicals that they are plain
Bible Christians, and that in order to be a biblical Christian
it is necessary to be an evangelical Christian. Put that way, it
may sound arrogant and exclusive, but this is a sincerely held
belief. Certainly it is the earnest desire of evangelicals to be
neither more nor less than biblical Christians. Their intention
is not to be partisan. That is, they do not cling to certain tenets
for the sake of maintaining their identity as a 'party'. On the
contrary, they have always expressed their readiness to modify,
even abandon, any or all of their cherished beliefs if they can
be shown to be unbiblical.

Evangelicals therefore regard as the only possible road to
the reunion of churches the road of biblical reformation. In
their view the only solid hope for churches which desire to unite
is a common willingness to sit down together under the authority
of God's Word, in order to be judged and reformed by it.

This being so, evangelicals cannot subscribe to the fashionable
ecumenical idea that each church has a fragment of the truth,
and that the truth cannot be recovered until all churches add
their bits and pieces of truth together. Dr J. I. Packer sums
this up with his customary lucidity: 'You cannot add to evangelical theology without subtracting from it. By augmenting it,
you cannot enrich it; you can only impoverish it. Thus, for

[5] It is because *evangelisch* means either 'Protestant' or 'Lutheran' that some
people are beginning in Germany to refer to a theologically evangelical
Christian not as *evangelisch* but as *evangelikal*.

example, if you add to it a doctrine of human priestly mediation, you take away the truth of the perfect adequacy of our Lord's priestly mediation. If you add to it a doctrine of human merit, in whatever form, you take away the truth of the perfect adequacy of the merits of Christ. . . . The principle applies at point after point. What is more than evangelical is less than evangelical. Evangelical theology, by its very nature, cannot be supplemented; it can only be denied.'[6]

This claim that evangelical theology is biblical theology means that it is the theology of the whole Bible. Evangelicals have sometimes been accused of making a selective use of Scripture to suit their own convenience. But if and when they have been guilty of this practice, they have contradicted their true character and witness. The evangelical testimony is to the whole of Scripture, as it unfolds what Paul termed 'the whole counsel of God'.[7] Indeed, since one important meaning of the word 'catholic' is 'loyal to the whole truth', one would dare even to say that, properly understood, the Christian faith, the catholic faith, the biblical faith and the evangelical faith are one and the same thing.

Evangelical means original
If evangelical theology is biblical theology, it follows that it is not a new-fangled 'ism', a modern brand of Christianity, but an ancient form, indeed the original one. It is New Testament Christianity. More than that, the distinctive doctrines on which evangelical believers insist are all to be found in the actual teaching of Jesus Himself. It is, in fact, on His teaching that I propose to concentrate in the later chapters of this book. I hope to show that the points at issue in Christ's controversies with His contemporaries, notably with the Pharisees and the Sadducees, are still burning issues today, and that evangelicals are simply trying to be faithful to the principles which He enunciated.

The same is true of the apostles who further elaborated these principles. It is our claim that the evangelical faith is the apostolic faith. At least we accept the unique authority of the

[6] From an address given to the Fellowship of Evangelical Churchmen on 20 March 1961, and subsequently published with the title *The Theological Challenge to Evangelicalism Today*.
[7] Acts 20:27.

apostles of Jesus Christ and desire to submit to their teaching.
We observe that they made their own instruction the rule by
which men's opinions were to be tested. Paul expected obedience
from his readers. He tells the Thessalonians to note and to shun
anybody who is not living 'in accord with the tradition that you
received from us' and who 'refuses to obey what we say in this
letter'.[8] Similarly, John, writing to a church or churches troubled
by false teachers, warned them that 'any one who goes ahead
and does not abide in the doctrine of Christ does not have
God; he who abides in the doctrine has both the Father and the
Son'.[9] It is likely that the false teachers were Gnostics who claimed
for themselves a special, esoteric enlightenment. In their opinion
they were the advanced thinkers, the progressives. They were
not stick-in-the-mud like the common herd of Christians. But
John is not impressed by their pretensions. A Christian's duty,
he insists, is not to advance but to 'abide', not to 'go ahead'
beyond the apostolic faith but to stay put in it.

This appeal of the New Testament authors to their readers
to be loyal to the primitive apostolic teaching is frequent and
urgent. In order to feel its cumulative force, it is necessary – even
if it may be thought tedious – to rehearse some of its principal
examples:

Paul: 'So then, brethren, stand firm and hold to the traditions
which you were taught by us, either by word of mouth or by
letter' (2 Thes. 2 : 15; *cf.* 3 : 6; Rom. 16 : 7).

'Now I would remind you, brethren, in what terms I preached
to you the gospel, which you received, in which you stand, by
which you are saved, if you hold it fast – unless you believed
in vain' (1 Cor. 15 : 1, 2; *cf.* 16 : 13; Phil. 4 : 9; Col. 2 : 6).

'But even if we, or an angel from heaven, should preach to
you a gospel contrary to that which we preached to you, let
him be accursed. As we have said before, so now I say again,
If any one is preaching to you a gospel contrary to that which
you received, let him be accursed' (Gal. 1 : 8, 9).

'O Timothy, guard what has been entrusted to you' (1 Tim.
6 : 20; *cf.* 4 : 6).

'Follow the pattern of the sound words which you have heard
from me . . .; guard the truth that has been entrusted to you . . .'
(2 Tim. 1 : 13, 14; *cf.* 2 : 2).

[8] 2 Thes. 3:6, 14.   [9] 2 Jn. 9.

'Continue in what you have learned and have firmly believed, knowing from whom you learned it' (2 Tim. 3 : 14; *cf.* Tit. 1 : 9).

Peter: 'You have been born anew . . . through the living and abiding word of God; for ". . . the word of the Lord abides for ever." That word is the good news which was preached to you' (1 Pet. 1 : 23–25).

'I intend always to remind you of these things, though you know them and are established in the truth that you have. I think it right, as long as I am in this body, to arouse you by way of reminder. . . . And I will see to it that after my departure you may be able at any time to recall these things' (2 Pet. 1 : 12–15).

Hebrews: 'Therefore we must pay the closer attention to what we have heard, lest we drift away from it' (2 : 1).

'Remember your leaders, those who spoke to you the word of God; consider the outcome of their life, and imitate their faith. . . . Do not be led away by diverse and strange teachings. . . .' (13 : 7, 9).

John: 'Beloved, I am writing you no new commandment, but an old commandment which you had from the beginning; the old commandment is the word which you have heard' (1 Jn. 2 : 7).

'Let what you heard from the beginning abide in you. If what you heard from the beginning abides in you, then you will abide in the Son and in the Father. . . . I write this to you about those who would deceive you. . . .' (1 Jn. 2 : 24, 26; *cf.* 3 : 11; 4 : 6; 2 Jn. 5, 6).

Jude: 'Beloved, . . . I found it necessary to write appealing to you to contend for the faith which was once for all delivered to the saints' (verse 3).

Revelation: '. . . to the rest of you in Thyatira, who do not hold this teaching [*i.e.* of 'the woman Jezebel, who calls herself a prophetess . . .'], who have not learned what some call the deep things of Satan, to you I say, I do not lay upon you any other burden; only hold fast what you have, until I come' (2 : 24, 25).

These passages speak with an impressive unanimity. The writers refer to a certain body of revealed teaching which is variously described as 'the good news', 'the faith' or (more fully) 'the faith which was once for all delivered to the saints', 'the truth', 'the sound doctrine', 'the traditions', 'the pattern of sound words', 'what you heard from the beginning' and 'the deposit'. This was the message which the apostles had 'preached', 'delivered', 'taught' and 'entrusted' to the church, so that the early Christians could be said to have 'heard', 'received', 'learned' and 'believed' it, to 'know' it and 'have' it, to 'stand' in it, to be 'established' in it and to be in the process of being 'saved' by it. Now the New Testament authors write to the churches to 'remind' them of this original message. They urge them to 'recall' it, not to 'drift' from it but to 'pay close attention' to it, to 'stand firm' in it, to 'follow' it, to 'continue' in it and let it 'abide' in them, to 'hold' it fast, to 'guard' it as a precious treasure and to 'contend' for it earnestly against all false teachers.

This harking back to the past fills many of our contemporaries with dismay. It seems to them to condemn the Christian church to stagnation and the Christian faith to sterility. They desire to move with the times, they say; to be modern in their views, not ancient; and to be flexible also, not set for ever in the same old mould. They would quote with approval the French proverb that 'only fools and dead men cannot change'.

Indeed, there has probably never been a generation more suspicious of the old and more confident in the new than the present generation. It is a generation in revolt against what it has inherited from the past (in many cases understandably and justifiably so). It hates tradition and loves revolution. Anything which savours of rigid institutionalism, of the *status quo* or of the establishment arouses its hot indignation. The most striking expression of this spirit of the age which I have seen was 'the great proletarian cultural revolution' in 1966 which was heralded as the new anti-bourgeoisie stage in China's revolutionary socialist movement. Some of the propaganda produced for foreign consumption included this statement: 'our people are out to eradicate all the old ideas, old culture, old customs and old habits of the exploiting classes and foster the new ideas, new culture, new customs and new habits of the proletariat.' This cultural revolution was summarized as a process of 'destroying the "four olds" and establishing the "four news" '.

Such a wholesale repudiation of what is old is, to say the least, extremely naïve. Nevertheless, the opposite tendency of resistance to all change is equally mistaken. Time does not stand still. History is change. Far from impeding progress, for example in scientific discovery and social justice, Christians should be in the vanguard of advance. That the Christian church has often been reactionary, clinging to intellectual prejudices no longer tenable, defending its entrenched positions of privilege and condoning the inequalities of the social order, has been one of its major denials of Christ. For such things we deserve to be criticized and need humbly to repent.

The Christian's welcome to change must be discriminating, however. It does not include the apostolic doctrine of the New Testament. Our responsibility towards this is not to abandon it but to hold it fast, not to modify it but to maintain it in its pristine purity.

Although the 'oldness' of the Christian faith is a stumbling-block to many, it is a stumbling-block which cannot be removed. Christianity is Christ Himself, together with the prophetic and apostolic witness to Christ. It depends on a historical event (the birth, life, death, resurrection, ascension and Spirit-gift of Jesus) and on a historical testimony by eyewitnesses. In the nature of the case neither the event nor the witness can be changed or superseded. We live in the twentieth century, but we are tethered to the first. What Jesus Christ said and did was unique and final. So is the interpretative teaching of the apostles, His chosen eyewitnesses and ambassadors. In Him, the Word made flesh, and in the apostolic witness to Him, God's self-revelation was brought to its completion.[1] This completed revelation, by God's providence preserved for us in Scripture, the church of every age is called to hold fast. It is in this sense that every Christian is (or should be) 'conservative', because it is his duty to conserve the truth which has been handed down to him from Christ and the apostles. In everything else, however – in social and ecclesiastical structures, in patterns of ministry and liturgical forms, in Christian living and missionary outreach, and in much else besides – the Christian is obliged to be as radical as Scripture commands and is free to be as radical as Scripture allows.

So Christianity is old, and is getting older every year. Yet it is also new, new every morning. As John put it: 'Beloved, I am writing you no new commandment, but an old commandment which you had from the beginning. . . . Yet I am writing

[1] *Cf.* Heb. 1:1–4; 2:1–4.

you a new commandment, which is true in him and in you, because the darkness is passing away and the true light is already shining.'[2] What he wrote about the commandment is equally applicable to the whole of Christianity. It is both old and new at the same time. We have considered its oldness. In what sense is it also new? John's straightforward answer is that it is new because it is true. For what is true is always new. It has about it a timelessness which keeps it for ever fresh. Again, it is new because it belongs to the new age. The darkness (of the old age), he says, is passing away, and the true light (of the new age) is already shining. So whatever belongs to the old age is old; they will pass away together. But whatever belongs to the new age is new; they will abide together for ever. We must investigate this 'newness' further.

First, what is old needs to be *freshly understood*. When we said that God's revelation reached its climax and completion in Christ and in the apostles' teaching about Christ, we neither said nor meant that we have no more to learn. The Holy Spirit has continued and still continues to teach the people of God. But His continuing instruction is rightly conceived in terms of illumination, not revelation. Revelation is the historical unveiling of God in Christ; illumination is the unveiling of men's minds to see what God has disclosed in Christ. God intends no new revelation for the church, but rather a progressive understanding of the old. Indeed, it is precisely this which He has given down the centuries. Step by step, often through painful conflict and controversy, the Holy Spirit of truth has enabled the church to increase its grasp of the biblical faith and so to clarify its belief and message. The history of the church is a history of debate in which the truths of Scripture have been successively defined so as to exclude the opinions of those who have questioned, obscured or denied them. This does not mean, however, that the church's formulations of doctrine (its creeds and confessions) possess the same unalterable infallibility as the scriptural doctrine itself. As Article XX of the Anglican Thirty-nine Articles expresses it: 'The Church hath . . . authority in controversies of faith: And yet it is not lawful for the Church to ordain any thing that is contrary to God's Word written. . . .'

Secondly, what is old needs to be *freshly applied*. Christianity

[2] 1 Jn. 2:7, 8.

is often dismissed as irrelevant. The fault does not lie with Christianity, however, whose truths and principles have an eternal validity, but with the church which has frequently failed to reapply them to the modern situation. Those who study Scripture carefully are constantly impressed with its contemporary relevance. And it is the task of Christian preachers and teachers to demonstrate this relevance. Preaching includes the application as well as the exposition of Scripture. To preach is to relate God's never-changing Word to man's ever-changing world. The fact that the oldness of Christianity is a stumbling-block to many brings an increased challenge to the church to indicate its true newness by delivering an ever fresh message from an ancient book.

Thirdly, what is old needs to be *freshly experienced*. The Jesus of history is the Christ of faith, whom we know and love, trust and obey. After every fresh experience of the saving power of Christ the Christian can say that He has 'put a new song in my mouth, a song of praise to our God'.[3] Perhaps the chief explanation of the almost incredible 'God is dead' theology is that the living God had 'gone dead' for its inventors, like a telephone line when a caller is cut off. But when a telephone conversation is thus interrupted, we do not immediately assume that the person at the other end has died! The truth is that everything old has to be freshened if it is to remain new. Old silver must be polished, old friendships kept in good repair, old memories revived, old resolutions repeated and (in the same way) old truths recovered.

Every Christian knows the tendency to spiritual staleness. Only by a fresh appropriation of our inheritance in Christ can the old faith be new to us and seem new to others. As P. T. Forsyth expressed it, the preacher 'must be original in the sense that his truth is his own, but not in the sense that it has been no-one else's. You must distinguish between novelty and freshness. The preacher is not to be original in the sense of being absolutely *new*, but in the sense of being *fresh*, of appropriating for his own personality, or his own age, what is the standing possession of the Church, and its perennial trust from Christ.'[4]

---

[3] Ps. 40:3.
[4] *Positive Preaching and the Modern Mind* by P. T. Forsyth (Independent Press, 1907), p. 60.

The history of the church has been tarnished by a recurrent failure to hold together the oldness and the newness of the Christian faith. Sometimes it has successfully maintained the old faith, but failed to relate it to the new world. At other times it has been determined to communicate with the new world, but failed in the process to preserve the old faith in its purity. We have considered how what is old must be ever freshly appropriated and applied; we must now emphasize the need, while striving to speak relevantly to modern man, to remain loyal to the old, the original, the apostolic faith.

Every true reform movement has involved a return at some point to the New Testament norm. The most notable example is the sixteenth-century Reformation, which was a radical attempt under God to purge the church of its medieval accretions and corruptions. The Reformers understood their task quite clearly. They were neither iconoclasts nor innovators. Their ambition was to reform the church by conforming it to the requirements of God's Word. As Lancelot Andrewes was to say at the beginning of the seventeenth century: *renovatores modo sumus, non novatores*, 'we are renovators not innovators'.[5]

It is particularly interesting to note that their recovery of original New Testament truth was nevertheless condemned by their opponents as a dangerous innovation. This charge they vigorously denied, asserting that on the contrary their doctrine was authentic because aboriginal, while it was the papists who were the innovators. Thus, Luther could write: 'We teach no new thing, but we repeat and establish old things, which the apostles and all godly teachers have taught before us.'[6] The English Reformers were equally clear. Hugh Latimer cried: 'But ye say, it is new learning. Now I tell you it is the old learning.'[7] Bishop John Jewel insists much on this point in his famous *Apology* (1562). For example, 'it is not our doctrine that we bring you this day; we wrote it not, we found it not out, we are not the inventors of it; we bring you nothing but what the old fathers of the church, what the apostles, what Christ our Saviour Himself hath brought before us'.[8]

[5] *Works*, III (Oxford, 1843), p. 26.
[6] *A Commentary on St. Paul's Epistle to the Galatians* (James Clarke, 1953), p. 53.
[7] *Works*, vol. I, pp. 30f.
[8] *Works*, vol. II, p. 1034.

The same controversy over what is old and what is new was revived by the liberal theology of the nineteenth century. In 1907 a Congregational minister named R. J. Campbell published a book entitled *The New Theology*. Influenced by the so-called 'new science' and especially by evolutionary theories, he expounded an almost pantheistic concept of God, denied the uniqueness of the incarnation (arguing that God was to some degree incarnate in every man) and repudiated the miraculous. Charles Gore, at that time Bishop of Birmingham, replied in the same year in *The New Theology and the Old Religion*.[9] 'I am sure', he wrote, '. . . that the self-disclosure of God which reached its culmination in Jesus Christ is final, and that by the very necessity of the case. That is to say, if Jesus Christ is God incarnate, no fuller disclosure of God in terms of manhood than is given in His person is conceivable or possible.'[1]

And now sixty years later history is repeating itself yet again. The evangelical quarrel with the modern fashion of radical theology, which boasts of a 'new reformation', a 'new theology', a 'new morality', even a 'new Christianity' is precisely this that, alas, it is what it claims to be! It is 'new'. It is not a legitimate reinterpretation of old first-century Christianity, for from this it deviates at many vital points. It is an invention of the twentieth century.

Evangelical believers, on the other hand, while recognizing the necessity of restatement and reinterpretation, are determined to remain loyal to the historic faith which they desire to restate and reinterpret. What is needed is a *translation* of the gospel into the language, idiom and thought forms of the modern world. But a genuine translation is never a fresh composition; it is a faithful rendering into another language of something which has already been written or said.

It is perverse, therefore, to accuse evangelicals of having introduced some new-fangled religion, when our whole aim is to recover primitive Christianity – not the religion of the Reformers merely, nor of the early church Fathers, but of the New Testament itself. When Dr Billy Graham was leading an evangelistic crusade in Los Angeles in August-September 1963,

[9] R. J. Campbell's book was published by Chapman and Hall, Charles Gore's by John Murray.
[1] Gore, p. vii.

Time magazine quoted a local episcopal clergyman as saying: 'I believe he's putting the church back 50 years.' Referring to this in an address to Los Angeles ministers, Billy Graham commented: 'Of course, I'm disappointed in a way. I was trying to set it back a thousand years.' He might have said 'one thousand nine hundred'!

Every Christian speaker and writer should be able to echo John Bunyan's opening 'Apology' for his *Pilgrim's Progress*:

> This book is writ in such a dialect
> As may the minds of listless men affect:
> It seems a novelty, and yet contains
> Nothing but sound and honest gospel strains.[2]

Indeed, every evangelical would wish to endorse Christ's own words that 'no one after drinking old wine desires new; for he says, "The old is better".'[3]

Evangelical means fundamental

If 'evangelical' is a word describing a theology that is biblical and therefore 'original' in the sense of primitive, it also lays stress on what is fundamental. One hesitates to use this word, because the closely related term 'fundamentalist' is now often used as an ecclesiastical smear-word. We do not relish it, because it is associated in many people's minds with obscurantism, emotionalism and other horrid forms of religious eccentricity and fanaticism. In its original use, however, not only were these regrettable overtones lacking, but it possessed a much-needed emphasis, namely loyalty to what is 'fundamental' in biblical Christianity.

The word 'fundamentalist' seems to have been used first in 1923 in connection with a series of tracts for the times which began to appear in America in 1909. Their publication was financed by two well-to-do brothers called Lyman and Milton Stewart. There were sixty-five booklets in the series, and altogether millions of copies were sold. They were entitled *The Fundamentals* and covered such fundamental themes as biblical

[2] *The Pilgrim's Progress* (first published 1678), Collins edition, 1953, p. 24.
[3] Lk. 5:39, RSV margin.

inspiration and authority (the first twenty booklets), the deity of Christ, His virgin birth and bodily resurrection, the Holy Spirit, sin, judgment and atonement, justification and regeneration, preaching, evangelism, the church and the return of Christ. The authors were drawn from North America and Britain, and included such well-known evangelical writers as B. B. Warfield, R. A. Torrey, A. T. Pierson, Dyson Hague, Robert E. Speer, James Orr, W. H. Griffith Thomas, Campbell Morgan and Bishops J. C. Ryle and Handley Moule.[6]

The Oxford English Dictionary has preserved the early meaning of 'fundamentalism' as 'strict adherence to traditional orthodox tenets . . . held to be fundamental to the Christian faith' and mentions biblical inerrancy only as an example. This is important. 'Fundamentalist' nowadays is an epithet usually reserved for somebody who is thought to have a cranky view of the Bible. He 'believes that every single word of the Bible is literally true', we are told, or that 'God inspired the authors as if they were a lot of tape-recorders', or something of the kind. Now an evangelical does believe in the divine origin and inspiration of Scripture (although he recognizes that parts of it are intended to be figurative, and he does not subscribe to a mechanical theory of inspiration). But the doctrine of biblical authority is only one of several fundamental Christian doctrines which he believes – doctrines about God, Christ and the Holy Spirit, about sin and salvation, about the church and the sacraments, about worship, morality and evangelism, about death and the life to come.

It is because the fundamentals of the faith are at stake that the evangelical cannot follow his natural inclination to withdraw from the field of controversy and spend the rest of his days on some remote island of tranquillity and peace. Nor can he accept the view expressed in some of the younger churches that these are purely western conflicts and divisions which should not be exported to Africa, Asia or Latin America. On the contrary, no church or individual Christian can avoid the pain of debate and decision about these issues, unless they are pre-

---

[6] To mark its jubilee in 1958 the Bible Institute of Los Angeles issued a two-volume work entitled *The Fundamentals for Today* (Kregel Publications). These volumes contain all the original sixty-five booklets, revised and edited by a committee under the direction of Dr Charles L. Feinberg.

pared to contract out of responsible Christian discipleship
altogether.

The evangelical insistence on fundamentals needs to be
explained and qualified in two ways.

First, it does not mean that we expect all Christians to dot
every 'i' and cross every 't' of our particular system. Our understanding of what is fundamental concerns what is plainly biblical.
However, we recognize that the Bible does not speak on every
issue with a clear and unmistakable voice. These matters,
therefore, including questions like the mode of baptism, the
character of the ministry and forms of worship, cannot be
regarded as fundamental. Indeed, any subject on which equally
devout, equally humble, equally Bible-believing and Bible-
studying Christians or churches reach different conclusions,
must be considered secondary not primary, peripheral not
central. We must not insist on these as fundamentals, but as
so-called *adiaphora* or 'things indifferent'. We must respect
each other's integrity and acknowledge the legitimacy of each
other's interpretations. We cannot do better than follow the
maxim which was enunciated by a certain Rupert Meldenius
at the beginning of the seventeenth century and quoted with
approval by Richard Baxter: '*In necessariis unitas, in nonnecessariis*
(or *dubiis*) *libertas, in omnibus caritas.*' That is, 'in fundamentals
unity, in non-fundamentals (or 'doubtful things') liberty, in all
things charity'.[5]

The second qualification is this: in contending for the fundamentals of the faith, evangelical believers are not contending
for any particular formulation of them. For example, it is a
mistake to suppose that the only war-cry of evangelicals is
'back to the Reformation'. Greatly as we admire the godly
scholarship and courage of the Reformers, and much as we
thank God for His grace in and through them, our regard for
them is not one of blind, unquestioning devotion. We do not

---

[5] It is not known who Rupert Meldenius was. Some think the name is a
pseudonym. The words quoted occur in a Latin treatise which, while upholding
Lutheranism, pleaded for peace in the church. It was published secretly
without any mention of date or place, probably in Germany between 1615
and 1630. The quotation soon became a proverb. In full it may be translated:
'If we would but observe unity in essentials, liberty in non-essentials, charity
in both (or 'all things'), our affairs would certainly be in the best possible
situation.'

believe in their infallibility. We would be prepared to dissent here and there from some of their views, confessions and formularies. We only desire to go 'back to the Reformation' in the sense that we believe this to be the general theological position to which going 'back to the Bible' would take us. The same applies to all other systematizations of evangelical theology. Systematic theologies are of great value. But we know that biblical truth is greater than all attempts to systematize it. In this connection evangelical Anglicans are fond of quoting some wise words of Charles Simeon. He was an evangelical stalwart in Cambridge at the beginning of the last century. Elected a Fellow of King's College in 1782, and Vicar of Holy Trinity for 53 years until his death in 1836, he stood firm (despite opposition which at times was fanatical) in his championship of evangelical truth. He lived in days when the Calvinist–Arminian controversy raged fiercely, but he steadfastly refused to take sides in any partisan way. In his preface to *Horae Homileticae* he wrote: 'The author . . . is no friend to systematizers in theology. He has endeavoured to derive from the Scriptures alone *his* views of religion; and to them it is his wish to adhere, with scrupulous fidelity; never wresting any portion of the Word of God to favour a particular opinion, but giving to every part of it that sense, which it seems to him to have been designed by the great Author to convey.

'He is aware that he is likely, on this account, to be considered by the zealous advocates of human systems as occasionally inconsistent; but if he should be discovered to be no more inconsistent that the Scriptures themselves, he will have reason to be satisfied. He has no doubt that there is a system in the Holy Scriptures (for truth cannot be inconsistent with itself); but he is persuaded that neither Calvinists nor Arminians are in *exclusive* possession of it.'[6]

Again, 'The truth is not in the middle, and not in one extreme, but in both extremes. . . . Sometimes I am a high Calvinist, at other times a low Arminian, so that if extremes will please you, I am your man; only remember, it is not *one* extreme that we are to go to, but *both* extremes.'[7]

[6] *Horae Homileticae* by Charles Simeon (1819), pp. 4, 5.
[7] From a letter dated July 1825 and quoted in *Charles Simeon* by Handley C. G. Moule (1892), IVP edition (1965), pp. 77, 78.

Thus Charles Simeon would warn us against adopting either one or other extreme or even the golden mean of Aristotle. He would have us hold fast to both extremes, so long as they are equally biblical, even if our human mind cannot reconcile or systematize them. For biblical truth is often stated paradoxically and the attempt to resolve all the 'antinomies' of Scripture is misguided because impossible. 'Don't you know, my dear brother,' he said to J. J. Gurney in 1831, when the latter saw his aged friend 'forgetful of the gout, dancing over the lawn' to meet him, 'that the wheels of your watch move in opposite directions? Yet they are all tending to one result.'[8]

Just so, when apparent opposites are encountered in the Bible, 'it is possible that the truly scriptural statement will be found, not in an exclusive adoption of either, nor yet in a confused mixture of both, but in the proper and seasonable application of them both.'[9]

This, then, is the claim which evangelical believers have always made. It is that evangelical Christianity is theological in its character, biblical in its substance, original in its history and fundamental in its emphasis. Some of its essential principles, as defended and maintained by Jesus Christ Himself, are set forth in the rest of this book.

[8] *Memoirs of the Life of the Rev. Charles Simeon* edited by William Carus (Hatchard, 1847), pp. 673-675.
[9] Carus, p. 180.

CHRIST THE CONTROVERSIALIST

1 RELIGION:
NATURAL OR SUPERNATURAL?

The popular image of Christ as 'gentle Jesus, meek and mild' simply will not do. It is a false image. To be sure, He was full of love, compassion and tenderness. But He was also uninhibited in exposing error and denouncing sin, especially hypocrisy. Christ was a controversialist. The Evangelists portray Him as constantly debating with the leaders of contemporary Judaism. The purpose of studying His controversies is to make sure that the principles on which He took His stand are those which we are seeking to maintain today.

The first controversy we shall consider was precipitated by a question which the Sadducees posed about the resurrection. It possesses a striking relevance for today, because it pinpoints the issue whether religion is natural or supernatural. Indeed it goes further than this. It concerns not only what kind of religion the Christian religion is, but what kind of God the Christian God is. So it is fundamental.

The Sadducees and their modern counterparts

But before we listen to the Sadducees' question, we must take a look at the Sadducees themselves. They were a small but influential Jewish party, which had originated during the days of the Maccabean dynasty. They were mostly educated, wealthy, aristocratic and resident in Jerusalem. The high-priestly families were Sadducees, so that Luke is quite correct to identify 'the Sadducean party' with 'the high priest and his colleagues'.[1] Politically, though influential, they were unpopular because they collaborated with the authorities of the Roman occupation. Theologically they were conservative, accepting the written

[1] Acts 5:17, NEB.

law (though in a very formal and prosaic way) and rejecting
the traditions of the elders which were so much loved by the
Pharisees. Thus, 'the Pharisees had an elaborate doctrine of
immortality, resurrection, angels, demons, heaven, hell, the
intermediate state and the Messianic kingdom, about all of
which the Sadducees were agnostic'.[2] Flavius Josephus, the
first-century Jewish historian, gave a terse summary of this
difference between the two major parties. The Pharisees, he
wrote, 'believe that souls have an immortal vigour in them',
whereas the Sadducees 'take away the belief of the immortal
duration of the soul', teaching instead 'that souls die with the
bodies'.[3]

This same basic theological distinction between the Pharisees
and the Sadducees is faithfully recorded by the Evangelists.
Mark describes the Sadducees as those 'who say there is no
resurrection'.[4] Similarly Luke comments in the Acts: 'the
Sadducees say that there is no resurrection, nor angel, nor
spirit; but the Pharisees acknowledge them all.'[5]

We might therefore refer to the Sadducees as the 'modernists'
of ancient Jewry. Although in one sense theologically conservative, since they acknowledged the authority of the law of Moses,
they yet read it *au pied de la lettre*. They were blind to the power
of the living God which it reveals. They virtually denied the
supernatural.

Their contemporary equivalents are those who have imbibed
the spirit of scientific materialism. Here are the kind of questions
which twentieth-century Sadducees are asking: 'Hasn't science
demonstrated that the universe is a closed, mechanistic system,
and therefore dispensed with any necessity for God?' 'Aren't
all the data of human experience to be explained in terms of
natural processes, so that we must repudiate even the possibility
of the *supernatural*?' 'Isn't religion itself a natural phenomenon,
having partly physiological and partly psychological causes,
so that what religion proves is not the existence of the God
believed in but the glandular disturbance or emotional disorder

[2] Article 'Pharisees' by Hugh M. Scott in Hastings' *Dictionary of Christ and
the Gospels* (vol. II, 1908), p. 351.
[3] From *The Works of Flavius Josephus*, translated by William Whiston (1737):
The Antiquities of the Jews xviii.1.3, 4 and *The Wars of the Jews* ii.8.14.
[4] Mk. 12:18.   [5] Acts 23:8; cf. 4:1, 2.

of the believer?' 'And even if we can still in some sense believe in God as the creator and controller of the natural order, we must surely now give up the old-fashioned notion that this God has ever intervened *supernaturally* in human history, let alone that He still does so?'

These are typical questions asked by modern Sadducees. How to answer them we must leave until we see how Jesus answered their ancient predecessors.[6] These original Sadducees came to Jesus and began: 'Teacher, Moses wrote for us . . .'. It will be noted that they referred to the Pentateuch, which they held in special veneration, and that they regarded its message as having a contemporary application ('Moses wrote *for us*'[7]). The particular legislation to which they were alluding is the law of levirate marriage.[8] By this law a woman who was widowed and childless was not to be married 'outside the family to a stranger', but to her brother-in-law, her deceased husband's brother, so that he might 'build up his brother's house'. This was the Mosaic background to the Sadducees' question. The New English Bible expresses Mark's version of what they said in this way:

> 'Now there were seven brothers. The first took a wife and died without issue. Then the second married her, and he too died without issue. So did the third. Eventually the seven of them died, all without issue. Finally the woman died. At the resurrection, when they come back to life' – a resurrection, the Sadducees implied, in which the Pharisees believe, but we don't[9] – 'whose wife will she be, since all seven had married her?'[1]

Without doubt the Sadducees thought they were being frightfully clever and that by their hypothetical case they had exposed what to them was the absurdity of the doctrine of the

---

[6] The controversy is recorded in Mk. 12:18–27; Mt. 22:23–33; Lk. 20:27–38.

[7] As a further example of the living relevance of the written revelation, compare Mk. 12:26 'have you not read . . . how God said *to him*' (*i.e.* Moses) with Mt. 22:31 'have you not read what was said *to you* by God'.

[8] Dt. 25:5ff. *Levir* is Latin for a husband's brother or a brother-in-law.

[9] The Sadducees quoted the brother-in-law's duty to 'raise up children for his brother' (v. 19). The Greek verb is that used of the resurrection. Conceivably the Sadducees were implying that the only resurrection they believed in was procreation, by which a man lives on in his posterity.

[1] Mk. 12:20–23, NEB.

resurrection. Their intention was to hold it up to ridicule. Their argument was that this life creates so many anomalies that to perpetuate it beyond the grave would be unthinkable. An after-life would simply magnify the problems of this life. Take the poor woman envisaged in the question. She would be claimed by seven men, all clamouring to possess her. Would she reject them all (which would hardly be fair to her) or all but one of them (which would be tough on the other six)? Or will polyandry be permitted in heaven so that she can enjoy all seven simultaneously? The Sadducees imagined that their problem had no solution. They thought they had impaled Jesus on the horns of a dilemma from which no escape was possible.

Jesus began and ended His reply with a clear statement of their error. 'You are wrong', He said (v. 24). 'You are quite wrong' (v. 27). I confess that I find His outspokenness very refreshing. Jesus did not compliment them, as we might have done, on getting hold of an important aspect of the truth, or on contributing a valuable insight to current theological debate. No. They were wrong, in fact 'greatly mistaken' (NEB), in grave and grievous error.

He then added the reason for their mistake. They were wrong, He said, because they were ignorant. 'You are mistaken, and surely this is the reason: you do not know. . . .' (v. 24, NEB). These educated aristocrats, priests and leaders of Israel, who believed in Moses' law and considered themselves extremely clever, were actually ignorant of two truths: 'you know neither the scriptures nor the power of God' (v. 24). Their ignorance of Scripture was the immediate cause of their mistake about the resurrection, but the ultimate, the fundamental cause was their ignorance of the power of God. We shall examine the causes of their error in this order (although Jesus expounded them in the opposite order). This means leaving verse 25 aside for the moment.

Ignorance of Scripture
We shall not elaborate on this in any detail, because the supremacy of Scripture is the subject of the next chapter. But some comment on it seems to be necessary now.

In general, Jesus traced the error of the Sadducees to their biblical ignorance. Most errors in the church today, especially those which precipitate unnecessary controversy, are similarly due to ignorance of or disrespect for the Scriptures. It is extremely significant that in His altercations with both Pharisees and Sadducees, Jesus regarded Scripture as the arbiter in the debate and the final court of appeal. When they came to Him with a question, He would commonly respond with a counter-question which referred them to Scripture. Thus, when a lawyer asked about eternal life, He replied: 'What is written in the law? How do you read?'[2] Again, when the Pharisees enquired His views on divorce, His immediate response was 'Have you not read?' and 'What did Moses command you?'[3] It is the same here with the Sadducees. 'Have you not read in the book of Moses . . .?' He asked.[4] So much was common ground between them. They had quoted Scripture; He quoted Scripture. They had referred to Moses; He referred to Moses also. In doing so, however, He had to complain of their misunderstanding. It was so great that it was tantamount to ignorance.

In particular, He quoted Exodus 3 : 6, where, in the passage about the burning bush, God described Himself to Moses as 'the God of Abraham, and the God of Isaac, and the God of Jacob'. This self-designation, Jesus added, carried with it the implication of their resurrection because 'He is not God of the dead, but of the living' (vv. 26, 27). The first point to notice is that the question at issue was not their survival merely, but their resurrection. Christ introduced His answer with the words 'as for the dead being raised' (v. 26). This is because, according to Scripture, the man God made is a single entity, a body-soul, whose destiny could not be fulfilled in the soul's immortality, but only in the body's resurrection also.

Then there is a second point to consider. Is Christ's argument fair? You might think that for God to call Himself 'the God of Abraham, Isaac and Jacob' implies no more than that He is the God of history, the God who revealed Himself successively to the patriarchs:

> God of our fathers, be the God
> Of their succeeding race.

But no. The words mean more than this, much more. The

argument rests not merely on the sentence 'I am the God of Abraham, Isaac and Jacob', still less on the verb and its tense 'I am' (for in any case there is no verb in the Hebrew), but on the whole context in which the sentence comes. The God who is speaking is both the eternally self-existing God who reveals Himself as 'I am that I am' and the covenant God of Abraham, Isaac and Jacob. He had made with Abraham 'an everlasting covenant, to be God to you and to your descendants after you',[5] and had confirmed it with Isaac and Jacob.[6] Further, His covenant promises were too extensive to be fulfilled in their lifetime, and they knew it. According to the Epistle to the Hebrews, 'they were strangers and exiles on earth', who 'desire a better country, that is, a heavenly one'.[7] So when God announced Himself to Moses as the God of Abraham, Isaac and Jacob, He meant not only that He had been their God centuries before, but that He was their God still and would be to the end, keeping covenant with them, sustaining them with His steadfast love. The God of ancient promise was the God of eternal fulfilment. 'He is not God of the dead, but of the living; for', as Luke adds, 'all live to him.'[8] The very object of their creation and election was that they might live to Him; it is inconceivable that such a purpose would not come to fruition but be terminated by death. The God of Abraham, Isaac and Jacob is Himself the living God, and the living God is the God of the living.

This, then, was the first answer which Jesus gave to the Sadducees' question. They were ignorant of the Scriptures. As Luke's version puts it: 'that the dead are raised, even Moses showed.'[9] Yet for all their proud boast of loyalty to Moses, they had rejected Moses' own testimony. Their minds had become blinded by prejudice or by rationalism or by the Greek culture they had absorbed. They no longer submitted to the revelation of God.

Ignorance of God's power

The more basic cause of the Sadducees' error, however, was another ignorance, not of the Word of God but of the power of God.

They seem genuinely to have supposed that their question

---

[5] Gn. 17:7.   [6] *Cf.* Ex. 2:24.   [7] Heb. 11:13–16.
[8] Lk. 20:38.   [9] Lk. 20:37.

about the law of levirate marriage would be sufficient by itself to discredit the notion of resurrection. In their opinion the problems which an after-life would create made it inconceivable. They hoped by the story of the woman with seven husbands to laugh the doctrine out of court; one can almost hear their suppressed chuckles.

One is tempted instead, however, to laugh at their incredible naïvety. For underlying their argument was this erroneous assumption, that if there were another life beyond death and resurrection, it would be *the same kind of life* as it had been before. It does not seem to have occurred to the Sadducees that God could create another order of being, a new and different life in which earth's insoluble problems would be solved. They underestimated the power of God.

The Pharisees might well have been made uncomfortable by the Sadducees' question, for the Pharisees' notion of the next life was extremely materialistic. For example, 'the earth will assuredly restore the dead, which it now receives in order to preserve them, making no change in their form, but as it has received, so will it restore them'.[1] Hence 'posing resurrection riddles was a favourite game of the Sadducees and often an embarrassment to the Pharisees'.[2] But such questions would not embarrass Jesus, since He knew that the resurrection life would by the power of God be entirely different. 'When they rise from the dead,' He said, 'men and women do not marry; they are like angels in heaven.'[3]

According to Luke the Lord Jesus went on to amplify this: 'The sons of this age marry and are given in marriage; but those who are accounted worthy to attain to that age and to the resurrection from the dead neither marry nor are given in marriage, for they cannot die any more, because they are equal to angels and are sons of God, being sons of the resurrection.'[4] Here Jesus was following familiar Jewish usage and dividing history into two ages, present and future, 'this age' and 'that age'. Further, He emphasized that the life of that age would be significantly different from the life of this age. 'The sons of this

[1] *Apocalypse of Baruch* 49:2, 3 and 50:1, 2.
[2] *The Gospel of Luke* (*The Century Bible*). Commentary by E. Earle Ellis (Nelson, 1966), p. 236.
[3] Mk. 12:25, NEB.   [4] Lk. 20:34–36.

age marry and are given in marriage.' On the other hand, 'those who are accounted worthy to attain to that age and to the resurrection from the dead' (none is worthy in himself, but some by God's grace will be 'accounted worthy') 'neither marry nor are given in marriage.' Why not? Because 'they cannot die any more'. Why not? 'Because they are equal to angels and are sons of God, being sons of the resurrection.'

In other words, the new age will be peopled by new beings living a new life under new conditions. Humans will be like angels. Mortals will have become immortal. Borrowing a phrase from the apostle Paul, they will have been 'raised imperishable'.[5] Consequently, the need to propagate the race will no longer exist. The creation command to 'be fruitful and multiply, and fill the earth'[6] will be rescinded. And in so far as reproduction is one of the chief purposes of marriage, humans will no longer marry. Not that love will cease, for 'love never ends'.[7] But sexuality will be transcended, and personal relationships will be neither exclusive in their character nor physical in their expression.

And all this – this new life under new conditions in the new age – will be due to the power of God, of which the Sadducees were ignorant.

The contemporary debate

The Sadducees have many successors, equally clever, equally foolish. Some of them argue in almost identical terms. They caricature the resurrection in order to discredit it. They speak of it in grossly materialistic terms, as if 'resurrection' were a synonym for 'resuscitation'. They imagine that by the resurrection Christians mean the miraculous material reconstruction of the earthly body which will then resume its former life and functions. They go on to ask incredulously what happens to people whose bodies are blown to bits (a common question during the two World Wars of this century) or whose ashes after cremation are scattered to the four winds. And they genuinely suppose that such questions will embarrass Christians and will permit them to dismiss the doctrine of the resurrection as an absurdity! They have never grasped that the resurrection body, according to the New Testament, although retaining some continuity

[5] I Cor. 15:52–54.   [6] Gn. 1:28.   [7] I Cor. 13:8.

with the earthly body, will be a different body, raised new and
glorious by the power of God. One can hear the apostle Paul
scolding them for their crude notions as he scolded the Corinthians who asked him, '*How* are the dead raised? With what kind
of body do they come?' 'You foolish man!' Paul replied. 'What
you sow does not come to life unless it dies. And what you sow
is not the body which is to be, but a bare kernel, perhaps of
wheat or of some other grain. But God gives it a body as he has
chosen, and to each kind of seed its own body. . . . So is it with
the resurrection of the dead. What is sown is perishable, what is
raised is imperishable. It is sown in dishonour, it is raised in
glory. It is sown in weakness, it is raised in power. It is sown a
physical body, it is raised a spiritual body.'[8]

Other modern Sadducees are the scientific materialists whom
I mentioned earlier. Their view of reality is limited to what their
five senses can grasp. Whatever cannot be empirically verified
they reject. They believe that the universe is a closed, self-
explanatory system, governed by so-called 'natural' laws. For
them this has two corollaries.

First, they can find no room for God. In the early centuries
of the age of science it was customary to distinguish between
natural law and divine action, the former being held to explain
most observable processes while allowing some latitude for
God in those areas where no natural law could (yet) be discerned.
According to this viewpoint the great God of creation is debased
into a mere 'God of the gaps'. One of the best examples of it
occurs in a letter which Isaac Newton wrote to the Master of
his College at Cambridge: 'the diurnal rotations of the planets
could not be derived from gravity, but required a divine arm
to impress it on them.'[9] In other words, 'natural law' (in this
case the law of gravity) is responsible for the orbiting of the earth
round the sun, but 'God' is responsible for its rotation on its
own axis. As Professor Coulson comments, 'This is asking for
trouble.' If God occupies only the gaps, then as scientific dis-
coveries increase and the gaps decrease, God is gradually
edged out of His own universe.

But the Christian's God has never been a 'God of the gaps',

[8] 1 Cor. 15:35-38, 42-44.
[9] Quoted by Professor C. A. Coulson in *Science and Christian Belief* (OUP,
1955), Fontana edition (1958), pp. 32, 33.

however much some Christians have portrayed Him as such. When the Marquis de Laplace 'was reproached by Napoleon for failing to mention God in his great treatise on celestial mechanics', he was right to reply, 'Sire, I have no need of that hypothesis.'[1] What he was denying by this statement was not God Himself, for he was a Christian man, but the use of God as a plug to stop gaps with. For the same reason Bishop Samuel Wilberforce was wrong, in his debate with T. H. Huxley at that famous British Association meeting in Oxford in 1860, to describe Darwin's theory of evolution as 'an attempt to dethrone God'.[2] It does not necessarily aim at any such thing, let alone succeed in the attempt. It is partly because Christians have often been misguided enough to defend some territory against the invasion of 'science' in order to preserve it for 'God' that the very notion of God has been so contemptuously dismissed by men like Julian Huxley: 'The concept of God as a supernatural personal being is only a stop-gap explanation, advanced to stop the gaps in pre-scientific thought.'[3] Surely we must agree with Professor Donald MacKay that this 'dispute deserved to die, because it was not really between science and Christianity at all, but between mistaken views of each'.[4]

Then there is a second deduction which scientific materialists draw from their view of the universe as ruled by 'natural laws'. They deny on a priori grounds the very possibility of the 'supernatural'. 'Miracles can't happen,' they say. So 'miracles don't happen'. The position they adopt is usually termed 'naturalist'; the very word 'supernaturalist' becomes in their vocabulary a term of reproach. If they make any Christian profession at all, the 'Christianity' they profess has been entirely shorn of the miraculous.

How are we to reply to such critics as these, who first eliminate God from the natural and then proceed to eliminate the supernatural altogether? We must repeat Christ's own words: 'you are wrong because you do not know the power of God.'

To begin with, the God of the Bible is the God of nature, who Himself has given and continues to give to nature its own con-

[1] Coulson, p. 41.   [2] Coulson, p. 27.
[3] Religion without Revelation by J. Huxley (Ernest Benn, 1927), p. 12.
[4] Science and Christian Faith Today by Donald M. MacKay (Falcon, 1960), pp. 3, 5.

sistent orderliness. The stop-gap theory of God was a convenient
device for explaining the inexplicable. It drew an arbitrary
distinction between what can and cannot (at the time of speaking) be rationally, scientifically explained, and then retained
God for the inexplicable and dismissed Him from the explicable.
If our concept of God is as mean as that, we deserve Julian
Huxley's stinging scorn: 'the god hypothesis is no longer of any
pragmatic value for the interpretation or comprehension of
nature, and indeed often stands in the way of better and truer
interpretation. Operationally, God is beginning to resemble not a
ruler but the last fading smile of a cosmic Cheshire Cat.'[5]

The truth is that no biblical Christian can accept the distinction
between natural law and divine action which lies at the root of
all this misunderstanding. For natural law is not an alternative
to divine action, but a useful way of referring to it. So-called
natural laws simply describe a uniformity which scientists have
observed. And Christians attribute this uniformity to the con-
stancy of God. Further, to be able to explain a process scientifically is by no means to explain God away; it is rather (in the
famous words of the astronomer Kepler) to 'think God's thoughts
after Him' and to begin to understand His ways of working.

The Bible itself should have protected us from regarding
God either as a stop-gap or as a machine-minder, for the God
of the Bible dwells not in gaps but in every place, whether
it appears to us full or empty. 'Do I not fill heaven and earth?
says the Lord.'[6] And the processes of nature are portrayed not as
automatic mechanisms but as due to His own personal activity.
Thus, God is said through Christ to be 'upholding the universe
by his word of power', so that 'in him all things hold together'.[7]
What is true of the whole universe is true of the planet on which
we live. 'The earth is the Lord's and the fullness thereof'; and
He has promised that 'while the earth remains, seedtime and
harvest, cold and heat, summer and winter, day and night,
shall not cease'.[8] Jesus Himself could affirm in the Sermon on
the Mount that it is God the Father who 'makes his sun rise
on the evil and on the good, and sends rain on the just and on the
unjust'.[9] He is the God of history as well as of nature, supervising

[5] *Religion without Revelation* (1927), 2nd edition (Parrish, 1957), p. 58.
[6] Je. 23:23, 24.   [7] Heb. 1:3; Col. 1:17.
[8] Ps. 24:1; Gn. 8:22; cf. Acts 14:17.   [9] Mt. 5:45.

the migration of tribes and establishing the frontiers of nations.[1] He 'gives to all men life and breath and everything', so that 'in him we live and move and have our being'.[2] He gives life to the lower creation also, feeds both animals and birds, and clothes the lilies of the field.[3]

True, all this is pre-scientific – even naïve – language. It eliminates second causes and ascribes the existence and continuance of all things, from the greatest to the least, to the direct, immanent activity of the living God. But it is still true. The scientific and the biblical ways of looking at nature do not contradict each other; they are complementary. Each explains something which the other does not explain. We must agree with Professor Coulson: 'Either God is in the whole of Nature, with no gaps, or He's not there at all. . . . If we cannot bring God in at the end of science, He must be there at the very start, and right through it. We have done wrong to set up any sharp antithesis between science and religion. . . . There is no other way out of our impasse than to assert that science is one aspect of God's presence. . . .'[4]

Once we are clear about this, we shall know how to confront materialists: 'It is on this issue that the Christian will take exception to the Scientific Humanists,' comments Professor Coulson. 'This does not mean that he denies their science: but it does mean that he deplores their narrow-mindedness. . . . A denial of God is practically always the result of shutting one eye. It may be for this reason that God gave us two.'[5]

So the God revealed in Scripture is not a magician or thaumaturge, whose every act is a miracle. He normally works according to the natural order which He has Himself established. At the same time, He is not imprisoned by nature or the laws of nature. It would be ridiculous to suppose that the creation now controls its Creator. He is able to deviate from His own uniformity, and the Bible says He has sometimes done so. These miracles are not evenly spread throughout Scripture, but appear in clusters. Their evident purpose was to authenticate a fresh stage of God's self-disclosure to His chosen people.[6] By specific,

1 Am. 9:7; Acts 17:26.   2 Acts 17:25, 28; cf. Dn. 5:23.
3 Ps. 104:27–30; Mt. 6:26–30.   4 Coulson, pp. 35, 44.
5 Coulson, pp. 103, 104.
6 For the purpose of miracles worked by Christ through the apostles, see, e.g., 2 Cor. 12:12; Heb. 2:3, 4.

supernatural acts of salvation, revelation and judgment He has made 'creative intrusions'[7] into His own world.

Christianity a resurrection religion

Take resurrection as an example, for this was the point at issue with the Sadducees. The *natural* process which God has established, partly by creation and partly by judgment, is birth, growth, decay, death and dissolution. This is the cycle of nature. It includes man: 'you are dust, and to dust you shall return.'[8] The very concept of 'resurrection' is therefore *supernatural*. At Christ's resurrection the natural process of physical decomposition was not only arrested, nor even reversed, but actually superseded. Instead of dissolving into dust, His body was transfigured into a new and glorious vehicle for His soul. Indeed, the resurrection of Jesus is presented in the New Testament as the supreme manifestation of the supernatural power of God. Paul's prayer for the Ephesian Christians was that the eyes of their heart might be enlightened to know the immeasurable greatness of God's power 'according to the working of his great might which he accomplished in Christ when he raised him from the dead . . .'.[9]

Now Christianity is in its very essence a resurrection religion. The concept of resurrection lies at its heart. If you remove it, Christianity is destroyed. Let me try to demonstrate these assertions.

The New Testament speaks of at least three separate resurrections.

First, *the resurrection of Christ*. About 36 hours after His death, His soul (which had been in Hades, the abode of the dead) and His body (which had lain on a stone slab in the sepulchre) were reunited. At the same time His body was 'raised'. That is to say, it was transformed into what Paul calls 'the body of his glory',[1] being invested with new and hitherto unknown powers. In this resurrection body Christ burst from the tomb, passed through closed doors, appeared to His disciples and disappeared, and finally, in defiance of the law of gravity, ascended out of sight.

[7] The expression is Dr J. I. Packer's. It occurs in *Guidelines* (Falcon, 1967), pp. 22, 23.
[8] Gn. 3:19.   [9] Eph. 1:18–20.   [1] Phil. 3:21, literally.

Secondly, *the resurrection of the body*. The New Testament teaches that the resurrection of Jesus from the dead supplies both the proof and the pattern of the resurrection of our body on the last day. As He rose, so we shall rise – in fact and in manner. The apostle Paul is quite clear about it: 'Just as we have borne the image of the man of dust [*i.e.* Adam], we shall also bear the image of the man of heaven [*i.e.* Christ].'[2] And, when Christ returns, He 'will change our lowly body to be like his glorious body'.[3] On that great day of Christ's return and our resurrection we shall be given bodies like His.

Thirdly, *the resurrection of sinners*. In affirming that Christianity is a resurrection religion, I do not mean only that Christians look back nineteen and a half centuries to the resurrection of Jesus Christ and on to the end when the general resurrection of the dead will take place. Between the past resurrection of Christ and the future resurrection of the body another resurrection is taking place – the present and spiritual (though not less supernatural) resurrection of sinners. Jesus Himself spoke of the reception of eternal life as a transition from death to life, a resurrection of the dead: 'Truly, truly, I say to you, he who hears my word and believes him who sent me, has eternal life; he does not come into judgment, but has passed from death to life. Truly, truly, I say to you, the hour is coming, *and now is*, when the dead will hear the voice of the Son of God, and those who hear will live.'[4] The apostle Paul explained this further: 'you he made alive, when you were dead through the trespasses and sins in which you once walked. . . . But God, who is rich in mercy, out of the great love with which he loved us, even when we were dead through our trespasses, made us alive together with Christ (by grace you have been saved), and raised us up with him, and made us sit with him in the heavenly places in Christ Jesus.'[5]

What exactly is this third resurrection? Is it a rather exaggerated and fanciful description of what happens when people turn over a new leaf? Indeed not. You cannot devalue a resurrection by the power of God into a reformation by the power of men! The two things are entirely different. What the gospel declares is that the process called 'becoming a Christian' is

[2] 1 Cor. 15:49.   [3] Phil. 3:21.
[4] Jn. 5:24, 25.   [5] Eph. 2:1–6.

actually a resurrection from the dead, a deliverance from the spiritual grave to which our sin and guilt had brought us. It is the bestowal of a new life, called 'eternal life', a life lived in fellowship with God, so that Christians are those who are 'alive from the dead'.[6] It is being quickened from death, raised to life, exalted to heaven. It is a miracle, as divine and supernatural an event as the resurrection of the body itself. It is not *against* nature. But it is altogether *beyond* nature, since no man can raise himself from death or give himself a new life. 'The condition of man after the fall of Adam is such, that he cannot turn and prepare himself, by his own natural strength and good works, to faith, and calling upon God.'[7] Once raised from spiritual death by God, the Christian lives in newness of life. Having been 'raised with Christ', he is determined to 'seek the things that are above, where Christ is, seated at the right hand of God'.[8]

These three resurrections are an integral part of the gospel which Paul preached. They are also present already in the teaching of Jesus. 'The Son of man must . . . be killed,' He said, 'and after three days rise again.'[9] In the same way all men will rise on the last day. Indeed, 'that the dead are raised, even Moses showed'.[1] And meanwhile 'the Son gives life to whom he will', quickening with eternal life those who are spiritually dead through sin.[2]

Further, all three resurrections are miracles, supernatural events, and are attributed to the power of God. Thus it was 'the immeasurable greatness of God's *power*' which raised Christ from the dead.[3] It is 'the *power* of Christ's resurrection' which Paul said he wanted increasingly to experience and which is available to all who believe.[4] And it will be the same divine power which, when Christ returns, 'will change our lowly body to be like his glorious body, . . . the *power* which enables him even to subject all things to himself'.[5]

The church of Jesus Christ is today facing a major crisis of faith. What is at stake is nothing less than the essential character

[6] Rom. 6:13; *cf.* 2 Cor. 5:15.
[8] Col. 3:1.
[1] Lk. 20:37.
[2] Eph. 1:19, 20.
[5] Phil. 3:21.

[7] Article X, *Of Free Will*.
[9] Mk. 8:31.
[2] Jn. 5:21ff.
[4] Phil. 3:10; Eph. 1:19, 20.

of Christianity: is the Christian religion natural or supernatural? Various attempts are being made to rid Christianity of its supernaturalism, to reconstruct it without its embarrassing miracles. But these efforts will be as fruitless as they are misguided. You cannot reconstruct something by first destroying it.

Authentic Christianity – the Christianity of Christ and His apostles – is supernatural Christianity. It is not a tame and harmless ethic, consisting of a few moral platitudes, spiced with a dash of religion. It is rather a resurrection religion, a life lived by the power of God. The power which raised Christ from the dead and will one day raise us is able meanwhile to give us a new life, to transform our character and conduct, or (in words taken from the Church of England Burial Service) 'to raise us from the death of sin unto the life of righteousness'.

C. S. Lewis once made an admirably succinct statement of the choice which lies before the church. Shortly after the beginning of World War II, in a letter to Sister Penelope, CSMV of Wantage, he wrote: 'To me the real distinction is not between high and low, but between religion with a real supernaturalism and salvationism on the one hand, and all watered-down and modernist versions on the other.'[6]

It is the old dilemma between Jesus Christ and the Sadducees. Still today the cynical modern Sadducee says, 'There is no resurrection.' Still today Jesus Christ replies, 'You are greatly mistaken, because you know neither the Scriptures nor the power of God.'

[6] *Letters of C. S. Lewis* edited by W. H. Lewis (Bles, 1966), p. 170.

AUTHORITY:
   TRADITION OR SCRIPTURE?

We have noted that Jesus Christ was constantly engaged in
controversy with the church leaders of His day. They were
critical of Him; He was even more outspokenly critical of them.
He did not hesitate when necessary to dissent from their views
in public or to warn the people of their false teaching. 'Take
heed and beware of the leaven of the Pharisees and Sadducees,'
He said to His disciples.[1] In the last chapter we considered His
debate with the Sadducees about the character of religion; in
this chapter we shall consider a debate He had with the Pharisees
about the source of authority.

After the question of religion itself, which involves the nature
of God's being and activity, the next most vital question is that
of authority. Whether we accept what any person teaches
depends on our assessment of his authority. It is therefore
perfectly understandable, and entirely justifiable, that the chief
priests, elders and scribes came to Jesus one day and asked
Him: 'By what authority are you doing these things, or who
gave you this authority to do them?'[2] Christ's quarrel with them
concerned the insincerity which He detected behind their
approach, not their actual question. Although their motives
were wrong, their question was right.

So today in Christendom. Although all churches hold much
belief in common, there are deep and wide divergences, especially
between churches calling themselves 'catholic' and 'orthodox'
on the one hand and those calling themselves 'reformed' on the
other, and between Christians styled 'liberal' or 'radical' and
those styled 'evangelical'. Granted the existence of these big
differences, how can we possibly know which church to believe

[1] Mt. 16:6.   [2] Mk. 11:28.

and follow? This query resolves itself into the question of authority. What people are really asking is a whole series of questions like these: By what authority do you believe what you believe and teach what you teach? By what authority do you accept certain doctrines and repudiate others? And who gave you this authority? Is it a matter of opinion, of one man's conviction against another's or one church's confession against another's? Or is there some criterion, some objective standard, by which the teaching of all churches and Christians may be assessed and judged? Is there an independent arbiter to settle disputes? Is there any final and authoritative court of appeal?

From these general questions we proceed to the particular one which is of crucial importance. It is this. All churches of every conceivable complexion assign some degree of authority to the Bible. But is Scripture the church's *sole* authority? Or may the church supplement the authority of Scripture with the authority of tradition? Of course the word 'tradition' in a Christian context signifies simply the 'handing down' of Christianity from one generation to the next. If what had been handed down were just the Bible itself, the words 'Scripture' and 'tradition' would be synonymous, and no problem about their relation would have arisen. But since in fact – and rightly – each generation has also interpreted the faith, attempting to elucidate and apply it, and has handed down to posterity both the faith (Scripture) and the interpretation (tradition), Scripture and tradition have come to be separated. For this reason it has become necessary to ask: what is the relation between Scripture and tradition?

Although this is a burning question today, it is not a modern problem. It was a bone of contention between the Pharisees and the Sadducees long ago. Josephus expressed it clearly: 'What I would now explain is this, that the Pharisees have delivered to the people a great many observances by succession from their fathers, which are not written in the law of Moses; and for that reason it is that the Sadducees reject them, and say that we are to esteem those observances to be obligatory which are in the written word, but are not to observe what are derived from the tradition of our forefathers.'[8]

[8] Josephus, *Antiquities* xiii.10.6.

The Pharisees' view of tradition

In the last chapter we watched Jesus take the part of the
Pharisees against the Sadducees and affirm that religion is not
natural but supernatural. In this chapter we shall watch Him
take the part of the Sadducees against the Pharisees and affirm
that authority is not in tradition but in Scripture. He was not
being partisan, however, and taking sides. For in both cases,
though His company was different, His position was the same,
namely an appeal to Scripture. He censured the Sadducees
for their ignorance of the Scriptures and attributed their error
to this ignorance. He censured the Pharisees that by their
traditions they were making 'God's word null and void'.[4]

It is necessary now to elaborate the comment of Josephus
quoted above. The Pharisees clung tenaciously to a body of
inherited traditions. They believed that these 'traditions of the
fathers', although handed down orally and not found in the
written law, had nevertheless been given to Moses on Mount
Sinai in addition to the law, and that by God Himself. In the
conviction of the Pharisees, therefore, there were two parallel
divine revelations, the written law and the oral tradition, equally
important and equally authoritative.

During the second century BC these oral traditions came to be
preserved in written form in the Mishnah. It has six divisions
containing laws about agriculture, festivals and marriage,
together with civil, criminal and ceremonial laws. It was supplemented later by the Gemara, which is a commentary on it.
The Mishnah and the Gemara together form the Jewish Talmud.

Several quotations could be given to illustrate the devotion
and reverence which the Jews felt for this corpus of tradition.
In one of the Rabbinic Targums (which are Aramaic para-
phrases of the Old Testament) God is even represented as
'busying Himself by day with the study of the Scriptures, and
by night with that of the Mishnah'.[5] At a later period the Rabbis
would say: 'The Scriptures are water; the Mishnah, wine;
but the Gemara, spiced wine.'[6]

---

[4] Mk. 7:13, NEB.
[5] *The Life and Times of Jesus the Messiah* by A. Edersheim (Longmans, 1883),
vol. II, p. 15.
[6] Quoted in *The Epistle of Paul to the Galatians* (*Tyndale New Testament Commentaries*). Commentary by Alan Cole (Tyndale Press, 1965), p. 50.

Thus the Pharisees tended to smother the Scriptures with a mass of tradition, whereas the tendency of the Sadducees was to undermine the authority of the Scriptures by their superficial interpretations. More simply, the Pharisees added to the Word of God, while the Sadducees subtracted from it. Both practices are equally wrong and dangerous.

We turn now to the details of Christ's controversy with the Pharisees over authority, as Mark records it:[7]

'Now when the Pharisees gathered together to him, with some of the scribes, who had come from Jerusalem, [2] they saw that some of his disciples ate with hands defiled, that is, unwashed. [3] (For the Pharisees, and all the Jews, do not eat unless they wash their hands, observing the tradition of the elders; [4] and when they come from the market place, they do not eat unless they purify themselves; and there are many other traditions which they observe, the washing of cups and pots and vessels of bronze.) [5] And the Pharisees and the scribes asked him, "Why do your disciples not live according to the tradition of the elders, but eat with hands defiled?" [6] And he said to them. "Well did Isaiah prophesy of you hypocrites, as it is written,

'This people honours me with their lips,
   but their heart is far from me;
[7] in vain do they worship me,
   teaching as doctrines the precepts of men.'

[8] You leave the commandment of God, and hold fast the tradition of men."

[9] And he said to them, "You have a fine way of rejecting the commandment of God, in order to keep your tradition! [10] For Moses said, 'Honour your father and your mother'; and, 'He who speaks evil of father or mother, let him surely die'; [11] but you say, 'If a man tells his father or his mother, What you would have gained from me is Corban' (that is, given to God) – [12] then you no longer permit him to do anything for his father or mother, [13] thus making void the word of God through your tradition which you hand on. And many such things you do." '

The occasion of this public controversy was that the Pharisees saw some of the disciples of Jesus eating food with hands 'defiled'

[7] Mk. 7:1–13. An abbreviated version of the same debate occurs in Mt. 15:1–9.

(v. 2). The Greek adjective *koinos* means 'common', *i.e.* 'ritually unclean'. Mark adds his own editorial comment that the disciples' hands were 'unwashed'. It is essential to understand that the issue was not one of medical hygiene, but of ceremonial purification. In the lengthy parenthesis of verses 3 and 4 Mark gives his Gentile readers a more elaborate explanation. 'The Pharisees, and all the Jews' (because these Pharisaic principles were popular), he writes, 'do not eat unless they wash their hands, observing the tradition of the elders.' Especially 'when they come from the market place', he adds, where they might contract all sorts of defilement and where the disciples may themselves just have been,[8] 'they do not eat unless they purify themselves'. Nor is this all. There are 'many other traditions which they observe', such as the ceremonial washing 'of cups and pots and vessels of bronze'.

Mark was certainly not exaggerating the Pharisaic insistence on hand-washing. Edersheim supplies chapter and verse for the strictness with which this tradition was enjoined.[9] 'To neglect it', he writes, 'was like being guilty of gross carnal defilement' and would lead inevitably (according to their teaching) to poverty or some worse calamity. Further, 'bread eaten with unwashen hands was as if it had been filth'.

So the Pharisees came to Jesus and said: 'Why do your disciples not live according to the tradition of the elders, but eat with hands defiled?' (v. 5). It is the Lord's reply which we are going to scrutinize carefully. To begin with, He had something to say about their views on purification, and applied to them a word of God spoken through Isaiah to Israel: 'This people honours me with their lips, but their heart is far from me; in vain do they worship me. . . .'[1] The vanity of their worship is that it was external. It was an affair of the lips, not the heart. We shall consider this more fully in later chapters about the essential inwardness of Christian morality and worship.

Jesus then went on to say something about their view of tradition. This is the subject on which we must concentrate now. In opposition to the opinions of the Pharisees He enunciated three important principles. First, that Scripture is divine, while

8 Mk. 6:56.
9 Edersheim, vol. II, pp. 9, 10.
1 Verses 6, 7 quoted from Is. 29:13.

tradition is human. Secondly, that Scripture is obligatory, while tradition is optional. Thirdly, that Scripture is supreme, while tradition is subordinate. We will consider these principles in turn.

Scripture divine, tradition human

What does Jesus say about tradition? The Pharisees referred to it as 'the tradition of the elders' (vv. 3, 5). But Jesus called it 'the precepts of *men*' (v. 7) and 'the tradition of *men*' (v. 8).

Now this immediately cut the ground from under the Pharisees' feet. As we have already seen, they believed that Scripture and tradition were equally ancient, equally Mosaic, equally divine. Christ did not share their view. On the contrary, He drew a sharp distinction between the two. On the one hand there was what '*Moses* said' (v. 10), and on the other what '*you* say' (v. 11). At first sight one might suppose that this was simply to set two Jewish teachers or schools of thought in opposition to each other, Moses and the elders. But this is not at all how Jesus saw the disagreement. To Him Moses and the elders were not comparable, for the elders were fallible men with human traditions, while Moses was the spokesman of God. So what '*you* say' is equivalent to '*your* tradition' (vv. 9, 13) or 'the tradition of *men*' (v. 8), whereas what '*Moses* said' is 'the commandment of *God*' (vv. 8, 9) and 'the word of *God*' (v. 13). To put this beyond question we máy observe that the phrase 'Moses said' in verse 10 is rendered in Matthew 15 : 4 'God said', and this was the consistent custom of Jesus and His apostles. For them 'Scripture says' and 'God says' were synonymous.[2]

Thus we have our Lord's own authority for distinguishing between Scripture and tradition as between God's Word written and all human interpretations and accretions.

Put another way, we may say that the only 'tradition' which Scripture recognizes is Scripture. For 'tradition' (*paradosis*) is what is handed down, and God's purpose has been that His Word, His unique revelation given to prophets and apostles, should be transmitted from generation to generation. So the

---

[2] See *The Inspiration and Authority of the Bible* by B. B. Warfield (Presbyterian and Reformed Publishing Company, 1948), chapter VII (pp. 299-348), from an article published in 1899.

apostle Paul wrote to Timothy: 'What you have heard from me . . . entrust to faithful men who will be able to teach others also.'[3] From Paul to Timothy, from Timothy to faithful men, and from them to others also. *This* is the true apostolic succession; it is the transmission of apostolic doctrine. By this written apostolic tradition the early church learned to judge all teaching, subjecting it to the test which Paul himself had commanded, namely whether it was 'in accord with the tradition that you received from us' (*i.e.* apostles).[4] As Dean Alford expressed it when commenting on 2 Timothy 2 : 2, 'Scripture has been God's way of fixing tradition, and rendering it trustworthy at any distance of time.'[5]

Therefore as Jesus distinguished between Moses and the elders, so we must distinguish between apostolic tradition (which is Scripture) and ecclesiastical tradition (which is the teaching of the church). We must also say with Him that the latter is human, but the former divine.

Scripture obligatory, tradition optional

When we seek to follow Christ in distinguishing between Scripture and tradition, we must be careful not to overstate the case. Jesus did not reject all human traditions out of hand, forbidding His disciples to cherish or follow any. What He did was to put tradition in its place, namely a secondary place, and then, provided that it was not contrary to Scripture, to make it optional.

This is what the Pharisees were failing to do. According to the second part of the quotation from Isaiah, they were 'teaching as doctrines the precepts of men'. The word used for 'doctrine' here is *didaskalia*, which H. B. Swete in his commentary defines as 'a definite piece or course of instruction'.[6] In other words, the Pharisees were taking their own inherited but human precepts and proceeding to teach them as authoritative doctrines. They were trying to enforce upon others what God had not prescribed. In so doing they were exalting their tradition into a position of authority equivalent to the revealed commandments of God, which was tantamount to saying that the observance of their traditions was necessary to salvation. But human traditions are not 'doctrines' which everybody is required to believe and obey.

Take the purification rituals of the Pharisees. There is nothing wrong with washing the vessels from which food is to be served or our hands before eating it. Hygienically it is a very laudable practice. Ceremonially, it is a pretty harmless one. It is certainly not contrary to Scripture. At the same time, it is not commanded by God in His Word, and so the Pharisees had no right to elevate it to the status of a divine requirement and make it obligatory.

The Pharisaic regulations about 'Corban' were similar. They had to do with the keeping of vows, and the law itself said that vows should be kept. But the Pharisees went beyond Scripture and laid down detailed rules so that, in certain situations, Jesus could say to them, 'you no longer permit' a man to follow a certain course (v. 12). This is a very tell-tale expression. It indicates that the Pharisees were setting themselves up as moral judges, commanding certain practices and prohibiting others. They were giving and withholding permission in matters of conduct, for which they had no mandate from God.

So Jesus insisted that those harmless traditions, which though not required by Scripture are yet not out of accord with Scripture, must nevertheless be regarded as optional. Because they are 'the precepts of men' they may never be taught 'as doctrines' and made obligatory. Men are free with regard to them. Since Jesus neither justified nor rebuked His disciples' breach of the Pharisees' ritual tradition, this 'implied at least an attitude of indifference towards traditionalism'.[7] What He resisted and condemned was the Pharisaic insistence on the observance of tradition, 'the attempt to enforce it as an essential'.[8]

This is the doctrine of the sufficiency of Scripture, which the Reformers understood very well. The Church of England expresses the matter clearly in her Articles. Article VI, *Of the Sufficiency of the holy Scriptures for Salvation*, reads: 'Holy Scripture containeth all things necessary to salvation: so that whatsoever is not read therein, nor may be proved thereby, is not to be required of any man, that it should be believed as an article of the Faith, or be thought requisite or necessary to salvation.'

[7] Edersheim, vol. II, p. 15.
[8] Swete. Comment on Mk. 7:3.

This does not mean that the church has no authority. Harmless traditions not contrary to Scripture are permissible, but they may not be made mandatory. Article XX, *Of the Authority of the Church*, reads: 'The Church hath power to decree Rites or Ceremonies. . . . And yet it is not lawful for the Church to ordain any thing that is contrary to God's Word written. . . . Wherefore, although the Church be a witness and a keeper of holy Writ, yet, as it ought not to decree any thing against the same, so besides the same ought it not to enforce any thing to be believed for necessity of Salvation.' The distinction is clear. Under no circumstances whatever has the church authority to decree anything 'against' Scripture. 'Besides' (*i.e.* in addition to) Scripture it may make rules, but only provided that it does not require or enforce them as necessary to salvation.[9]

Perhaps I could illustrate the principle from the practice of the Church of England. It is traditional in the Church of England for the candidate for baptism to be signed with the sign of the cross on his forehead, in token that thereafter he will 'not be ashamed to confess the faith of Christ crucified'; for the bride to receive a ring from the bridegroom during the marriage ceremony; for the coffin to be brought into church during the burial service; and for ministers to wear certain robes during public worship. None of these customs is commanded in Scripture. At the same time, they are not contrary to Scripture. Therefore they are permissible, provided that they are not invested with divine authority or enforced upon people as essential to salvation.

What is true of churches is equally true of individual Christians. We may value certain traditions, either of belief or practice. For example, we may have worked out a distinctive prophetic programme which, because it is an elaboration of Scripture, belongs to the category of tradition, or we may have accepted for ourselves a certain discipline regarding prayer, Bible reading, attendance at the Lord's Supper, fasting, or Christian giving. Provided that our tradition is not contrary to Scripture, we

---

[9] Similarly the Westminster Confession refers to 'some circumstances concerning the worship of God, and government of the Church, common to human actions and societies, which are to be ordered by the light of nature and Christian prudence, according to the general rules of the word, which are always to be observed' (I.6).

have liberty to hold it ourselves as a private opinion or a private regulation. But we have no liberty to attempt to make our traditions binding on others, lest we are found 'teaching as doctrines the precepts of men'. We must give other people the liberty to reject them.

Scripture supreme, tradition subordinate

The third principle which Jesus enunciated, namely regarding the supremacy of Scripture, He developed from the teaching of the Pharisees about Corban.

'Corban' is a transliterated Hebrew word, fairly common in the Old Testament, for a gift or offering which is consecrated to God. When something was pronounced 'Corban', however, it was not necessarily given then and there for the service of God in the Temple; it could be so designated in intention rather than fact. 'The meaning might simply be, and generally was, that it was to be regarded like Corban.'[1] So the Jewish tradition grew up that things thus designated were inalienable; they could not be diverted to any other purpose. (This explains the uproar when Pilate used Corban money to build his famous aqueduct.) Further, when the word 'Corban' was used in a formula of making a vow, the vow was regarded as absolutely binding. Indeed, the Pharisees 'expressly stated that such a vow was binding even if what was vowed involved a breach of the law'.[2]

Now the case supposed in this controversy of Christ with the Pharisees is of a young man who, either piously or rashly, has taken a vow about his money. He has designated it as 'Corban' and thus (according to the tradition) has alienated it from any other use, even the support of his parents in their old age. Edersheim refers to an actual discussion in the Mishnah whether the command to honour one's parents could invalidate such a vow.[3] A negative decision was given. To the Lord Jesus, however, the opposite was obviously right. Indeed, to Him the issue was simple because Moses had settled it by a clear command and warning (v. 10). The command was 'Honour your father and your mother'[4] and the warning 'He who speaks evil of father or mother [how much more he who *does* evil to them?]',

---

[1] Edersheim, vol. II, p. 19.   [2] Edersheim, vol. II, p. 20.
[3] Edersheim, vol. II, pp. 20, 21.   [4] Ex. 20:12.

let him surely die'.[5] '*But you*', Jesus continues, emphasizing the contrast between the teaching of the Pharisees and the teaching of Moses, 'you say that if a man has alienated his wealth by a vow',[6] then 'he need not honour his father'.[7] In this way 'you no longer permit him to do anything for his father or mother, thus making void the word of God through your tradition which you hand on'. Further, 'many such things you do' (vv. 12, 13). That is, the same principle of negativing Scripture by tradition could be illustrated by other examples from your practice.

It may be helpful at this point to state Christ's second and third principles side by side. The second is that traditions which are not in conflict with Scripture (like the washing of hands and vessels) are permissible if optional. The third principle is that traditions which are in conflict with Scripture (like the Corban vow which led to the dishonouring of a man's parents) must be firmly rejected. For Scripture is always supreme and tradition must always be subordinate.

Three times Jesus repeats this third principle, in order to put it beyond doubt. Verse 8: 'You leave the commandment of God, and hold fast the tradition of men.' Verse 9: 'You have a fine way of rejecting the commandment of God, in order to keep your tradition!' Verse 13: 'thus making void the word of God through your tradition which you hand on.' In each case Jesus sets the traditions of men and the commandments of God in opposition, and forbids us to 'leave', 'reject' or 'make void' God's Word in order to 'keep' or 'hold fast' our tradition. In fact, we should do the exact reverse. Our duty is to 'keep' or 'hold fast' God's Word, and if necessary 'leave' and 'reject' our traditions in order to do so. This is even clearer in Matthew's version of this incident, where the key concept is that of 'transgression', the infringement of a law or rule. The Pharisees asked: 'Why do your disciples *transgress* the tradition of the elders?' Jesus replied: 'And why do you *transgress* the commandment of God for the sake of your tradition?'[8]

The offence of the Pharisees should now be clear. True, it was not their intention. They claimed that the oral tradition was a 'fence for Torah', that is to say, a protective bulwark to preserve the integrity of the law; 'but in actual fact it tampered

[5] *Cf.* Ex. 21:17.   [6] A paraphrase of v. 11.
[7] Mt. 15:5.   [8] Mt. 15:2, 3.

with the Law.'[9] Further, in practice they seem to have preferred their own traditions, so that Rabbi Jochanan could say 'words of Soferim (sc. the scribes) . . . are more beloved than words of Torah (sc. the law)'.[1]

This tendency Jesus firmly opposed. When Scripture and tradition are in collision, He insisted, Scripture is supreme over tradition. God's Word about the honour due to parents must take precedence over man's tradition about Corban vows. On many occasions Jesus expressed and applied this same principle. His reverent acceptance of the divine origin and supreme authority of the Old Testament Scriptures is beyond question. In the Sermon on the Mount, for example, and in His teaching about sabbath observance and divorce, He went back behind accumulated tradition and appealed direct to God's Word written. To Him Scripture was always the final court of appeal. 'Have you not read?' He would ask. 'What is written in the law?' What is written and may be read, *i.e.* the teaching of Scripture, must arbitrate in every controversy and settle every dispute.

We are now in a position to put together the three principles which Jesus expounded in this debate with the Pharisees. He taught the divinity,[2] the sufficiency and the supremacy of Scripture. That is, He affirmed Scripture's sufficiency without the addition of any binding traditions, and its supreme authority by which all traditions must be judged. And the foundation on which He built these two truths is the divine origin and inspiration of Scripture, tradition being the word of men, but Scripture the Word of God.

We turn now from biblical principle to historical illustration.

The Reformers and the supremacy of Scripture
The relation between Scripture and tradition was one of the principal issues of the Reformation. Both sides accepted the

---

[9] *The Gospel according to St. Mark (Cambridge Greek Testament).* Commentary by C. E. B. Cranfield (CUP, 1959), pp. 233, 236.
[1] Quoted by Swete in his comment on Mk. 7:9.
[2] This is not bibliolatry. I use the term in one of its accepted dictionary meanings ('divine quality, virtue or power'), with special reference to the Bible's divine origin as God's Word written.

divine inspiration and authority of the Bible. This was not a point of contention between them. The issue was whether Scripture had *sole* authority, whether its teaching was sufficient for salvation without any unbiblical accretions, and whether it was supreme over even the most ancient traditions of the church.

Rome said 'no'. Like the Pharisees she relied much on what she termed 'unwritten traditions'. Indeed there is great similarity between the Roman and the Pharisaic views of tradition. Both Pharisees and Roman Catholics believed their tradition to be as inspired as Scripture. The Pharisees traced theirs back to Moses, while the Roman Catholics traced theirs to Christ. Thus, a Rabbi could declare in the Mishnah: 'Moses received the (oral) Law from Sinai, and delivered it to Joshua and Joshua to the elders, and the elders to the prophets and the prophets to the men of the great synagogue.' Similarly, Rome asserted that her traditions had been 'received by the Apostles from the mouth of Christ Himself, or from the Apostles themselves, the Holy Ghost dictating'.[3] The Fourth Session of the Council of Trent in 1546 pronounced on the matter. 'Scripture and tradition are to be received by the Church as of equal authority,' it said. Again, the Council 'receives and venerates with equal affection of piety and reverence' both Scripture and tradition. Consequently the Church of Rome did not reform herself according to Scripture or purge out of her system those traditions about (for example) the Virgin Mary, the Mass, the priesthood, purgatory and indulgences which had grown up over the centuries but which Scripture either did not teach or actively contradicted.

The Reformers were of a different mind. *Sola Scriptura* was one of the rocks on which they built. They knew that the early church had had good reason to fix and close the canon of the New Testament. The fixing of the canon (by which the church did not invest the biblical books with an extraneous authority but simply acknowledged their own inherent authority) indicated that there was a clear line to be drawn between apostolic tradition and ecclesiastical tradition, and that the apostolic traditions of the New Testament books were the 'canon', the

[3] *The Creeds of Christendom* by Philip Schaff (6th edition, Harper, 1931), vol. II, p. 80.

78   CHRIST THE CONTROVERSIALIST

standard or measuring rule, by which the traditions of the
church must always be tested. They also knew that the early
church Fathers understood this. 'All contention which the old
fathers had with heretics was for the Scriptures', wrote Cranmer,
'. . . but for things which are not contained in the Scriptures
they never accused any man of heresy.'[4] That is, Scripture
was their rule.

This same issue between Scripture and tradition was mentioned
by Hugh Latimer in his famous 'Sermon of the Plough', preached
outside St Paul's Cathedral on 18 January 1548. In it he described the devil as 'the most diligent bishop and prelate in all
England', who is 'never out of his diocese' but is 'the diligentest
preacher in all the realm'. And where the devil is resident,
Latimer continued, 'and hath his plough going', 'there away
with books and up with candles, away with Bibles and up with
beads, . . . up with man's traditions and his laws, down with
God's tradition and His most holy word'.[5]

The reformed Church of England teaches clearly in its Articles
both the sufficiency and the supremacy of Scripture. It does
so not just in the plain statements of Articles VI and XX already
quoted, but by their frequent biblical allusions and by applying
these two principles throughout. Again and again they affirm
the acceptance of some doctrine because it 'may be proved
by most certain warrants of holy Scripture', and equally the
repudiation of another because it is 'a fond [i.e. foolish] thing
vainly invented, and grounded upon no warranty of Scripture,
but rather repugnant to the Word of God'.[6]

The reformed Church of Scotland also teaches the same
doctrine plainly: 'The whole counsel of God, concerning all
things necessary for his own glory, man's salvation, faith, and
life, is either expressly set down in scripture, or by good and
necessary consequence may be deduced from scripture: unto
which nothing at any time is to be added, whether by new
revelations of the Spirit, or traditions of men.'[7]

Not only is Scripture (in all essential matters) sufficient of

[4] Cranmer, Works, I, p. 52.
[5] Sermons of Hugh Latimer, Parker Society Edition (CUP, 1844), pp. 70, 71.
[6] These phrases are taken from Articles VIII and XXII respectively, but
similar expressions occur frequently.
[7] Westminster Confession I.6.

itself without supplementary traditions; it is also the means by which the truth and value of all traditions are to be assessed: 'The supreme Judge, by which all controversies of religion are to be determined, and all decrees of councils, opinions of ancient writers, doctrines of men, and private spirits, are to be examined, and in whose sentence we are to rest, can be no other but the Holy Spirit speaking in the scripture.'[8]

But these documents of the Reformation and of the Counter-Reformation from which I have quoted belong to the sixteenth and seventeenth centuries. What about today? Do the Roman and the Reformed Churches still stand in this matter where they stood three or four hundred years ago?

Present-day trends in the Church of Rome

We shall consider first the position of the Church of Rome. One of the two most important documents emanating from the Second Vatican Council (1963–1965) is the *Dogmatic Constitution on Divine Revelation*, which contains in six chapters the Council's teaching about revelation itself, its transmission, the inspiration and interpretation of Scripture, the Old Testament, the New Testament, and Scripture in the life of the church.

Much of it is extremely welcome. For one thing, it includes an outspoken reaffirmation of the plenary inspiration of Scripture. According to paragraph 11, the Church of Rome 'holds that the books of both the Old and New Testament in their entirety, with all their parts, are sacred and canonical because, having been written under the inspiration of the Holy Spirit . . ., they have God as their author . . .'. 'Therefore, since everything asserted by the inspired authors or sacred writers must be held to be asserted by the Holy Spirit, it follows that the books of Scripture must be acknowledged as teaching firmly, faithfully, and without error that truth which God wanted put into the sacred writings for the sake of our salvation.'

Another excellent feature of this *Dogmatic Constitution* is the new encouragement which it gives to Bible study. For centuries the laity of the Roman Catholic Church have been discouraged from reading the Scriptures, and even in some cases forbidden to do so. But now Scripture has been set free in the Church, with incalculable consequences. Paragraph 22: 'Easy access to

[8] Westminster Confession I.10.

sacred Scripture should be provided for all the Christian faithful.' A footnote comments: 'This is perhaps the most novel section of the Constitution. Not since the early centuries of the Church has an official document urged the availability of the Scriptures for all.'[9]

In the paragraph which follows theologians are urged to 'devote their energies . . . to an exploration and exposition of the divine writings', so that 'as many ministers of the divine word as possible will be able effectively to provide the nourishment of the Scriptures for the people of God . . .'.

The last paragraph (26) concludes: 'In this way, therefore, through the reading and study of the sacred books, let "the word of the Lord run and be glorified" (2 Thess. 3 : 1) and let the treasure of revelation entrusted to the Church increasingly fill the hearts of men.' Indeed, the Council expresses the hope that there will be 'a new surge of spiritual vitality from intensified veneration for God's Word, which "lasts for ever" . . .'.

Thus the Church of Rome, the most conservative of all the churches, for all her insistence that she is *semper eadem*, and despite the recent reactionary statements and reaffirmations of the Pope quoted earlier, has a biblical yeast at work in her ancient dough, whose full fermentation she may find herself unable to stop. We shall see!

Nevertheless, at least on the surface, Vatican II appears to reassert the teaching of the Council of Trent that Scripture and tradition are on a par as two separate and independent parts of the divine revelation. Paragraph 10: 'Sacred tradition and sacred Scripture form one sacred deposit of the Word of God, which is committed to the Church.' Paragraph 21: 'The Church . . . has always regarded the Scriptures together with sacred tradition as the supreme rule of faith, and will ever do so.'

At the same time, under the surface, a significant if subtle change of stance may be detected. In his Introduction to the Constitution the Very Rev. R. A. F. Mackenzie tells us that 'drama was not lacking in the document's history'. Apparently the preliminary draft submitted by the Theological Commission to the Council was so severely criticized in the first session in November 1962 that Pope John appointed a new joint com-

[9] *The Documents of Vatican II* edited by Walter M. Abbott and J. Gallagher (Chapman, 1966), pp. 125, 126.

mission to recast the text. This revised text, further amended after its presentation to the third session, was approved almost unanimously at the fourth session in 1965.

The chief difference between the first draft and the final document concerns the relation between Scripture and tradition. The original draft's first chapter was entitled 'Two Sources of Revelation', referring to Scripture and tradition. In the final document, however, two chapters are substituted for this one, the first on revelation itself and the second on its transmission, in which Scripture and tradition are 'not explicitly distinguished as separate "sources" '.[1] Instead, they are likened to two streams issuing from the same source. Paragraph 9: 'there exist a close connection and communication between sacred tradition and sacred Scripture. For both of them, flowing from the same divine wellspring, in a certain way merge into a unity and tend towards the same end.' What this seems to mean is that alongside Scripture there flows the second stream of the Church's traditional understanding of Scripture. So, in a sentence added at the last minute at Pope Paul's request,[2] 'it is not from sacred Scripture alone that the Church draws her certainty about everything which has been revealed'. 'Therefore both sacred tradition and sacred Scripture are to be accepted and venerated with the same sense of devotion and reverence.'

This last phrase, being a quotation from the Council of Trent, may give the regrettable impression that nothing has changed. Yet there is at least a change of emphasis. Pope Paul's sentence actually says, not that Rome draws her dogmas from both Scripture and tradition (which is what Trent said), but that she 'draws her certainty about everything which has been revealed' from tradition as well as Scripture. In this case the place of tradition is subsidiary after all, for as a means to certainty it is not an alternative source to Scripture but a parallel, interpretative stream. We are told that this question (whether tradition is a separate source or a subsidiary stream) 'was much debated in the Council' and that 'the majority of the Fathers preferred not to decide it one way or the other'.[3]

Yet a decision must be made on this issue sooner or later. The Roman Church cannot for ever sit on the fence. As it is, the tension between the two opinions is apparent in the Con-

[1] Abbott, p. 107.   [2] Abbott, p. 117, note.   [3] Abbott, p. 115, note.

stitution, and some of its statements seem to be mutually contra-dictory. Professor Frederick C. Grant quite properly writes in his 'Response' to the document: 'If only the Constitution had said something about the claims made for such doctrines as the Assumption of the Blessed Virgin, as based upon sound tradition, it would have clarified the minds of many inquirers. And it might have started a "dialogue" destined to open the whole question of the criteria of true tradition, and the tests by which extra-biblical teaching should be re-evaluated, and if possible reinstated in the category of "pious opinion" where it belongs (many of us think), not in the category of dogma.'[4]

One further point needs to be added. Even if tradition is relegated to a subsidiary position, as not additional to Scripture but interpretative of Scripture, although this is a gain from Trent, it does not go far enough. Theologically, we must go further (as Christ did) and say that all non-biblical tradition is fallible and needs to be corrected by Scripture. Pragmatically it is not helpful to maintain that tradition is the church's authori-tative interpretation of Scripture, for how do we know which traditions are true and which false? There were rival Rabbinic schools in Christ's day, and His appeal was direct to Scripture in order to determine the truth. There have been rival Catholic traditions too. So, for help in discerning the true from the false, the genuine from the spurious, the Roman Church appeals to the *magisterium* which it believes Christ has given it, the teaching office vested ultimately in the Pope whose *ex cathedra* utterances are regarded as infallible. Hence Pope Pius IX could dare to claim 'I am tradition'. This effectively subordinates Scripture to tradition again and puts final authority back in the hands of the church. But we must insist upon the contrary, as the Lord Jesus did, namely that ultimate authority is in Scripture, in God speaking through Scripture, for whereas tradition is oral, open and often self-contradictory, Scripture is written, fixed and always self-consistent.

Meanwhile, we may and must be thankful for those tentative concessions to the primacy of Scripture, which emerge from the Constitution like the first snowdrops heralding the end of the freeze and the beginning of spring. They at least make it possible for us, in debate with Roman Catholics, to appeal from tradition

4 Abbott, p. 132.

to Scripture. We can now challenge them to demonstrate that their tradition is in fact a legitimate elucidation of Scripture, and neither an accretion which may be dispensed with nor a contradiction which must be rejected.

Present-day trends in Protestant churches

So much for the Church of Rome. What about the churches of the Reformation? Unfortunately, the Protestant churches of the mid-twentieth century are not speaking on this issue with a clear, unequivocal voice. Indeed, we are faced with the anomaly that, just as the Roman Catholic Church is beginning to acknowledge the Reformation doctrine of the supremacy of Scripture, the Reformed churches appear to be drifting away from their Reformation mooring.

For example, the Consultation on Church Union (COCU) which has been taking place in the United States between eight large Protestant denominations, and which may secure a united American Protestant Church of some twenty-four million members, stated in 1966: 'we can no longer lean solely on Scripture as the source of divine truth, but must take greater cognizance of the great store of Christian tradition.' This is a confused and confusing statement. To take cognizance of the rich store of Christian tradition is good and right. But in order to do this there is no need to stop leaning solely on Scripture as 'the source of divine truth'.

I am glad to say that the Church of England's official position is better than this. Although it is sometimes said in Anglican circles that Scripture, tradition and reason form a 'threefold cord' which restrains and directs the Church, and although there are not lacking those who regard these three as having equal authority,[5] yet official pronouncements continue to uphold the primary, the supreme authority of Scripture, while accepting the important place of tradition and reason in the elucidation of Scripture. Thus, the report on the Bible issued by the 1958 Lambeth Conference contained this heartening statement: 'The

[5] For example, the Anglo-Catholic authors of *Catholicity*, a Study in the Conflict of Christian Traditions in the West, being a Report presented to the Archbishop of Canterbury in 1947 (Dacre Press, 1947), wrote of the possibilities of a synthesis of different views 'by a single appeal to Scripture, Tradition and sound learning that goes beyond the partisan positions' (p. 51).

Church is not "over" the Holy Scriptures, but "under" them, in the sense that the process of canonization was not one whereby the Church conferred authority on the books but one whereby the Church acknowledged them to possess authority. And why? The books were recognized as giving the witness of the Apostles to the life, teaching, death, and resurrection of the Lord and the interpretation by the Apostles of these events. To that apostolic authority the Church must ever bow.'[6]

During the revision of the Church of England's Canons in the 1950s, Draft Canon A 5 was submitted to Convocation in this form: 'The doctrine of the Church of England is grounded in the Holy Scriptures and in the teachings of the ancient Fathers and Councils of the Church agreeable to the said Scriptures, and in particular is to be found in the Thirty-nine Articles of Religion, the Book of Common Prayer, and the ordinal.' On 21 May 1957 Canon T. L. Livermore proposed an amendment, that the words 'such teaching' replace the words 'the teachings' and the words 'as are' be inserted after the word 'Church'. The purpose of the amendment was to put beyond doubt that Scripture was the primary authority and tradition secondary. The amendment was carried unanimously in the Upper House and with one dissentient in the Lower House. The Archbishop of Canterbury then told Convocation that he had been thinking of proposing an amendment of his own, namely to insert a full stop after 'the Holy Scriptures'. Although this amendment was not put to Convocation, a comma was later added, and Canon A 5 now begins: 'The doctrine of the Church of England is grounded in the Holy Scriptures, and in such teachings of the ancient Fathers and Councils of the Church as are agreeable to the said Scriptures. . . .'[7]

The tension which continues to exist in the churches regarding this matter may be illustrated from the negotiations for union between the Church of England and the Methodist Church. When the first report was published in 1963 it was found that four prominent Methodist members of the Committee had found themselves unable to sign the report. The objections of the dissentients were largely theological, and one objection was concerned with the relation between Scripture and tradition.

[6] *The Lambeth Conference 1958* (SPCK, 1958), part 2, p. 5.
[7] See *The Chronicle of Convocation* (1957), No. 1, pp. 11–20.

'The discussion of this fundamentally important subject [*i.e.* in the Report]', they wrote, 'does not recognize adequately the pre-eminent and normative place of Scripture, or set out satisfactorily its relation to tradition.'[8]

Actually the 1963 Report did contain a useful statement about the supremacy of Scripture: 'Holy Scripture is and must always be the supreme standard of faith and morals in the Church because it embodies the testimony of chosen witnesses to God's saving action. . . . Tradition, in the sense of the handing down of the faith from one generation to another, is both inevitable and inescapable. But what is to be handed down, without perversion or addition or alteration, is in the first place the apostolic testimony of Scripture. The formulation of the canon is a sufficient sign that the early Church intended to distinguish between the apostolic tradition and all later tradition, and to insist that the apostolic tradition as witness to the work of God in Christ should be the norm of all other tradition'.[9]

Commenting on this statement, the final report entitled *Anglican–Methodist Unity* clarified and strengthened its position thus: 'These assertions have the effect of establishing holy Scripture as the sole and authoritative source of "all doctrine required of necessity to eternal salvation", and as the norm and standard of doctrinal and ethical teaching, of worship, and of practice for the Church in every age.'[1] Tradition on the other hand, 'venerable and valuable though it is', and 'however high and holy', 'can never stand by itself. . . . The products of the traditionary process must be tested by the Scriptures to which they claim to be subservient, and wherever they are found deficient they must be reformed.'[2]

Some practical conclusions
So far we have concentrated on biblical principle (as expounded by Jesus in controversy with the Pharisees) and historical illustration (drawn from various official statements both ancient and modern). A practical conclusion is necessary, in order

---

[8] *Conversations between the Church of England and the Methodist Church* (SPCK and Epworth, 1963), p. 57.
[9] *Conversations*, pp. 15, 17.
[1] *Anglican–Methodist Unity, The Scheme* (SPCK and Epworth, 1968), p. 18.
[2] *The Scheme*, p. 19.

to earth our discussion of the church's principle of authority in the realities of every day. I will make three suggestions about the place of tradition.

First, we must distinguish more clearly between tradition and Scripture. Most of us Christian people have a set of cherished beliefs and practices, probably inherited from our parents or learned in childhood from the church. Too many of us have accepted them uncritically *en bloc*. And evangelical believers are by no means free of this tendency. For example, our 'touch not; taste not; handle not'[3] has often been 'smoke not, drink not, dance not'. I am not expressing an opinion on whether we should or should not engage in these habits. What I am saying is that Scripture contains no explicit pronouncement about them. These prohibitions belong therefore to 'the traditions of the evangelical elders'; they are not part of the Word of God. No Christian can escape the responsibility of trying to think biblically and to decide conscientiously about such ethical questions as these. He then has liberty to refrain or to practise at his discretion. But he has no liberty either to impose his traditions on others or to stand in judgment on others if they disagree with him. We need to say to ourselves again and again, as Christ taught the Pharisees, that 'Scripture is obligatory, but tradition optional'.

Secondly, we must value tradition for what it is, and not for what it is not. In our anxiety to assert the supremacy of Scripture, evangelicals have often been scornful of tradition. But we should not despise or reject all tradition indiscriminately. Some traditions are the church's formulations of biblical truth. The creeds and confessions of Christendom belong to this category of tradition. And very valuable they are. Indeed, we believe that the Holy Spirit Himself has guided this historical development of tradition. Professor James Orr argued in his book *The Progress of Dogma*[4] that, as the church clarified its mind down the centuries in doctrine after doctrine, the chronological order was the logical order, beginning with necessary prolegomena and with God Himself, moving on to the relations between the three Persons of the Trinity and between the two natures of Christ, then to the great doctrines of man, sin, grace, the atonement and salvation. Is it not right to trace the hand of the Holy

[3] Col. 2:21, AV.   [4] Hodder and Stoughton, 1901.

Spirit in this process of developing understanding? One reason for rejecting the theological radicalism which wants to replace the 'outworn' categories of ancient formularies with something quite new is precisely that it shows little respect for tradition (in the sense of historical theology) and therefore for the work of the Holy Spirit. Having said this, however, we must add that even this hallowed historical tradition is not sacrosanct like Scripture. For, though in the production of both the Holy Spirit has been active, His work of revelation (in the authors of Scripture) and of illumination (in the interpreters of Scripture) must be distinguished. Ecclesiastical creeds and confessions are not infallible. They may be criticized and amended as the Holy Spirit causes further light to break upon us from Scripture. The only unalterable formulations of truth are the biblical formulations themselves.

Thirdly, we must rigorously subordinate tradition to Scripture. This applies to both churches and individuals.

Every church should be engaged in continuous self-reformation, scrutinizing its traditions in the light of Scripture and where necessary modifying them. This is particularly true in the case of churches desiring to unite. Evangelicals hold different views regarding the nature of Christian unity and whether the visible, organic union of churches is a desirable goal. But all would agree that no movement towards reunion can be pleasing to God or beneficial to the church which is not at the same time a movement towards reformation. True unity will always be unity in truth, and truth means biblical truth. If only church leaders would sit down with their Bibles, would distinguish clearly between apostolic traditions (which are biblical) and ecclesiastical traditions (which are not), and would agree to subordinate the latter to the former by requiring the former of each other but giving each other liberty over the latter, immediate and solid advance could be made.

It is this distinction, already outlined, on which Professor Oscar Cullmann has been so strongly insisting. 'There is . . . a difference between apostolic tradition and ecclesiastical tradition,' he writes, 'the former being the foundation of the latter. They cannot, therefore, be coordinated.'[5] The distinction is

[5] Chapter IV, 'The Tradition' (1953) in *The Early Church* by Oscar Cullmann (SCM Press, 1956), pp. 79, 80.

due to the uniqueness of the apostolate, which the early church plainly recognized: 'The fixing of the Christian canon of Scripture means that *the Church itself*, at a given time, traced a clear and definite line of demarcation between the period of the apostles and that of the Church, between the time of foundation and that of construction, between the apostolic community and the Church of the bishops, in other words, between apostolic tradition and ecclesiastical tradition. Otherwise, the formation of the canon would be meaningless' (p. 89). The result of this recognition, issuing in the fixing of the canon, has been to give the church 'a *norm* or *criterion*' (p. 83) by which to judge all post-apostolic teaching. The church's teaching ministry is not thereby abolished, but humbly self-limited. 'The teaching-office of the Church did not abdicate in this final act of fixing the canon, but made its future activity dependent on a superior norm' (p. 91).

Let me relate this principle to current reunion proposals. The great bugbear in these schemes is the so-called 'historic episcopate', that is to say, episcopacy understood in Catholic terms as a historic succession from the apostles. Now quite apart from the question whether such an episcopate is 'historic' (as is claimed) either in origin or in unbroken continuity, it is certainly a non-biblical tradition. *Episkopē* (pastoral oversight) is required by Scripture, and is set forth there as a gift of God to His church; but monarchical episcopacy in the historic or Catholic sense is not. Therefore churches would be right to insist on the former, but not the latter.

The question has been the chief bone of contention both in the Anglican–Methodist unity scheme and in the conversations between the Church of England and the Church of Scotland. The Scots are quite right to argue that they already have in their presbyters a perfectly scriptural form of *episkopē*; there is no justification for trying to impose on them another and a particular form of episcopacy which they do not want.

Dr Ian Henderson, formerly Professor of Systematic Theology in Glasgow University, wrote an extremely outspoken book on this subject. He gave it the title *Power without Glory* and the subtitle 'A study in ecumenical politics'.[6] Chapter 13 is called 'Ecumenicity and Anglican Imperialism'.[7] Professor Henderson agrees that the Church of England is 'one of the great indigenous

[6] Hutchinson, 1967.   [7] *Power without Glory*, pp. 97–106.

churches of Christendom', but adds that 'in the fantasy world of ecclesiastical power mythology, the Church of England bishops are the successors of the apostles'. Hence what he describes as the Church of England's 'ruthless series of take-over bids', which 'in ecumenical terminology . . . are called Church unions'. 'Basically then', he continues, 'Anglican diplomatic policy is the extermination of all Protestant (*i.e.* non-episcopally ordained) ministers', and he attributes the policy to arrogant English nationalism, 'one of the most grotesque manifestations of 20th century racialism'. Now I confess that I find Professor Henderson's tone polemical and his language at times intemperate. I also doubt if he is correct to ascribe either nationalist or racialist motives to the Anglican episcopate! Nevertheless, his basic thesis is incontrovertible.

Anglican evangelicals may regard the historic episcopate as an acceptably biblical form of *episkopē* (though it has by no means always conformed to the scriptural ideals of pastoral oversight). They may also value it as a symbol of continuity and a focus of unity in the church. But to acknowledge its potential value as a domestic institution is one thing; to insist upon it as a non-negotiable condition of union with all other churches is quite another. Those who do this are not only hindering the church's advance to unity but infringing a principle which the church's Lord laid down. They are teaching as a doctrine a precept of men. They are failing to subordinate tradition to Scripture.

It is easy to point an accusing finger at others, however; easy to see the speck of sawdust in the eye of others and miss the log in our own. The need to subordinate tradition to Scripture is not only the corporate affair of churches; it is the individual Christian's responsibility also. It is urgently necessary for us to study the Scripture with greater industry and humility, with a view to submitting our whole mind, will and life to what God has said in His Word. Only so can we 'learn . . . to live according to scripture'.[8]

[8] 1 Cor. 4:6.

Jesus had two controversies with the Jews about Scripture. The first, which we considered in the last chapter, concerned its nature as God's Word written, and in consequence its supremacy over the traditions of men and its sufficiency for salvation without them. His second controversy, to which we turn our attention in this chapter, was concerned principally with its function, the purpose for which God had given it to His people.

Jesus Christ accorded to Scripture a very exalted position. He clearly asserted its divine origin and authority. But He also warned us of the possibility of over-exalting it (as the Jews were doing) by making it an end in itself. The God-ordained purpose of Scripture is to point and lead people to Christ. It was never intended as an end in itself, but as a means to that end.

This further controversy of Christ (about the true function of Scripture) is relevant to the theological debate of our time. As we have seen, many people have too 'low' a view of Scripture; they do not accept it (as Jesus did) as the written Word of God. At the same time, there are others whose view of Scripture is too 'high'. They regard Scripture with an almost superstitious reverence. They become so absorbed in Scripture itself that they lose sight of its purpose, which is to manifest Christ to them. They earn for themselves the title 'bibliolater' or 'Bible-worshipper', for they behave as if Scripture and not Christ were the object of their devotion.

Now evangelicals have, or should have, an extremely high view of the divine inspiration of Scripture (a view as high as Christ's own view, in fact). But we must be careful not to incur the charge of bibliolatry, or if we find ourselves thus accused we must be able to refute the charge. We must demonstrate clearly in our behaviour and attitude that our ultimate pre-occupation is not with Scripture itself, but with the Christ to whom Scripture bears witness.

This is how Jesus reproached His contemporaries:

'You search the scriptures, because you think that in them you have eternal life; and it is they that bear witness to me; yet you refuse to come to me that you may have life.'[1]

In these verses Jesus gave a succinct summary of both the divine origin and the practical purpose of Scripture.

Scripture's divine origin

'It is they that bear witness to me', He said, and in so saying implied that their witness is divine.

In order to grasp the force of this, we have to see it in its context. Most of John 5, from which our quotation is taken, is devoted to the nature of the testimony which is borne to Christ and which warrants our faith in Him. The chapter begins on a sabbath day in Jerusalem, beside the Sheep Gate pool called Bethesda or Bethzatha. Here Jesus healed a paralysed man who had been ill for thirty-eight years. 'Rise,' He said to him, 'take up your pallet, and walk.' The Jews immediately raised objections. First, they reproached the man for unlawfully carrying his pallet on the sabbath (v. 10). Then they reproached Jesus for having unlawfully healed him on the sabbath (v. 16).

In the discourse which follows Jesus enlarged on His claim to be working in collaboration with His Father (v. 17). The divine work on which He was engaged was twofold – giving life to the dead (v. 21) and judging (v. 22). Everyone who hears and believes, He declared, then and there receives eternal life and will escape judgment; he has already passed out of death into life (v. 24).

Having made this astonishing claim, the Lord Jesus went on to repeat it yet more forcefully. Already the dead were hearing His voice, He maintained, and those who were hearing were receiving life and emerging from their spiritual graves (v. 25). That is, a sifting process was going on, because the Father had given to the Son both to have life in Himself and authority to execute judgment (vv. 26, 27). Further, on the last day, *all* in the tombs ('all' is emphatic) would hear His voice and come

[1] Jn. 5:39, 40.

forth. Then the sifting of judgment would be brought to completion, for some would rise 'to the resurrection of life', others 'to the resurrection of judgment' (vv. 28, 29).

This twofold claim of Jesus (to have authority to give life and to execute judgment) had tremendous implications, which the Jews were not slow to grasp. It is not surprising to read that they sought to kill Him for what they supposed to be blasphemy (v. 18). For life-giving and judging are both divine prerogatives. Yet Jesus dared to say that they had been committed to Him. Already at that time He was quickening some and judging others, He said; and on the last day His work as Life-giver and Judge would reach its consummation.

But could men credit His claims? It is to this question that Jesus now proceeds. He begins by clearing Himself of all proud or independent pretensions. He is not acting on His own authority, but on God's, He says. Nor is He seeking His own will, but God's (v. 30). In the same way (v. 31) He does not rely on His own testimony (for nobody can be a witness in his own cause), but on God's. Verse 32: 'There is another who bears witness to me, and I know that the testimony which he bears to me is true.' This *allos* ('another') is God the Father. True, there were other human witnesses and still are. There was John the Baptist (v. 32), 'a burning and shining lamp' (v. 35). There was John the fourth Evangelist also, whose whole Gospel is a testimony to Christ.[2] But so far-reaching were the claims of Jesus that He needed stronger testimony than that of men. He needed *divine* testimony.

And this is what He claimed to have. 'Not that the testimony which I receive is from man. . . . But the testimony which I have is greater than that of John. . . . And the Father who sent me has himself borne witness to me' (vv. 34, 36, 37).

What, then, is the Father's testimony to the Son? What form has this divine witness taken? Jesus explains that it is a twofold testimony – in works and in words. First, in works. 'The works which the Father has granted me to accomplish, these very works which I am doing, bear me witness that the Father has sent me' (v. 36; *cf*. 14 : 10, 11). So the mighty works of Jesus, because they were done by the Father's power, were the first part of the Father's witness to Him. But the Father's

[2] Jn. 20:31.

testimony takes a second form too. 'And the Father who sent me has himself borne witness to me' (v. 37), not now indirectly through the works, but in some way directly, 'Himself'. Further, He 'has borne witness to me' (a perfect tense), which implies that it is a past witness whose validity continues into the present. How? Not in voice ('his voice you have never heard'), nor in vision ('his form you have never seen'), but in a written word which could be received, but alas! 'you do not have his word abiding in you', which is evident because 'you do not believe him whom he has sent' (vv. 37, 38). 'You search the scriptures . . .; and it is they that bear witness to me; yet you refuse to come to me. . . .' (vv. 39, 40). Thus, the Scriptures are the Father's word which does not abide in them, the Father's testimony which they have read but rejected.

Christ's view of Scripture

Looking back over the chapter which we have surveyed, the sequence of thought is plain. Jesus was advancing great claims when He said He had authority to quicken and to judge, for these are activities of God. When challenged, He said He had testimony enough to substantiate His claims, neither self-testimony, nor human testimony, but divine. And this divine testimony was borne to Him partly through the mighty works which the Father had given Him to do, but especially through the written word of Scripture.

This, then, was Jesus Christ's view of the Scriptures. Their witness is God's witness. The testimony of the Bible is the testimony of God. And the chief reason why the Christian believes in the divine origin of the Bible is that Jesus Christ Himself taught it.

Moreover, He taught it consistently. He adopted towards the Scriptures of the Old Testament an attitude of reverent assent and submission, and He maintained this position throughout His life and ministry, including the post-resurrection period. According to John He said 'scripture cannot be broken',[3] and according to Matthew 'not an iota, not a dot, will pass from the law until all is accomplished'.[4] He accepted the statements of Scripture without question, believing them to be true. He predicted with confidence His rejection by His own people,

[3] Jn. 10:35.   [4] Mt. 5:18.

His sufferings, death and resurrection, because thus it was written. He obeyed the requirements and applied the principles of Scripture in His everyday life. He voluntarily accepted a position of humble subordination to what Scripture said. The word *gegraptai* ('it stands written') was enough to settle any issue for Him.[5] He understood His mission in the light of Old Testament prophecy, recognizing and declaring Himself to be both Daniel's Son of man and Isaiah's suffering Servant of the Lord. At least from the age of 12 He felt the compulsion of Scripture upon His soul, an inner constraint to fulfil the role which Scripture portrayed for Him. Thus, 'Did you not know that I must be in my Father's house?' 'He began to teach them that the Son of man must suffer many things, and be rejected . . ., and be killed, and after three days rise again.' 'The Son of man goes as it is written of him.' 'Behold, we are going up to Jerusalem, and everything that is written of the Son of man by the prophets will be accomplished.'[6] No wonder the apostle Paul could later write that He 'became obedient unto death'.[7] When Peter tried to avert His arrest in the garden, Jesus rebuked him: 'Do you think that I cannot appeal to my Father, and he will at once send me more than twelve legions of angels? But how then should the scriptures be fulfilled, that it must be so?'[8]

Further, what He Himself believed and practised with regard to the authority of Scripture He expected others to believe and practise also. In debate with religious leaders, as we have seen, it was to Him axiomatic that Scripture must be the court of appeal. His great complaint against the Jews was, 'Have you not read?' Ignorance of Scripture had caused the Sadducees to err, and disregard for Scripture the Pharisees; while to some of His own disciples after the resurrection He had to say: 'O foolish men, and slow of heart to believe all that the prophets have spoken! Was it not necessary that the Christ should suffer these things and enter into his glory?' Then, Luke adds, 'beginning with Moses and all the prophets, he interpreted to them in all the scriptures the things concerning himself'.[9]

And all this personal submission to Scripture and this commendation of Scripture to others were due to His belief that

[5] *E.g.* Mt. 4:4, 7, 10.
[7] Phil. 2:8.
[9] Lk. 24:25–27; *cf.* vv. 44–47.

[6] Lk. 2:49; Mk. 8:31; 14:21; Lk. 18:31.
[8] Mt. 26:53, 54.

what Scripture said God said. He referred to the human authors, but took it for granted that behind them all was a single divine Author. He could equally say 'Moses said' or 'God said'.[1] He could quote a comment of the narrator in Genesis 2 : 24 as an utterance of the Creator Himself.[2] Similarly He said, 'Well did Isaiah prophesy of you hypocrites, as it is written', when what He went on to quote is the direct speech of the Lord God.[3] It is from Jesus Himself that the New Testament authors have gained their conviction of the dual authorship of Scripture. For them it was just as true to say that 'God spoke of old to our fathers by [i.e. through] the prophets'[4] as it was to say that 'men moved by the Holy Spirit spoke from God'.[5] God did not speak in such a way as to obliterate the personality of the human authors, nor did men speak in such a way as to corrupt the Word of the divine Author. God spoke. Men spoke. Neither truth must be allowed to detract from the other.

So Jesus Christ endorsed the authority of the Old Testament. There is no occasion on which He contradicted it, or gave the slightest hint that He questioned its divine origin. His only condemnation was of men's ignorance and perversion of it.[6] He also made provision for the writing of the New Testament, by appointing the Twelve (to whom after the resurrection He added Paul) to be His 'apostles' or special delegates, giving them three years' intensive training and eyewitness experience, investing them with His personal authority, sending them out to teach in His name and promising them an extraordinary inspiration of the Spirit to bring to their remembrance what He had taught them and to lead them into all the truth.

So the Christian accepts the Bible because of Christ. Christ Himself thought of Scripture in terms of a divine word or testimony.

Returning to John 5 : 39, 40, the quarrel which Jesus had with the Jews was not over their *view* of Scripture, but over their *use* of it. They too accepted its divine *provenance* (although

---

[1] E.g. Mk. 7:10; Mt. 15:4.
[2] Mt. 19:4, 5.
[3] Mk. 7:6; cf. Is. 29:13.
[4] Heb. 1:1.
[5] 2 Pet. 1:21.
[6] For the scribal misinterpretations which He rejected, see Mt. 5:21-48, and a comment about them in chapter 5 of this book.

God's word was not 'abiding' in them, v. 38). But they misunderstood its purpose. We need now to consider what the
Jews were doing and then what they ought to have been doing.
In this way we shall see contrasted with one another the wrong
and the right use of Scripture.

The wrong use of Scripture

First, what the Jews were actually doing is an example of the
wrong use of Scripture.

'You search the scriptures,' Jesus said (v. 39). The mood of
the Greek verb could be imperative (AV 'Search the Scriptures'),
but it is more likely to be indicative. The Revised Version,
Revised Standard Version and New English Bible all take it
thus and understand Jesus to have been making a statement,
not issuing a command. But what is wrong with searching the
Scriptures? We shall see.

The Jews of that day were meticulous students of Scripture.
They knew that they were greatly privileged to have been
'entrusted with the oracles of God'.[7] God had not dealt thus
with any other nation; the nations did not know His ordinances.[8]
So Israel prized the Scriptures highly, rejoicing at God's Word
'like one who finds great spoil',[9] valuing it more 'than gold,
even much fine gold' and finding it 'sweeter also than honey
and drippings of the honeycomb'.[1]

This led them to 'search' the Scriptures. The Greek word is
used in the New Testament of God and Christ searching men's
hearts and of the Holy Spirit searching God's depths.[2] It expresses the most painstaking perseverance. Surely then, one
may ask, this was a wholly estimable procedure? Is it not right
and necessary to search the Scriptures? Would it not be good
if we ourselves were as zealous in our study of Scripture as they
were? Yes indeed. It is not for this that Jesus criticized them.

Their mistake comes to light when we read the rest of Christ's
sentence: 'You search the scriptures, because you think that in
them you have eternal life.' The complaint of Jesus is expressed
not so much in the words 'you search' as in the words 'you
think'. He does not reproach them because they searched the

[7] Rom. 3:1, 2.   [8] Ps. 147:19, 20.
[9] Ps. 119:162.   [1] Ps. 19:10.
[2] Rom. 8:27; Rev. 2:23; 1 Cor. 2:10.

Scriptures, but because they regarded their search as an end in itself. They misunderstood Scripture's God-intended function, which is to point beyond itself to Christ.

Archbishop Temple comments that 'the word for *search* does not suggest spiritual penetration but meticulous analysis': Westcott adds that it indicates 'that minute, intense investigation of Scripture which issued in the allegorical and mystical interpretations of the *Midrash*'. The scribes, for example, whose task it was to copy and teach the sacred text, subjected it to the closest scrutiny. They weighed its every syllable. They went so far as to count up the number of words, even letters, of each book. And they gave themselves all this labour, not only for the sake of accurate copying but because they foolishly imagined that eternal life consisted in such accurate knowledge.[3] Like some modern Bible commentators and Bible readers, they became so engrossed in the *words* that they lost sight of the *truth* which the words expressed. They were not concerned about the *message* of Scripture (they did not understand this, let alone embrace and obey it), but only about *meanings*. If they could but search and know and memorize and quote the Word of God, they reckoned that they had eternal life.

Westcott gives an example of this emphasis on head-knowledge: 'Hillel used to say . . . more Torah (sc. law), more life (Prov. 3 : 1 ff.) . . . He who has gotten to himself words of Torah has gotten to himself the life of the world to come.' As the New English Bible renders verse 39: 'You study the scriptures diligently, supposing that in having them you have eternal life.' These contemporaries of Jesus were not like those noble Jews of Beroea who were not content merely with searching the Scriptures daily, but engaged in this task in order 'to see if these things [*i.e.* which Paul was preaching] were so'.[4] No doubt they intended, if they were convinced, to put their trust in the Christ whom Paul was proclaiming. But the Jews to whom Jesus spoke had no such excellent reason for searching the Scriptures. They simply searched the Scriptures. They imagined that to possess Scripture was tantamount to possessing life. Their study was an end in itself. In this they were grievously deceived.

[3] For this Jewish confidence in the mere possession of sacred knowledge, *cf.* Rom. 2:17–20.
[4] Acts 17:11.

The right use of Scripture

Having considered what the Jews were doing (or the wrong use of Scripture), we are in a position now to turn to what they should have been doing (or the right use of Scripture). The next phrase of our Lord's speech makes this clear: 'it is they that bear witness to me; yet you refuse to come to me that you may have life.' In these words the divinely ordained purpose of Scripture is made plain. Far from being an end in itself, Scripture is a means to the end of finding life in Christ. It therefore bears witness to Christ, so that people will come to Christ for life. Yet the Jews had missed both these points.

First, they should have seen Christ in Scripture. We have already seen that the biblical testimony is *divine* testimony; we must now see that it is divine testimony *to Christ*. Indeed, the three Persons of the Trinity are all involved in Scripture, for Scripture is the Father's testimony to the Son through the Spirit.

Jesus was, of course, referring to the Old Testament. The Old Testament is a book of hope, of unfulfilled expectation. From beginning to end it looks forward to Christ. Its many promises through Abraham, Moses and the prophets find their fulfilment in Christ.[5] Its law, with its unbending demands, was man's 'custodian until Christ came', keeping him confined and under restraint, even in bondage, until Christ should set him free.[6] Its sacrificial system, teaching day after day that without the shedding of blood there could be no forgiveness, prefigured the unique bloodshedding of the Lamb of God.[7] Its kings, for all their imperfections, foreshadowed the Messiah's perfect reign of righteousness and peace. And its prophecies are all focused upon Him. Thus Jesus Christ is the seed of the woman who would bruise the serpent's head, the posterity of Abraham through whom all the families of the earth would be blessed, the star that would come forth out of Jacob and the sceptre that would rise out of Israel.[8] Jesus Christ is also the priest after the order of Melchizedek, the king of David's line, the servant of the Lord God who would suffer and die for the sins of the people, the Son of God who would inherit the nations, and the Son of man, coming with the clouds of heaven, to whom would be given

---

[5] *Cf.* 2 Cor. 1:20.   [6] See Gal. 3:23 – 4:7.
[7] Heb. 9:22.   [8] Gn. 3:15; 12:1–3; Nu. 24:17.

dominion, glory and a kingdom, that all peoples, nations and languages should serve him for ever.[9] Directly or indirectly Jesus Christ is the grand theme of the Old Testament. Consequently He was able to interpret to His disciples 'in all the scriptures the things concerning himself'.[1]

The contemporaries of Jesus were greatly favoured in that they were allowed to witness the fulfilment of accumulated prophecy. 'Blessed are your eyes,' Jesus could say to His disciples, 'for they see, and your ears, for they hear. Truly, I say to you, many prophets and righteous men longed to see what you see, and did not see it, and to hear what you hear, and did not hear it.'[2] But the unbelieving Jews did not see Him. They did not even see Him in Scripture. For all their zealous searching of the Scriptures, they missed the Scriptures' chief subject.

If Christ is the heart of the Old Testament, this is even more obvious in the New. The Gospels recount His earthly career, His virgin birth and sinless life, His gracious words and mighty works, His sinbearing death, His glorious resurrection and ascension. The book of Acts describes His gift of the Spirit on the Day of Pentecost, and what He continued to do and to teach by His Spirit through His apostles. The Epistles unfold more fully the unparalleled glory of His divine-human Person, saving work and coming kingdom, and tell us how we should live in the light of these truths. The Revelation lifts our eyes beyond earth and history, up to heaven where Christ is seen to share God's eternal throne and on to the end when He will come again in majesty, take His power and reign. Yet there are some people who read the whole Bible, New Testament as well as Old, without realizing that its principal purpose is to bear witness to Jesus Christ!

The Bible is full of Christ. Some of the old English commentators used to put it like this: Just as in England every road, lane and path, linking on to others, will ultimately lead you to London, so in the Bible every book, chapter and verse, linking on to others, will ultimately lead you to Christ.

The Jews' two mistakes

Thus the first tragedy about those Jewish contemporaries of

---

[9] Ps. 110:4; Je. 23:5, 6; Is. 52:13 – 53:12; Ps. 2:7–9; Dn. 7:13, 14.
[1] Lk. 24:27.   [2] Mt. 13:16, 17.

Christ is that they searched the Scriptures, the very Scriptures which bear witness to Christ, but failed to see the Christ to whom the Scriptures bear such constant testimony.

The second tragedy is this: they should have come to Christ for life. We have seen that the Bible is testimony to Christ. But what is the purpose of this biblical testimony to Him? It is not just that we should look at Him, but that we should go to Him in order to receive life from Him. The true function of Scripture is to testify to Christ so plainly and powerfully that first we see Him, and secondly we believe in Him for life. Thus life comes through faith, and faith comes through testimony.

John himself emphasizes this towards the end of his Gospel: 'these [i.e. signs] are written that you may believe that Jesus is the Christ, the Son of God, and that believing you may have life in his name.'[3] The apostle Paul writes something almost identical to Timothy: 'the sacred writings . . . are able to instruct you for salvation through faith in Christ Jesus.'[4] So Christ and His apostles teach the same sequence of events. 'Salvation' or 'life' is in Christ. Therefore the Scriptures set Christ forth as the Saviour, the Giver of life, in order to elicit our faith in Him.

The Jews should have come to Christ to receive life. But they did not. It is partly that they were blind: 'You think' – and think wrongly – Jesus said, that life is in the Scriptures. But it is especially that they were stubborn: 'you will not come to me to receive life.' These words of Christ are very revealing, this 'you think' and 'you refuse'. They show that the controlling factor in our behaviour is not only our reason and our understanding, but our will. Perhaps these Jews were using theology to rationalize their sinful unwillingness to come to Christ.

We can now see the tragic folly of their second mistake. They were using the Scriptures as an end instead of as a means to an end. Their view of Scripture was academic instead of practical. They imagined they could find eternal life in the Scriptures, whereas eternal life is to be found only in the Christ to whom the Scriptures testify. As Marcus Dods has put it: 'they do not give life . . .; they lead to the Lifegiver.'[5] Since

[3] Jn. 20:31.   [4] 2 Tim. 3:15.
[5] *The Gospel of John* (*The Expositor's Greek Testament*). Commentary by M. Dods (Hodder and Stoughton, 1897), *ad loc.*

they bear witness *concerning* (Gk. *peri*) Christ, it is only reasonable that we should go *to* (Gk. *pros*) Christ.

A simple illustration may help to show the extreme stupidity of the Jews, and of all readers of the Bible who never look beyond it to Christ. Supposing we decide one day to go on a family picnic to a beauty spot such as Box Hill in Surrey. We get into the car and drive off in the direction of the destination which we have chosen. After a while we come to the signpost marked 'Box Hill'. What now? Do we immediately stop the car, get out and have our picnic round the signpost? Of course not. The idea is ridiculous. We follow the signpost to Box Hill and have our picnic there.

Now the Bible is a signpost – not to Box Hill, but to Calvary's Hill, where Christ died for sinners. It thus shows us the way to God, to forgiveness, to heaven, to holiness, because it points us to Christ who is the way to all these. True, we often gather round the Scriptures in Christian fellowship. But we do not stop there. We do not have our picnic round the signpost. Christ, not the Bible, is the object of our faith and the centre of our fellowship.

So evangelical Christians are not bibliolaters. If we value the Scriptures very highly (which we do), this is not for themselves, but because they are the Father's testimony to Christ. A young man treasures his sweetheart's photographs and letters, but only because they speak to him of her. So too Christians love the Bible, because it is Christ's portrait and speaks to us of Him.

To suppose that salvation lies in a book is as foolish as supposing that health lies in a prescription. When we are ill and the doctor prescribes some medicine for us, does he intend that we should go home with the prescription, read it, study it and learn it by heart? Or that we should frame it and hang it on our bedroom wall? Or that we tear it into fragments and eat the pieces three times a day after meals? The absurdity of these possibilities is obvious. The prescription itself will not cure us. The whole purpose of a prescription is to get us to go to the chemist, obtain the medicine prescribed and drink it. Now the Bible contains the divine prescription for sin-sick souls. It specifies the only medicine which can save us from perishing. In brief, it tells us of Jesus Christ who died for us and rose again.

But we do not worship the Bible as if it could save us; we go to Christ. For the overriding purpose of the Bible is to send us to Christ and persuade us to drink the water of life which He offers.

What Christ said about the Scriptures is equally true of the sacraments, namely Baptism and the Lord's Supper. Their function and purpose are the same. Both the Scriptures and the sacraments are God-given signposts (the Scriptures in written words, the sacraments in visible words or pictures) directing our attention away from themselves to Christ. Verbally in Scripture, visually in sacrament, Jesus Christ is set forth as the only Saviour of sinners. But neither Scripture nor sacrament is an end in itself. Both are means to an end, namely that we find salvation (understood in its full New Testament sense) in Christ. Thus both are means of grace, *media* through which God's grace is offered to us, because they exhibit Christ to us and kindle our faith in Him. Indeed, 'the sacraments function as a means of *grace* because, and only because, God uses them, as He uses His Word, as a means to *faith*'.[6] So the evangelical should steadfastly repudiate any *ex opere operato* view of either Scripture or sacrament. Neither the reading of the Bible, nor the receiving of Baptism or Holy Communion brings any automatic blessing. God's Word read and preached does not benefit a congregation unless it 'meets with faith in the hearers'.[7] Nor are the sacraments beneficial to the unbelieving. Since they are 'visible words', they also must be met with faith. Indeed, 'in such only as worthily receive the same they have a wholesome effect or operation'.[8] And 'worthy' reception means believing reception.

To become engrossed in a book on the one hand, or in bread, wine and water on the other, is therefore to overthrow the God-ordained function of both Scripture and sacrament. It is just as possible to have superstitious views of the Bible as it is

[6] Dr J. I. Packer in an article on the sacraments published in *Church Gazette*, September/October 1962.
[7] Heb. 4:2; *cf.* Rom. 10:17.
[8] Article XXV, *Of the Sacraments. Cf.* Westminster Confession XXVII.3: 'The grace which is exhibited in or by the sacraments, rightly used, is not conferred by any power in them.' It depends rather 'upon the work of the Spirit, and the word of institution; which contains . . . a promise of benefit to worthy receivers'.

to have superstitious views of the consecrated elements at Communion. But we should not fall into this trap. This is not to say that we do not value both Scriptures and sacraments very highly. We do. We do not forget that both have a divine origin and appointment. But we also remember that God has given us both in order to display Christ before the eyes of our heart, to attract our attention to Him and to draw out our faith in Him. Scripture and sacrament alike are Christ-conscious, not self-conscious.

When somebody first handles a pair of binoculars, having never seen such a thing before, he is very likely to misuse them by looking *at* them, not realizing that their purpose is to look *through* them in order to see and appreciate better the beauties of the countryside. So people misunderstand the purpose of Scripture and sacrament. They are binoculars for the magnification of Jesus Christ. We are to look through them, not at them. Our gaze is to be on Christ.

The need for obedience

How, then, shall we avoid making the same foolish mistakes as the Jews of our Lord's day? It would be salutary to remind ourselves of certain simple facts.

First, it is not enough to *possess* a Bible. It is extraordinary how much primitive superstition lurks in the human heart. There are people whose only acquaintance with the Bible is that they have a copy on a bookshelf somewhere. They suppose that its presence there somehow adds sanctity to the home. Maybe it has sentimental value because it is a family heirloom or Sunday School prize or Confirmation present. Some speak of it with bated breath as the 'Holy Bible'. If it wasn't so bulky, they might even carry it around with them for luck, like a charm.

Next, it is not enough to *read* the Bible, or hear it read in church. Neither public nor private Bible reading is to be an end in itself. There is neither merit nor profit in the reading of Scripture for its own sake, but only if it effectively introduces us to Jesus Christ. There is no special value in reading it as great literature either. The Bible was never 'designed to be read as literature'; it was designed by God as a testimony to Christ to persuade us to go to Him. Whenever the Bible is read, in private, in family prayers or in church, what is needed is an eager expectation that through it we may meet Christ.

Thirdly, it is not enough to *study* the Bible. Some Christians 'search the scriptures' today, like the Jews of old. They find it a fascinating textbook. They pride themselves on their biblical knowledge and excel in tracing the biblical allusions in cross-word puzzle clues. Like Apollos they are 'mighty in the scriptures'. They have read it many times from cover to cover and committed large portions of it to memory. Fine! But an accumulation of Bible knowledge is one thing; a growing personal knowledge of Jesus Christ, whom to know is eternal life, is quite another.

No. What is required is that we *obey* the Bible. The best way to honour this book as God's book is to do what it says. And if we do what it says, we shall keep coming to Christ for the supply of all our needs. We shall never be satisfied to search the Scriptures; we shall search for Christ in the Scriptures and go on searching until we find Him. Then He will never need to address to us the kind of rebuke which He administered to His Jewish contemporaries and say: 'You search the Scriptures. You are a member of the Scripture Union and you read your portion every day. You even memorize verses and call yourself a Bible student. But you will not come to *me* for life.'

At the Charles Simeon centenary in Cambridge Dr Christopher Chavasse, Bishop of Rochester, summed up the centrality of Christ in Scripture with these words: 'The Bible . . . is the portrait of our Lord Jesus Christ. The Gospels are the Figure itself in the portrait. The Old Testament is the background, leading up to the divine Figure, pointing toward it, and absolutely necessary for the composition as a whole. The Epistles serve as the dress and accoutrements of the Figure, explaining and describing it. And then, while by our Bible reading we study the portrait as a great whole, the miracle happens! The Figure comes to life! And, stepping from the canvas of the written word, the everlasting Christ of the Emmaus Story becomes Himself our Bible teacher to interpret to us in all the Scriptures the things concerning Himself.'

From the verses in John 5 which we have been considering Jesus indicates that the Scriptures have both a divine origin and a practical purpose. We learn their divine origin from Christ's testimony to them. We learn their practical purpose from their testimony to Christ. There is therefore between Christ (the living Word) and Scripture (the written Word) this reciprocal testimony. Each bears witness to the other. Because Christ bears witness to Scripture, we believe it. Because Scripture bears witness to Christ, we go to Him.

4 SALVATION: MERIT OR MERCY?

Two of the most fundamental issues of religion concern authority and salvation, the source of authority and the way of salvation. That is, two questions every religious person is bound to ask are, first, how can I know what to believe, and secondly, how can I be reconciled to God? These questions are to some extent common to all religions. The very fact that they are asked presupposes a degree of common understanding about man's limitations – of mind (since he is finite, how can he know God?) and of character (since he is sinful, how can he reach God?).

The divine initiative

The Christian answer to both questions is to direct the enquirer's attention to God Himself, and to affirm that God has taken the initiative to do for man what man could not do for himself. By what authority can I know what is true? Answer: because God has spoken. By what means can I be saved? Answer: because God has acted. The Christian word for this divine initiative is 'grace'. Grace is God's love to the undeserving. Grace is love that cares and stoops and rescues. Before going any further it seems right to consider certain aspects of this double divine initiative of grace.

First, the divine initiative belongs in one sense to the past. It began in eternity, progressively unfolded in the history of the nation God chose to be His people, and culminated in the coming of Jesus Christ. In Him God's initiative reached its climax, in one sense one could say its conclusion.

This truth regarding the finality of God's initiative in Christ is conveyed by one word of the Greek Testament, namely the adverb *hapax* and *ephapax*. It is usually translated in the Author-

ized Version 'once', meaning not 'once upon a time' but 'once
for all'. The Grimm-Thayer *Lexicon* comments that 'like the
Latin *semel* it is used of what is so done as to be of perpetual
validity and never need repetition'. It is applied in the New
Testament to both revelation and redemption. Thus, Jude
refers to 'the faith which was *once for all* delivered to the saints'.[1]
The apostles Paul and Peter, on the other hand, and the unknown
author of the Epistle to the Hebrews, use the word *hapax* to
describe the atoning death of Christ. For example, 'the death
he died he died to sin, *once for all*'.[2] 'Christ also died for sins
once for all.'[3] Again, 'he has appeared *once for all* at the end of the
age to put away sin by the sacrifice of himself. And just as it is
appointed for men to die *once*, and after that comes judgment,
so Christ, having been offered *once* to bear the sins of many,
will appear a second time. . . .'[4]

Thus we may say that God has spoken once for all and Christ
has suffered once for all. This means that the Christian revelation
and the Christian redemption are both alike in Christ complete.
Nothing can be added to either without being derogatory to
Christ, either to the unique glory of His divine-human Person
or to the absolute adequacy of His saving work. These are the
two rocks on which the Protestant Reformation was built –
God's revealed word without the addition of human traditions
and Christ's finished work without the addition of human
merits. The Reformers' great watchwords were *sola scriptura* for
our authority and *sola gratia* for our salvation.

Secondly, the divine initiative belongs in another sense to the
present also. Although what God said and did in Christ was
finished in the past, it is not *buried* in the past. Although it is
final, it is also contemporary. For the fruits of God's finished
word and work in Christ may be gathered and enjoyed today.
Indeed, it is the peculiar work of the Holy Spirit in these New
Covenant days to do this very thing, namely to apply to believers
in the present the riches of Christ's word and work in the past.
What God finished in Christ once He administers now through
the Spirit. It is the Holy Spirit who illumines our minds to
grasp what God has said in Christ. It is the same Spirit who
kindles our faith to grasp what God has done in Christ.

[1] Jude 3.   [2] Rom. 6:10.
[3] 1 Pet. 3:18.   [4] Heb. 9:26–28.

Nevertheless, it must be emphasized that what the Spirit speaks He speaks through what has been spoken, and what the Spirit does He does through what has been done. There is no fresh revelation, but a progressive understanding of what God revealed in Christ (and in the apostolic witness to Christ). There is no fresh redemption, but a progressive appropriation of what God achieved in Christ.

Thirdly, the divine initiative in both spheres (revelation and redemption) and in both their aspects (finished and contemporary) is supernatural. This is why we began in chapter 1 with the question whether the Christian religion is natural or supernatural. It was an essential preliminary to our subsequent questions about authority and salvation. What God said and did in the historical Christ involved events which were unashamedly and inescapably supernatural. The incarnation, including the virgin birth as the way God chose to effect it, the mighty works, the atonement, the resurrection, the ascension and the descent of the Spirit – these cannot be explained in natural or humanistic terms. And the same is true of what God says and does through the Spirit today. If we understand the truth as it is in Jesus, this is not because of any superior native intelligence of our own, but because of divine illumination: 'Flesh and blood has not revealed this to you, but my Father who is in heaven'; '. . . he who had set me apart before I was born . . . was pleased to reveal his Son to me'; 'it is the God who said, "Let light shine out of darkness," who has shone in our hearts to give the light of the knowledge of the glory of God in the face of Christ'; 'no one can say "Jesus is Lord" except by the Holy Spirit'.[5] Similarly, if we have become new people in Christ, redeemed and recreated, it is not because of any human resolve or effort of our own, but because of divine grace: 'For by grace you have been saved through faith; and this is not your own doing, it is the gift of God – not because of works, lest any man should boast. For we are his workmanship, created in Christ Jesus for good works . . .'; 'All this is from God, who through Christ reconciled us to himself. . . .'[6]

Having considered some of the parallels between authority

[5] Mt. 16:17; Gal. 1:15, 16; 2 Cor. 4:6; 1 Cor. 12:3.
[6] Eph. 2:8–10; 2 Cor. 5:18.

and salvation, and the same divine initiative of grace operative
in both, we are now able to concentrate our attention on salvation.

Salvation and justification

The subject of salvation is crucial. In his book *Christianity Rightly
So-called*[7] the American author S. C. Craig suggests three distinctive characteristics of true Christianity. The vital one is that
Christianity 'presents itself as a redemptive religion'. Dr Craig
is right. His point cannot be gainsaid. Christianity is a religion
of salvation.

Of course we all know that the word 'salvation' is out of fashion
today. There are some in the church too squeamish to use it.
But the fact that it causes many either amusement or embarrassment only demonstrates how far the contemporary church
has drifted from biblical religion. The whole Bible is a *Heilsge-
schichte*, the story of salvation. Salvation in Christ is the one theme
which runs through Scripture from beginning to end, the living
God taking action in His grace to seek and to save mankind.

What, then, is 'salvation'? It is a great word. It urgently
needs to be set free from those narrow concepts to which it has
often been reduced. Salvation is not a synonym for forgiveness.
It is bigger and broader than that. It denotes God's total plan
for man, and it includes at least three phases. Phase one is our
deliverance from the guilt and judgment of our sins, our free
and full forgiveness, together with our reconciliation to God
and our adoption as His children. Phase two is our progressive
liberation from the downdrag of evil, beginning with our new
birth into the family of God and continuing with our transfor-
mation by the Spirit of Christ into the image of Christ. Phase
three is our final deliverance from the sin which lingers both in
our fallen nature and in our social environment, when on the
last day we shall be invested with new and glorious bodies and
transferred to a new heaven and a new earth in which righteousness dwells.

Further, these three phases, or tenses, of salvation (past,
present and future) are associated in the New Testament with
the three major events in the saving career of Jesus, His death,
His resurrection and subsequent gift of the Spirit, and His

[7] Tyndale Press, 1946.

return in power and glory. Paul calls them justification, sanctification and glorification.

We shall now restrict ourselves to the first phase, 'justification',
and consider how Christ handled the subject in another of His
controversies with the Pharisees. We saw in chapter 2 how He
accused them of 'making void the word of God through their
tradition'. In this chapter we shall see how they were just as
adept at making void God's work of redemption. Christ's quarrel
with them now is not that they had an exaggerated respect
for their own traditions, but that they had an exaggerated
confidence in their own merits. His criticism of them comes
out clearly in His parable of the Pharisee and the publican.[8]

> 'He also told this parable to some who trusted in themselves
> that they were righteous and despised others: 10 "Two
> men went up into the temple to pray, one a Pharisee and the
> other a tax collector. 11 The Pharisee stood and prayed thus
> with himself, 'God, I thank thee that I am not like other men,
> extortioners, unjust, adulterers, or even like this tax col-
> lector. 12 I fast twice a week, I give tithes of all that I get.'
> 13 But the tax collector, standing far off, would not even lift
> up his eyes to heaven, but beat his breast, saying, 'God,
> be merciful to me a sinner!' 14 I tell you, this man went down
> to his house justified rather than the other; for every one who
> exalts himself will be humbled, but he who humbles himself
> will be exalted." '

Perhaps the best approach to an understanding of this parable
is to begin at the end with the word *dedikaiōmenos*, 'justified'
(v. 14). It is with this single word that Jesus summed up the
great blessing which the publican received and the Pharisee
missed. True, we normally associate the vocabulary of justification with the apostle Paul. But Paul's teaching is already adum-
brated here, and it is quite wrong to attempt to drive a wedge
between Jesus and Paul in this (or any other) doctrine. There
are two further occurrences in Luke's Gospel of the verb 'to
justify', both relating to self-justification: the first of the lawyer
who was 'desiring to justify himself' and the second of the
Pharisees whom Jesus similarly described as 'those who justify
yourselves before men'.[9]

That Jesus should have used the vocabulary of justification

8 Lk. 18:9-14.   9 Lk. 10:29; 16:15.

is not in the least surprising, because it occurs quite frequently
in the Old Testament. 'Justification' is a legal word, a technical
term borrowed from the lawcourts. It is best understood from
its opposite, 'condemnation'. The Old Testament magistrates
were instructed to justify the righteous and to condemn the
wicked; that is, to pronounce the innocent man innocent and
the guilty man guilty. And they were told that 'he who justifies
the wicked, and he who condemns the righteous are both alike
an abomination to the Lord'.[1]

This Old Testament background is sufficient to indicate with
what horror and indignation the Pharisees will have heard
Jesus say that the sinful publican 'went down to his house
justified rather than the other'. How could Jesus countenance
such a miscarriage of justice? Was He not daring to ascribe
to God an action which Scripture had said was an abomination
to God? Had God not categorically stated in Exodus, 'I will
not justify the wicked'? How then could anybody possibly say
that He 'justifies the ungodly'? – which, incidentally, is exactly
what Paul says in Romans that He regularly does.[2]

These are fundamental questions about salvation. The answer
to them is supplied in embryo in the parable and fully developed
in the rest of the New Testament. To understand it, before we
study the parable itself, we need to look at the two men who
figure in it. They are representative of two groups with whom
throughout His public ministry Jesus was in constant touch.

The Pharisee and the publican contrasted
The 'publicans', or tax collectors, were widely despised on both
political and moral grounds. Being in the employment of the
hated Romans, they were regarded as political collaborators.
And they tended to rely for their livelihood on whatever extra
they could extort from their hapless victims beyond the tax
or custom they were entitled to levy.

The Pharisees, on the other hand, were almost as universally
popular as the publicans were despised. Their views on religion
and ethics were accepted by the great majority of their com-
patriots. Both politically and morally they were as strict as
the publicans were lax. They refused to compromise with the

[1] Dt. 25:1; Pr. 17:15.   [2] Ex. 23:7, AV; Rom. 4:5.

Roman occupation, and they were determined to keep themselves free from all defilement as they understood it. 'On entering the order, they took two vows . . . one to tithe everything eaten, bought or sold; the other not to be guest of the '*am-hā'āres* (*i.e.* the common people) and to observe all ceremonial purification.'[3] They 'preached the keeping of the Law, and the coming world of blessedness as the reward of obedience. . . . All this made the Pharisees more and more proud, formal and uncharitable. They despised the common people.'[4] An example of their confidence in their own righteousness for salvation is found in the so-called *Psalms of Solomon*: 'To do right and wrong is in the work of our hands'. Again, 'he who works righteousness obtains life from the Lord'.[5]

In the parable which Jesus told, the two actors have much in common. Both were men. Both 'went up into the temple to pray'. Both stood to pray, as the Jews normally did. Both prayed. Both began their prayer with the same word, 'God'.

But there the similarities between them ended. When we look below the surface they were separated from each other by four major differences.

First, they had an entirely different *opinion of themselves*. This was expressed in their prayers. The Pharisee said, 'God, I . . . I . . . I . . . I . . . I . . .'. Five times he used the personal pronoun in his brief utterance. The publican also used the personal pronoun – once – but not in the nominative. He did not regard himself as a *subject* who had done or could do anything to win the divine favour, or who even had a right to address God at all. He saw himself rather as the needy *object* of the divine mercy: 'God, be merciful to *me* a sinner!'

The opinion which each man cherished of himself is further illustrated by the fact that each placed himself in a category by himself. The Pharisee's words, literally translated, begin: 'God, I thank Thee that I am not like the rest of men.' Luke has prepared us a little for this egregious arrogance by his editorial introduction: 'He also told this parable to some who had placed their confidence upon themselves that they were righteous and despised everybody else.'[6] That this was not an

[3] Scott, p. 352.   [4] Scott, p. 353; *cf.* Jn. 7:49.
[5] Scott, p. 354. The references are *Psalms of Solomon* 9:7–15; 13:9; 14:1–6.
[6] Lk. 18:9, literally.

exaggerated sentiment for Jesus to have put into the mouth of a
Pharisee is plain from the Talmud. There we can read of a
certain Rabbi Simeon ben Jochai who used to say, 'I have seen
the children of the world to come, and they are few. If there are
three, I and my son are of their number; if they are two, I and
my son are they.'[7]

The publican too regarded himself as unique – not in virtue,
however, but in sin. 'God, be merciful to me, *the* sinner,' he
said, using the definite article. So vividly aware was he of his
own shortcomings that he made no odious comparisons between
himself and others. He was conscious only of his personal need
for mercy. This is the language of true penitence. The apostle
Paul, the converted Pharisee, was the same. He called himself
'the foremost of sinners', whom Christ Jesus had come to save.[8]

Thus the Pharisee sought to draw God's attention to what he
regarded as his outstanding, his incomparable, merit. The
publican, on the other hand, refrained from going into details;
to call himself 'the sinner' was enough.

Secondly, their different opinion of themselves was reflected
in their different *posture in prayer*. True, both men 'stood' in
customary Jewish fashion. But their stance was not the same.
The Pharisee stood erect, proud and ostentatious, and though
he called upon God in words, he was actually praying 'towards
himself'.[9] The publican, however, was seen 'standing far off'.
Presumably he had not thought it appropriate to enter the
Temple. He did not consider himself fit to stand in God's house.
Probably he stayed outside, in one of the Temple courts. There
he 'would not even lift up his eyes to heaven, but beat his breast,
saying, "God, be merciful to me a sinner!"' Though with a
notable economy of words, Jesus seems to indicate that every
part of the publican's body expressed his humble penitence.
His feet kept their distance from the holy place; like Moses
at the burning bush he knew himself unfit to come near.[1] His
eyes looked down to the ground in shame; he could have echoed
Ezra's prayer, 'I am ashamed and blush to lift my face to thee,
my God'.[2] His hands struck his breast mournfully, in acknowledgment of his guilt, 'as the Jews still do in the most solemn

[7] Edersheim, vol. I, p. 540.   [8] 1 Tim. 1:15, 16.
[9] Gk. *pros heauton* (v. 11).   [1] Ex. 3:4, 5.
[2] Ezr. 9:6.

part of their confession on the Day of Atonement'.[3] And his mouth uttered words of deep contrition and penitence.

In view of their different opinion of themselves expressed in their different posture, it is no surprise to read, thirdly, of their different *standing before God*. 'I tell you,' Jesus concluded with deliberate emphasis, 'this man went down to his house justified rather than the other.' The Pharisee was condemned, while the publican was justified. In their present standing and their final destiny they were as different as heaven and hell.

And this was due to the fourth and fundamental difference between these men, namely their different *object of confidence*.

In order to understand this truly, it is important to realize that each man in the parable gave an assessment of himself which (at least externally in the Pharisee's case) was accurate. They were not lying or even exaggerating. The Pharisee was what he said he was, both religious and righteous. As for his religion, he had gone into the Temple to pray, he fasted, and he tithed his money. And these three – prayer, fasting and alms-giving – were accepted as the three chief religious duties. Jesus Himself in the Sermon on the Mount made it clear that He expected His own disciples to pray, to fast and to give.[4] The Pharisee even went beyond the requirements of the law. According to the law it was obligatory for the Jew to fast twice a year (on the Day of Atonement and the day commemorating the destruction of Solomon's Temple); the Pharisee fasted 'twice a week'. According to the law it was obligatory for the Jew to tithe his produce, that is the fruit of his ground and of his cattle; the Pharisee could claim 'I give tithes of all that I get'. By doing so he was faithfully observing one of his vows, for it was said of the Pharisee in the Mishnah that he 'tithes all that he eats, all that he sells, and all that he buys'.[5]

As for the Pharisee's righteousness, there is no need to doubt that he was telling the truth when he declared himself neither an extortioner, nor unjust, nor an adulterer. He had not broken the commandments of God about honesty and immorality – at least not in deed, externally.

So, in both religion and morals, this Pharisee in Christ's story will have appeared to his contemporaries (as indeed he appeared to himself) a wholly admirable person.

[3] Edersheim, vol. II, p. 292.   [4] Mt. 6:1–18.   [5] Edersheim, vol. II, p. 291.

The publican, on the other hand, was despicable. He styled himself 'a sinner', 'the sinner'. And there is no reason to doubt that he too was exactly what he said he was. He was politically and morally disreputable.

Then how in the name of justice can Jesus have declared the righteous Pharisee condemned and the unrighteous publican justified?

We begin to get an answer to our question when we notice this: the Pharisee was not condemned because he was righteous, but because he was self-righteous. His righteousness in any case was external only. 'God knows the heart.'[6] If the Pharisee could have seen his heart, he would have known immediately that he was no fit object for his own confidence.

Similarly, the publican was not justified because he was a sinner but because, having acknowledged that he was a sinner, guilty and deserving of judgment, he cried to God for mercy.

In a word, both men were sinners, deserving judgment. But only one admitted it and called on God to have mercy on him. This is why Jesus could even have said to the Pharisees: 'Truly, I say to you, the tax collectors and the harlots go into the kingdom of God before you.'[7] Not because they were tax-collectors and harlots (sin in itself is no condition of eligibility for God's kingdom), but because they humbled themselves in recognizing their sin, repented and believed.

So this fourth difference between the Pharisee and the publican was the really basic one. It concerned the object of their confidence for salvation. The Pharisee 'trusted in himself that he was righteous and despised others' (v. 9). The publican forgot others, so conscious was he of his own guilt, and relied utterly on the mercy of God.

Indeed, the more one contemplates these two men, the more clear it becomes that they had entirely opposite notions of the proper ground of a man's confidence for his standing before God. So exaggerated was the Pharisee's view of his own righteousness, that he considered himself a proper subject not for prayer, still less for penitence, but actually for *thanksgiving*! 'God, I thank thee,' he began. Taken out of their context and considered in themselves, these words make a promising beginning to any prayer. If only he had continued 'I thank Thee that

[6] Lk. 16:15.   [7] Mt. 21:31.

Thou art such a great God', or 'that Thou hast given me everything richly to enjoy', all would have been well. Instead, he
thanked God for his own merits. As Edersheim expressed it,
'his thanksgiving referred not to what he had received, but to
the sins of others by which they were separated from him, and
to his own meritorious deeds by which he was separated from
them'.[8] A similar self-righteousness was found in Rabbi Simon
who even claimed that, if Abraham's righteousness had redeemed all generations up to his time, he would redeem by his
own merits all that followed him until the end of the world![9]

What of the publican's confidence? He was without doubt
ashamed of his past and sincerely anxious to be a better man.
But it did not occur to him to plead his prayer or penitence or
future resolve or sincerity as grounds for acceptance with God,
or to make them the objects of his confidence. No. He had sinned
against God. He had offended God. Only divine mercy could
save him from divine judgment, from the judgment he knew he
deserved. And in this mercy of God he put his trust, knowing
from the Old Testament that the Lord is 'merciful and gracious,
slow to anger, and abounding in steadfast love'.[1]

The difference between them was this: the Pharisee appealed
for justice on the ground of his supposed merit, while the publican
acknowledged his entire lack of merit and appealed for mercy
alone. Jesus summed up this contrast by one of His favourite
epigrams: 'every one who exalts himself will be humbled, but
he who humbles himself will be exalted' (v. 14).

Mercy not merit

It is not without significance that the parable is immediately
followed (in vv. 15–17) by the incident of the infants who were
brought to Jesus. When the disciples saw it, being themselves
by no means entirely free from the spirit of Pharisaism, they
rebuked the adults who brought them. They had not yet learned
that the humble dependence of a little child was the indispensable
condition of acceptance with God and precisely what the
Pharisees lacked. So Jesus called the disciples to Him and said,
'Let the children come to me, and do not hinder them; for
to such belongs the kingdom of God. Truly, I say to you, whoever

[8] Edersheim, vol. II, p. 290.   [9] Edersheim, vol. I, p. 540.
[1] Ex. 34:6; Ps. 103:8–13.

does not receive the kingdom of God like a child shall not
enter it.'[2]

Thus Jesus continued to teach, emphasizing the givenness,
the freeness of salvation. The so-called 'unmerciful servant' in
the parable was so heavily in debt to his master that 'he could
not pay'; his master then out of pity 'released him and forgave
him the debt'.[3] So the forgiveness of God is a gift to be received,
not a reward to be merited. 'If you knew the gift of God,' He
had said earlier to the Samaritan woman, 'and who it is that
is saying to you, "Give me a drink," you would have asked
him, and he would have given you living water.'[4] And again,
this time to the Jews who did not believe in Him: 'Do not labour
for the food which perishes, but for the food which endures
to eternal life, which the Son of man will give to you. . . .'
'What must we do, to be doing the works of God?' they went
on to ask. Jesus replied, 'This is the work of God, that you
believe in him whom he has sent.'[5] It is the same contrast as
He draws in the parable of the Pharisee and the publican.
Eternal life is a gift, not a wage. It is free, not earned. Not by
'doing' or 'labouring' does it become ours, but by 'receiving' or
'believing'. The way of salvation is by faith, not works.

The same fundamental distinction between the two objects
of confidence or boasting (human merit and divine mercy)
finds its most striking New Testament illustration in the career
of Saul of Tarsus, the Pharisee who became a Christian. 'We . . .
glory in Christ Jesus,' he writes, 'and put no confidence in the
flesh',[6] thus setting in opposition the two stages of his career,
first as Saul the Pharisee who put his confidence in the flesh,
and now as Paul the Christian who glories in Christ Jesus alone.
By 'the flesh' he meant everything he was in himself and by
himself – what his parents and teachers had made him and
what he considered he had succeeded in making himself. To
put the matter beyond dispute, he separates out for us the various
elements which together made up his 'flesh' – his Jewish ancestry,
his Hebrew education, his religion, sincerity, zeal and righteousness.[7] They were exactly the things of which every Pharisee
was proud. But then: 'whatever gain I had, I counted as loss
for the sake of *Christ*. Indeed I count everything as loss because

---

[2] Lk. 18:16, 17.   [3] Mt. 18:23-35.   [4] Jn. 4:10.
[5] Jn. 6:27-29.   [6] Phil. 3:3.   [7] Phil. 3:4-6.

of the surpassing worth of knowing *Christ Jesus* my Lord. For *his* sake I have suffered the loss of all things, and count them as refuse, in order that I may gain *Christ* and be found in *him*, not having a righteousness of my own, based on law, but that which is through faith in *Christ*, the righteousness from God that depends on faith. . . .'[8] The sixfold reference to Christ stands out in bold relief. He had been trusting in himself that he was righteous; he came to put his trust in Christ. Or, as we might equally well express it, he came to rely on the mercy of God displayed in Christ, since there is no substantial distinction between the publican's faith in God's mercy and Saul's faith in Christ.

The significance of Christ's death

Nor is there any distinction in this matter of saving faith between the publican and us – except that we know far more about God's mercy than the publican ever knew. For we live after the death of Christ in which the mercy of God was supremely exhibited. Therefore today the object of the penitent sinner's confidence for acceptance with God is not divine mercy in general but, in particular, Jesus Christ and Him crucified. For although God's mercy is seen in the whole saving career of Jesus, and although in that saving career His birth, life, death, resurrection, ascension and gift of the Spirit belong inseparably together, yet the New Testament states that what He did to put away our sins was to die. It was on the cross that He bore them in His own body, paying their penalty. It is His 'blood', the symbol of the laying down of His life, which can cleanse us from them today. And only because He died our death is it possible for us to have life. Only because He was made a curse for us can we inherit a blessing. Only because He endured our condemnation may we be justified – if we pray the publican's prayer.[9]

Although it is not until the New Testament Epistles that the full implications of the death of Jesus are drawn out, yet the nature and the necessity of it were already plain in His own mind.

[8] Phil. 3:7–9.
[9] For some plain New Testament teaching about the 'substitutionary' nature of Christ's death, that He died in our place, bringing us life through His death, blessing through His curse, justification through His condemnation, see, *e.g.*, 2 Cor. 5:14, 15 and 18–21; Gal. 3:10, 13, 14; Rom. 8:1, 3; 1 Pet. 2:24.

He made at least two unequivocal statements about the aim
and object of His death. First, He said He had come 'to give
his life as a ransom for many'.[1] Secondly, He referred to the
Communion cup as His 'blood of the (new) covenant', which
would be 'poured out for many for the forgiveness of sins'.[2]
Thus it was by the shedding of His blood in a violent, sacrificial
death that the promised new covenant between God and man
would be established, whose terms would include both the
forgiveness of sin and deliverance from sin. Since this was to be
the epoch-making achievement of His death, it is small wonder
that it loomed so large in His mind. He *must* suffer, He kept
repeating, as it stood written of Him in Scripture. This was the
'hour' for which He had come into the world. At the same time,
He would undergo this death voluntarily, and nothing would
deflect Him from His purpose. As the Good Shepherd, He would
lay down His life for His sheep. No man would take His life
from Him. He would lay it down of His own accord. He had
power to lay it down, and He had power to take it again.[3]
Moreover, through His death He would draw all men, including
the Gentiles, to Himself. Just as a grain of wheat must fall into
the earth and die before it can bear much fruit, so He would
die in order to multiply.[4]

So positive was Jesus about the centrality of His death in the
purpose of God that He instituted His special Supper for its
perpetual commemoration. It is highly significant that the only
regular ritual act instituted and commanded by Jesus sets
forth supremely His death. It is His *death*, His body given and
blood shed, which the bread and wine were intended to signify.
In issuing the command to 'do this in remembrance' of Him,
He intended that His atoning death should be kept before every
generation, indeed 'placarded' before their very eyes. This
according to Paul is the function of preaching.[5] It is one of the
functions of Communion also. The ministry of both word and
sacrament makes Christ's death contemporary, presenting it
anew not to God (for the sacrifice itself was offered on the cross
once for all) but to men (for its benefits are always freshly
available).

Further, when during His ministry Christ presented Himself

[1] Mk. 10:45.   [2] Mt. 26:28.   [3] Jn. 10:11, 18.
[4] Jn. 12:24, 32.   [5] See Gal. 3:1.

to men as the object of their faith, it was as their sacrificed
Saviour that He did so. Two striking examples will suffice.
First, 'as Moses lifted up the serpent in the wilderness, so must
the Son of man be lifted up, that whoever believes in him may
have eternal life.'[6] Secondly, 'Truly, truly, I say to you, unless
you eat the flesh of the Son of man and drink his blood, you have
no life in you; he who eats my flesh and drinks my blood has
eternal life. . . .'[7] Saving faith, therefore, is gazing at the Son
of man lifted up on the cross; it is eating the flesh and drinking
the blood of the divine victim who has offered Himself as a
sacrifice for sin.

These vivid metaphors of Jesus do more than illustrate the
object of saving faith (Christ crucified); they also demonstrate
that there is no merit in faith itself. For there is no virtue in the
eye, but only in Him who is gazed upon. And there is no virtue
in the mouth, but only in Him on whom we feed. Richard
Hooker expressed this lucidly: 'God doth justify the believing
man, yet not for the worthiness of his belief, but for His worthiness
who is believed.'[8]

The sacraments of the gospel
If there is no saving merit either in our good works or in our
faith, there is no saving merit in the mere reception of the
sacraments either. The sacraments dramatize salvation; they
do not and cannot by themselves convey it. However, as drama
they set forth both the character and the condition of salvation.

Take its character first. Baptism is a purification rite. The
waters of baptism stand for that 'heavenly washing'[9] and that
gift of the Spirit which together constitute salvation and which
Christ died to purchase for us. Similarly, the bread and wine
of Communion are visible, tangible emblems of Christ's body
given and blood shed on the cross for our sins. The message
which both sacraments preach is the gospel of salvation through
Christ crucified.

The sacraments emphasize the condition of salvation as well
as its character. What does the candidate for baptism do?
Nothing, precisely nothing! Instead, something is done to him.

[6] Jn. 3:14, 15.   [7] Jn. 6:53, 54.
[8] *Definition of Justification,* chapter xxxiii.
[9] An expression which occurs in the Church of England 1662 Baptism Service.

If the baptism is by immersion, he is plunged beneath the water; if it is by affusion, water is poured or sprinkled upon him. In either case he is a passive recipient. Nowhere in the New Testament does any man ever baptize himself. Instead, he submits to baptism. From the first baptisms on the Day of Pentecost right up to the present day the same word has gone forth: 'Repent, and *be baptized* every one of you in the name of Jesus Christ for the forgiveness of sins; and you shall receive the gift of the Holy Spirit.'[1] Jesus Christ is the sole giver of forgiveness and of the Holy Spirit. So the penitent sinner is baptized in His name, to signify his believing acceptance of Christ's gifts.

It is the same in the Lord's Supper. The drama in the Upper Room did not have one actor and eleven in the audience. The apostles were themselves participants also; they were not mere spectators. What was their part? Just to receive what Christ gave them. He broke the bread; they ate it. He took the cup; they drank it. He thus gave the church both a permanent symbol of His dying sacrifice in the bread and wine, and in the eating and the drinking a permanent illustration of saving faith. The Lord's Supper portrays visibly that great word of Jesus already quoted, 'he who eats my flesh and drinks my blood has eternal life'.[2]

Let me repeat that the sacraments dramatize salvation and do not in themselves automatically convey it. Augustine called them *verba visibilia*, 'visible words', and Hooker 'signs to which are annexed promises'. Therefore it is not by the mere outward administration of water in baptism that we are cleansed and receive the Spirit, nor by the mere gift of bread and wine in Communion that we feed on Christ crucified, but by faith in the promises of God thus visibly expressed, a faith which is itself meant to be illustrated in our humble, believing acceptance of these signs. But we must not confuse the signs with the promises which they signify. It is possible to receive the sign without receiving the promise, and also to receive the promise apart from the receiving of the sign. This is unquestionably taught in the formularies of the church. Take Holy Communion first. On the one hand, 'the Wicked, and such as be void of a lively faith, although they do carnally and visibly press with their teeth (as Saint Augustine saith) the Sacrament of the Body

[1] Acts 2:38.   [2] Jn. 6:54.

and Blood of Christ, yet in no wise are they partakers of Christ.'[3] On the other hand a sick person who is prevented from receiving the sacrament is to be instructed that 'if he do truly repent him of his sins, and stedfastly believe that Jesus Christ hath suffered death upon the Cross for him, and shed his Blood for his redemption, earnestly remembering the benefits he hath thereby, and giving him hearty thanks therefore, he doth eat and drink the Body and Blood of our Saviour Christ profitably to his Soul's health, although he do not receive the Sacrament with his mouth'.[4]

The same is true of baptism. As the Westminster Confession expresses it: 'Although it be a great sin to contemn or neglect this ordinance, yet grace and salvation are not so inseparably annexed unto it, as that no person can be regenerated or saved without it, or that all that are baptized are undoubtedly saved.'[5]

The Oxford English Dictionary is therefore right to say that the word 'evangelical' is 'applied to those Protestants who hold that the essence of the Gospel consists in the doctrine of salvation by faith in the atoning death of Christ, and deny the saving efficacy of either good works or the sacraments'.

Justification and its fruits

The biblical way of salvation is clear. As with the Pharisee and the publican, as with Saul and Paul, so too with us: God accepts us sinners not because of any work or supposed merit of our own, but because of His own mercy, on the ground of Christ's finished work in which by grace we put our trust.

John Berridge, the eighteenth-century Vicar of Everton in Bedfordshire, is a good and more modern example of the same continuing alternative. In his book *Christian World Unmasked*, a dialogue between two imaginary characters about the way of salvation, he writes this: 'Once I went to Jesus as a coxcomb,[6] and gave myself fine airs, fancying, if He were something, so was I; if He had merit, so had I. I used Him as a healthy man

[3] Article XXIX, *Of the Wicked which eat not the Body of Christ in the use of the Lord's Supper.*
[4] Third rubric following the service for *The Communion of the Sick* in the 1662 Book of Common Prayer.
[5] Chapter XXVIII, *Of Baptism*, 5.
[6] According to Professor Garmonsway's *Penguin English Dictionary* (1965), a coxcomb is a 'conceited swaggering fop'.

will use a walking-staff – lean an ounce upon it, and vapour with it in the air. But now He is my whole crutch; no foot can stir a step without Him. He is my all, as He ought to be if He will become my Saviour, and bids me cast all my care on Him.'[7] John Berridge also wrote his own epitaph for his own grave-stone. It describes the main stages of his spiritual pilgrimage. It reads as follows:

HERE LIE
THE EARTHLY REMAINS OF

JOHN BERRIDGE,
LATE VICAR OF EVERTON,
AND AN ITINERANT SERVANT OF JESUS CHRIST,
WHO LOVED HIS MASTER AND HIS WORK,
AND AFTER RUNNING ON HIS ERRANDS MANY YEARS
WAS CALLED TO WAIT ON HIM ABOVE.

READER,
Art thou born again?
No salvation without new birth!
I was born in sin, February 1716.
Remained ignorant of my fallen state till 1730.
Lived proudly on faith and works for salvation till 1754.
Was admitted to Everton Vicarage, 1755.
Fled to Jesus alone for refuge, 1756.
Fell asleep in Christ, January 22, 1793.[8]

Quaint, even a trifle eccentric, John Berridge's testimony may seem, but his theology and his experience should be shared by every Christian believer. Jesus Christ, the sinbearing Saviour, must be the only 'crutch' on which we also lean, the only 'refuge' to which we flee.

Now this trust in the finished work of Christ, which is the way of justification, results in two further blessings on which evangelical Christians have always joyfully insisted. The first is 'the priesthood of all believers'.

In Old Testament days the priests were a distinct caste, enjoying privileges which were denied to the people as a whole.

---

[7] Quoted by J. C. Ryle in *Five Christian Leaders of the Eighteenth Century* (Banner of Truth Trust, 1960), p. 138.
[8] *Five Christian Leaders*, p. 132.

In particular, they offered the sacrifices which the people might
not offer and they enjoyed access to God in Tabernacle or
Temple, while the people stayed outside. This priest–people
distinction is done away in Christ. He offered one sacrifice
for sins for ever and then entered the presence of God. Now
He makes all His people 'priests'.[9] As such, 'we have confidence
to enter the sanctuary' – all of us, from the greatest to the least
without distinction – 'by the blood of Jesus'.[1] Moreover, though
there is no further sacrifice for sin to offer, since Christ's single
sin-offering was sufficient for the putting away of all sin, yet
there are sacrifices of praise, thanksgiving and dedication which
as 'a holy priesthood' we should be offering to God continuously.[2]

If the priesthood of all believers is the first fruit of justification,
'assurance' is the second, that is to say, the God-given certainty
that through Christ our sins have been forgiven, we have peace
with God and He has given us eternal life. Such assurance is
not presumption, for it does not rest upon ourselves and our own
imagined merit, but only on the completed work of Christ
who bore our sins and purchased our salvation.

Some objections
However, the way of salvation which Jesus Christ and His
apostles proclaimed, as a mercy-gift not a merit-award, despite
its great and wonderful blessings, has had many outspoken
critics. It seems right, therefore, at the close of this chapter
to weigh some of the chief objections to it which have been
lodged.

1. It is said to be *dishonest*. The dishonesty is thought to
belong not to God's part in the transaction, but to ours. 'How
can we take our place beside that publican,' it is asked, 'and
echo his talk about being a miserable sinner, unless we cross
our fingers and put our tongue in our cheek?' 'This is the exaggerated language of the religious past,' the objector continues.
'It no longer rings true today.'

No? Then all I can say is that it should. If I cannot take the
publican's prayer upon my lips and mean it, it simply shows that

[9] See, *e.g.*, 1 Pet. 2:5, 9; Rev. 1:6.
[1] Heb. 10:19.
[2] 1 Pet. 2:5; Heb. 13:15; Rom. 12:1.

I am still a Pharisee. But once the Holy Spirit has done His work of convincing us sinners of our sins, we will have no difficulty about the publican's humble, penitential language. Humility is nothing but the truth. Humility is a synonym for honesty, not hypocrisy. It is not an artificial pretence about myself, but an accurate assessment of myself. To be sure, we find it hard enough to see ourselves as other people see us. But when we begin to see ourselves as God sees us – defiant of His authority, rebellious against His love, self-centred and proud – then we shall recognize that we are under His just judgment for our sin and that the language of the publican, far from being dishonest, is the only possible language to use.

2. It is said to be *morbid*. 'Your doctrine of justification puts a most regrettable emphasis on sin,' we are told. 'Even if it is not dishonest to identify ourselves with the publican, it is not healthy. You seem to require us to wallow in sin. Sin seems to be your obsession. You are almost pathological about it.'

On the contrary, evangelical Christians who take the subject of sin seriously and seek to be faithful to the biblical doctrines of sin and salvation are only being realists. Declension from evangelical Christianity has often been due to making light of sin. But 'fools make a mock at sin'.[3] The gravity of sin, according to Scripture, is that it is the assertion of self against God, our Creator, Lord and Judge, and against our neighbour whom we are meant to love and serve. Besides, if nothing could put away sin but the death of God's Son, it must be grave indeed. It is the false prophets who heal the wound of God's people lightly, 'saying, "Peace, Peace," when there is no peace'.[4]

3. It is said to be *selfish*. That is, 'Talk about *sin* is morbid, talk about *salvation* is selfish,' people say. 'You Christians are only interested in saving your own skins.'

This objection is so superficial that it hardly deserves consideration. But let me ask this: is it selfish to consult a doctor when you are ill? or to escape from a building when it's on fire? It seems rather to be straightforward common sense. Whether it is selfish or not depends on how we use the life which is thereby given back to us. The Christian who has received

[3] Pr. 14:9, AV.   [4] Je. 8:11.

salvation by the mercy of God finds himself in the grip of Christ's love, with no alternative but to spend the rest of his life in the service of God and man.[5]

4. It is said to be *unjust*. 'Salvation by mercy alone, irrespective of any merit, just isn't fair. The Pharisee *was* righteous. The publican *was* a sinner. It is shocking that Jesus declared the publican righteous when he wasn't. It represents a serious miscarriage of justice.'

But the Pharisee was righteous only in an external sense, as we have already seen. Underneath, and unacknowledged, he was just as much a sinner as the publican. Both men were sinners. Neither had loved God with all his being or his neighbour as himself. Yet only one acknowledged the truth about himself and cried to God for mercy. This was part of Christ's quarrel with the Pharisees: 'Woe to you, scribes and Pharisees, hypocrites! for you are like whitewashed tombs, which *outwardly* appear beautiful, but within they are full of dead men's bones and all uncleanness. So you also *outwardly* appear righteous to men, but within you are full of hypocrisy and iniquity.'[6] Again, 'You are those who justify yourselves before men, but God knows your hearts . . .'.[7]

So, then, if it is justice for which you are asking, both men, indeed all men, must be condemned. Only by the sin-bearing death of Christ has God provided a basis upon which He can declare the unrighteous righteous without compromising His own righteousness. Because of the cross God is able to prove 'that he himself is righteous and that he justifies [*i.e.* declares righteous] him who has faith in Jesus'.[8] To receive what we have ourselves merited would mean condemnation; God offers us what Jesus Christ has merited for us – justification.

5. It is said to be '*antinomian*', to undermine morality and promote lawlessness. 'Evangelical doctrine is extremely dangerous,' our detractors say. 'If a sinner can be saved irrespective of any character, conduct or effort of his own, the chief incentive to righteousness is removed. Indeed, sin and slackness are encouraged, and social progress is impeded.'

[5] See 2 Cor. 5:14, 15; NEB, 'The love of Christ leaves us no choice . . .'.
[6] Mt. 23:27, 28.   [7] Lk. 16:15.   [8] Rom. 3:26.

The argument is as old as Paul's day.[9] If salvation is by grace alone without merit, his critics were evidently protesting, 'why not continue in sin that grace may abound?' So this is a somewhat antiquated objection! Paul's answer to it, as cogent today as it was then, is that salvation involves union with Christ. It is 'in Christ' that God accepts us. And if anyone is in Christ, he is a new creation; the old life is finished, and a new life has begun.[1] Put another way, this union with Christ, effected by God through faith and sealed in baptism, is union with Him especially in His death and resurrection. Further, His death was a death to sin; so, 'how can we who died to sin still live in it?' The very idea is a contradiction in terms. And His resurrection brought Him into 'newness of life' in which we too must walk, since we have been spiritually raised with Him. Indeed, once we have grasped what (through union with Christ) has happened to us, we shall continuously 'consider ourselves dead to sin and alive to God in Christ Jesus', and live accordingly.

Therefore, although we cannot be saved by works, we also cannot be saved without them. Good works are not the way of salvation, but its proper and necessary evidence. A faith which does not express itself in works is dead, James insists;[2] it is not a real or living or saving faith at all. The language of genuine faith is: 'I by my works will show you my faith.'[3] In Paul's words, it is 'faith working through love'.[4] Thus Paul and James do not contradict each other. It is only their emphasis which differs. Paul stresses the faith which issues in works, James the works which issue from faith.

6. It is said to be *inhuman*, to belittle humanity. 'Evangelical doctrine is an insult to man,' some say. 'It portrays him as anaemic and flabby, feebly giving up the struggle, and looking helplessly to someone else to do for him what he ought to do by himself. Surely, at the very least, man is given a free choice and by choosing Christ is co-operating in his own salvation?'

However, Jesus Himself was quite clear that the people He had come to seek and save were 'lost';[5] indeed, that is why He

[9] For Paul's argument summarized in this paragraph, see Rom. 6:1–11.
[1] See 2 Cor. 5:17.
[2] Jas. 2:14–17; *cf.* Eph. 2:8–10, '. . . not because of works . . . for good works . . .'.
[3] Jas. 2:18.   [4] Gal. 5:6.   [5] *E.g.* Lk. 19:10.

128 CHRIST THE CONTROVERSIALIST

had come to seek and to save them. As Paul was later to write, if our acceptance with God could be achieved by our own obedience to the law, 'then Christ died to no purpose'.[6] To imply this is to insult Christ, which would be worse even than insulting man. But the doctrine of human inability and of free and undeserved mercy does not insult man. The authors of the report *Catholicity* express their opinion that Orthodox Protestantism is guilty of 'two radical errors', one of which is such a doctrine of man's total depravity as involves 'the complete destruction of the *imago Dei* in human nature'.[7] But this is a mistaken criticism. Whatever some Protestant theologians may have written, no biblical Christian can deny that man is still 'made in the likeness of God', since James says he is.[8] The divine image in man is marred, but it is not destroyed. Nevertheless, it is marred at every point. This is the meaning of 'total depravity' – the totality referring to extent rather than degree. We do not therefore deny that man still bears the image of God, though defaced, nor that in the new birth the image is restored.[9] What we do deny is that man can achieve his own salvation or even contribute to it. This may be humiliating to man, but it is a fact.

We also deny that man in his natural and unredeemed state can be invited to worship God. For he has nothing whatever to offer until he has first received. This is why the movement of both gospel sacraments, like the movement of the gospel itself, is primarily towards man in grace. Further, in the Lord's Supper we do not and cannot in any sense offer Christ or participate in His self-offering; instead we receive Him, spiritually and by faith. It is only after we have received, and because of it, that we offer ourselves, our souls and bodies, as a living sacrifice to God. As Bishop Ridley put it in the written reply he made during his trial: 'Christ made one perfect sacrifice for the sins of the whole world, neither can any man reiterate that sacrifice of His; and yet is the Communion an acceptable sacrifice to God of praise and thanksgiving.'

[6] Gal. 2:21.
[7] *Catholicity*, A Study in the Conflict of Christian Traditions in the West, being a Report presented to Archbishop Fisher (Dacre Press, 1947), pp. 22–25.
[8] Jas. 3:9.
[9] Eph. 4:24; Col. 3:10.

Apart from this responsive offering of ourselves, sacrificial language is quite inappropriate in connection with the Communion Service, and our Anglican Reformers carefully eliminated it from the Prayer Book. They replaced 'altar' by 'Holy Table' or 'Communion Table', and retained 'priest' only because the English word is a contraction of 'presbyter' and translates *presbyteros* (elder), not *hiereus* (sacrificing priest). For the officiant at Holy Communion is not a priest who makes a sacrifice on an altar; he is a minister who serves supper from a table. And the people come primarily as beggars, like the publican. We declare ourselves unworthy even to gather up the crumbs under Christ's table. The giving of ourselves to His service is subsequent to, and entirely dependent upon, our reception of the divine largesse.

All six objections are, in the last resort, rationalizations. The real reason why the doctrine of justification by grace alone through faith alone is unpopular is that it is grievously wounding to our pride. It removes all ground for boasting. 'Then what becomes of our boasting? It is excluded.'[1] Instead, 'Let him who boasts, boast of the Lord'.[2] The gospel of free grace forces us to admit that we are 'poor in spirit', spiritually bankrupt, totally unable to purchase our own salvation, indeed 'wretched, pitiable, poor, blind, and naked'.[3] It places us just where we do not want to be, beside the outcast publican, crying 'God, be merciful to me a sinner'. Professor Nathaniel Micklem of Mansfield College, Oxford, put it thus: 'The ultimate scandal (*i.e.* stumbling-block) of evangelical religion . . . lies not in dogma or symbolism but in its intolerable offence to human pride. "Nothing in my hand I bring; simply to Thy cross I cling" – it is *that* which the man of taste and culture cannot bring himself to say; he feels no need of so utter a salvation; to him therefore it is nonsense or mere mythology that the majesty of God should take a Servant's form. . . . That is what the Master said: "the publicans and the harlots go into the kingdom before you"; that is the reason for the aversion of men of taste to evangelical religion.'[4]

[1] Rom. 3:27.   [2] 1 Cor. 1:31.   [3] Mt. 5:3; Rev. 3:17.
[4] Quoted from *Christendom*, a quarterly review, Autumn 1936 by J. K. van Baalen in *The Chaos of Cults* (Pickering and Inglis, 1957), p. 352.

Yet we cannot escape this stumbling-block, for it is central to biblical Christianity. Luther was right to call justification by faith 'the principal article of all Christian doctrine, which maketh true Christians indeed'.[5] And Cranmer endorsed it: 'This faith the Holy Scripture teacheth: this is the strong rock and foundation of Christian religion; this doctrine all old and ancient authors of Christ's Church do approve: this doctrine advanceth and setteth forth the true glory of Christ, and beateth down the vain glory of man: this doctrine whosoever denieth is not to be reputed [i.e. counted] for a true Christian man, nor for a setter-forth of Christ's glory, but for an adversary of Christ and His gospel, and for a setter-forth of men's vainglory.'[6]

The Second Vatican Council did not give its attention to the doctrine of salvation. Yet even so, if justification is indeed 'the principal article of all Christian doctrine', it is surprising to find no reference to it at all in *The Documents of Vatican II*. In the voluminous index of forty-four pages the word does not occur. There is some mention of 'salvation', however, including some welcome statements about both the centrality of the cross and the necessity of faith. Thus, the *Declaration on the Relationship of the Church to Non-Christian Religions* contains this: 'It is . . . the duty of the Church's preaching to proclaim the cross of Christ as the sign of God's all-embracing love and as the fountain from which every grace flows.'[7] And this is written on the origin of faith: 'Since no one can be saved who has not first believed, priests . . . have as their primary duty the proclamation of the gospel of God to all. . . . For through the saving Word the spark of faith is struck in the hearts of unbelievers, and fed in the hearts of the faithful.'[8]

Turning now to the Church of England, and speaking for myself, I am profoundly thankful that its services express so clearly the doctrine of justification by grace, and man's humble

---

[5] *Commentary on Galatians* (James Clarke, 1953), p. 143.
[6] From the 'Homily on Salvation' (1547) in *Book of Homilies and Canons*, pp. 25, 26. *Cf.* Article XI, *Of the Justification of Man*: 'We are accounted righteous before God, only for the merit of our Lord and Saviour Jesus Christ by Faith, and not for our own works or deservings: wherefore, that we are justified by Faith only is a most wholesome Doctrine, and very full of comfort. . . .'
[7] Abbott, p. 667.
[8] Abbott, pp. 538, 539. From the *Decree on the Ministry and Life of Priests*.

dependence on divine mercy. In his Litany Cranmer has cast every worshipper willy-nilly in the role of the publican, for he puts into our lips the repeated suffrage, 'Have mercy upon us miserable sinners.' At the Lord's Supper, at which we commemorate the mercy of God in the death of Christ, we say: 'We do not presume to come to this Thy Table, O merciful Lord, trusting in our own righteousness, but in Thy manifold and great mercies.' And after receiving Communion we ask God to receive and accept us, 'not weighing our merits, but pardoning our offences, through Jesus Christ our Lord'. I confess that I love to see a communicant kneeling at the rail. This is my brand image of a Christian. Not a soldier brandishing a sword, not an athlete stripped for the race, not a farmer braving wind and rain, with his hand on the plough and never looking back – though all these are true. But a penitent sinner, with knees bent, head bowed and downcast eyes, but with open, empty hands uplifted to receive a gift.

I do not know any more striking expression of this than was once given by Charles Simeon. At one of his weekly tea-parties in Cambridge somebody asked him: 'What, Sir, do you consider the principal mark of regeneration?' This was Simeon's reply: 'The very first and indispensable sign is self-loathing and abhorrence. Nothing short of this can be admitted as an evidence of a real change. . . . I want to see more of this humble, contrite, broken spirit amongst us. It is the very spirit that belongs to self-condemned sinners. . . . This sitting in the dust is most pleasing to God. . . . Give me to be with a broken-hearted Christian, and I prefer his society to that of all the rest. . . . Allow me to state to you what have sometimes been my feelings while seated in this chair by myself, shut in with God from the world around me. . . . I find myself with my God, instead of being shut up in an apartment in hell, although a hell-deserving sinner. Had I suffered my deserts, I should have been in those dark abodes of despair and anguish. There I should have thought of eternity – eternity! without hope of escape or release. From all this I am delivered by the grace of God, though I might have been cut off in my sins, fifty-four years ago. While engaged in these thoughts they sometimes overpower me. Were I now addressing to you my dying words, I should say nothing else but what I have just said. Try to live in this spirit of self-abhorrence, and let it habitually mark your life and conduct.'[9]

Whether we agree or disagree with Simeon in this, it is a good test whether our religion is truly evangelical or not.

This great evangelical principle of a free salvation, illustrated by Christ in His parable and recovered from oblivion at the Reformation, has again fallen into desuetude in the church. Lip-service is still paid to it, but it is scarcely preached. The man in the street is ignorant of it; so largely is the man in the pew.

Yet it is basic and distinctive to Christianity. All the other religions of the world are essentially systems of human merit. Even those which teach the mercy of God emphasize that He is merciful to the meritorious. Only Christianity announces that God is merciful to the undeserving, to sinners, who have no merit but the merit of Christ to plead, and no argument but the humble, believing cry, 'God, be merciful to me a sinner!'

[9] Carus, pp. 651, 652.

5 MORALITY: OUTWARD OR INWARD?

So far we have considered four major topics of controversy between Jesus Christ and the contemporary Jewish leaders: religion, authority, Scripture and salvation. We have seen how, in opposition to the Pharisees and Sadducees, Jesus taught that religion is not natural but supernatural (a life lived by the power of God), that authority is not in tradition but in Scripture (because tradition is human, Scripture divine), that Scripture is not an end in itself but a means to an end (pointing us to Christ that we may find life in Christ), and that salvation is due not to man's merit but to God's mercy.

The fifth topic of controversy is morality. Logically it comes next, because in a sense it is part of salvation, since 'salvation' includes sanctification as well as justification, holiness of life as well as acceptance with God. What, then, is the nature of the good life? And how can it be attained? How in any given situation can we know which action would be right and which wrong? What is it which makes us clean or unclean in God's sight?

The old and the new morality

These are important questions, and the answers given by the Pharisees were widely divergent from those given by Jesus Christ. They are still a field of controversy today, especially in the debate between the so-called 'old morality' and the so-called 'new morality'. It is necessary to look into this a little in order to see whether Christ's controversy with the Pharisees throws any light on the contemporary debate.

First, some definitions and explanations. The 'old' morality is commonly called 'prescriptive', because in it the rules are

largely laid down before you begin, whereas the 'new' morality
is called 'situational' because (according to this way of thinking)
it is the situation itself, not any pre-fixed rules, which will guide
your behaviour. The advocates of the new (or situational)
morality reject the old (or prescriptive) for two principal reasons.
First, because it is *authoritarian*. It is a morality revealed in
divine laws and buttressed by divine sanctions, so that right
conduct is imposed by an external authority called 'God'.
A situational ethic, on the other hand, they say, commends
itself by no authority but its own inherent reasonableness.

Secondly, they reject it because it is *absolute*. Laws are inflexible
things, they argue, and life is too complicated to be governed
by rigid rules. The new morality, on the other hand, is guided
by love, and love can adapt itself to 'the actual concrete relationship in all its particularity'.[1]

The new moralists do more than expound their position;
they go on to claim both Jesus Christ and the apostle Paul
as its champions. They maintain that Jesus Himself out of love
broke the law on a number of occasions, especially with regard
to the sabbath. And they like to quote some of Paul's epigrams
such as 'we are not under the law' or 'Christ is the end of the
law' or 'love is the fulfilling of the law'. Believing that they
have both dominical and apostolic warrant for their position,
they do not hesitate to repudiate the category of law from the
field of Christian ethics.

At this stage only one point needs to be made, namely that we
do not find in the life and teaching of Jesus such a neat antithesis between law and love as the new moralists describe.
The antithesis they pose is a false antithesis, and they force us
to make a choice which the Bible neither makes nor asks.[2]
Certainly Jesus made love pre-eminent. This is common ground.
But in doing so He did not reject law. What He rejected was the
scribal misinterpretations of the law, not the law itself. On the
contrary, He obeyed it in His own life. He stated plainly that
He had come not to abolish the law, but to fulfil it. He also

[1] *Honest to God* by J. A. T. Robinson (SCM Press, 1963), p. 114.
[2] In *Christian Morals Today* (SCM Press, 1964) Dr J. A. T. Robinson actually
modifies the position he had expounded in chapter 6 of *Honest to God* (1963).
He writes now of two 'polarities' – fixity and freedom, law and love, authority
and experience – and adds that there should be between them no 'sterile
antagonism' but rather a 'proper tension' (pp. 20, 22).

boldly echoed God's word in Ex. 20:6 ('those who love me and keep my commandments') by insisting that His disciples must love Him and keep His commandments.[3]

The Pharisees' obsession

One of the mistakes of the new moralists is their failure to distinguish between 'law' and 'legalism'. Legalism is a wrong use of law, by which it is perverted into either a way of salvation or a merely external code or both. What Jesus repudiated was Pharisaic legalism, not Mosaic (*i.e.* divine) law. His opposition to the morality of the Pharisees was not that their view of the law was authoritarian (imposed from above), nor that it was absolute (and therefore inflexible), but that it was external. In practice, they were reducing the law's absolute and authoritative demands. They were attempting to make the law less daunting and more manageable by codifying it into a set of man-made rules. As a result, their observance did not come from the heart, which is what primarily concerns God.

Let us look at Mark's record of the controversy:[4]

'Now when the Pharisees gathered together to him, with some of the scribes, who had come from Jerusalem, [2] they saw that some of his disciples ate with hands defiled, that is, unwashed. [3] (For the Pharisees, and all the Jews, do not eat unless they wash their hands, observing the tradition of the elders; [4] and when they come from the market place, they do not eat unless they purify themselves; and there are many other traditions which they observe, the washing of cups and pots and vessels of bronze.) [5] And the Pharisees and the scribes asked him, "Why do your disciples not live according to the tradition of the elders, but eat with hands defiled?" [6] And he said to them, "Well did Isaiah prophesy of you hypocrites, as it is written,

'This people honours me with their lips,
  but their heart is far from me;
[7] in vain do they worship me,
  teaching as doctrines the precepts of men.'

[8] You leave the commandment of God, and hold fast the tradition of men." . . .
[14] And he called the people to him again, and said to them,

[3] Jn. 14:15, 21; *cf.* 1 Jn. 5:3.   [4] Mk. 7:1–23.

"Hear me, all of you, and understand: [15] there is nothing outside a man which by going into him can defile him: but the things which come out of a man are what defile him." [17] And when he had entered the house, and left the people, his disciples asked him about the parable. [18] And he said to them, "Then are you also without understanding? Do you not see that whatever goes into a man from outside cannot defile him, [19] since it enters, not his heart but his stomach, and so passes on?" (Thus he declared all foods clean.) [20] And he said "What comes out of a man is what defiles a man. [21] For from within, out of the heart of man, come evil thoughts, fornication, theft, murder, adultery, [22] coveting, wickedness, deceit, licentiousness, envy, slander, pride, foolishness. [23] All these evil things come from within, and they defile a man." '

We began to study this passage in chapter 2, in order to illustrate our Lord's view of the relation between Scripture and tradition. The occasion of the controversy was that the Pharisees saw some of Jesus' disciples, perhaps on their return from the market-place (6 : 56), eating 'with hands defiled, that is, unwashed' (vv. 1, 2). Mark goes on to explain to his Gentile readers (vv. 3, 4) that the Pharisees – and indeed 'all the Jews', following popular Pharisaic teaching – were punctilious in 'observing the tradition of the elders', particularly in the matter of purifying themselves by washing their hands before eating, and by washing cups, pots and vessels as well. After this explanation Mark continues his narrative. The Pharisees came to Jesus and asked (v. 5): 'Why do your disciples not live according to the tradition of the elders, but eat with hands defiled?' It is important to note that in the Pharisees' query two separate questions were combined. The first was general as to why the disciples of Jesus did not conform to the ancient traditions; the second concerned a particular tradition regarding purification and why the disciples did not observe it.

In the discourse which follows Jesus answers both questions. He begins by quoting Isaiah 29 : 13 as a prophecy of Pharisaism. In it the two subjects are touched upon. God roundly rebukes His Pharisaic people both for their worship (which is a homage of lips, not heart) and for their teaching (which is an instruction in the traditions of men, not in the commandments of God). Taking this Old Testament verse as His text Jesus proceeds

to preach a sermon, in which He expounds and illustrates this
double theme. First, He speaks about the place of tradition, and
secondly, about the nature of defilement and therefore of purification. First (in vv. 6–13) He subordinates tradition to Scripture, as we saw in chapter 2. Secondly (in vv. 14–23) He insists
that the defilement and therefore the purification which really
matter are inward and moral, not outward and ritual. What
defiles men in God's sight is not the food which enters their
stomach, but the sin which comes out of their heart.

The portrait of the Pharisees which the Evangelist paints
here is accurate and fair. These Pharisees of the first century AD
were descended from the *Hasidim* ('pious people') of a century
or two earlier. The word 'Pharisees' means 'separated ones',
and was applied to them 'when they withdrew from the Sadducee
court party of the Maccabean rulers and John Hyrcanus (135–
105 BC)'.[5] They were determined to resist the incoming tide of
Greek influence. Fundamental to their position was this principle, that they 'regarded nature and spirit as so related that
impurity could pass from one to the other'. Thus, 'a bad man's
body was impure, and to touch it would bring uncleanness
to another man's soul'.[6] This principle naturally led them to
devise complicated ritual regulations, which were later collected
in the six divisions of the Mishnah. 'Their aim was in daily life
to be as ceremonially pure as the priests were in the temple.'[7]

Prominent among these rules regarding ceremonial purification was the matter of hand-washing. 'He who lightly
esteems hand-washing', went one tradition, 'will perish from the
earth.' This emphasis was universal among them. Edersheim
describes the strictness with which the rituals were observed,
and points out that Hillel and Shammai, the two great rival
teachers who flourished shortly before Christ, although they
disagreed on many points, yet agreed about the ordinance of
hand-washing and on the 'eighteen decrees' which were intended to purify the Jews from defiling contact with Gentiles.[8]

It is no wonder, therefore, that, seeing the disciples of Jesus
eat without washing their hands, and hearing His subsequent
teaching, 'the Pharisees were offended'.[9]

[5] Scott, p. 351.   [6] Scott, p. 354.   [7] Scott, p. 351.
[8] Edersheim, vol. II, pp. 9–14.   [9] Mt. 15:12.

What did Jesus say? The next paragraph (vv. 14–23) is divided into two parts, the first being His words to the crowd, and the second to the disciples. To the crowd He said, 'Hear me, all of you, and understand: there is nothing outside a man which by going into him can defile him; but the things which come out of a man are what defile him' (vv. 14, 15). By these words He establishes the fundamental principle: what defiles a man, rendering him unclean in the sight of God, is what comes out of him, not what goes into him. This principle Jesus later elaborated to His disciples privately (vv. 17–23), in answer to a question they asked Him. After expressing His sorrow that His own disciples seemed to share the people's lack of understanding, He went on: 'Do you not see that whatever goes into a man from outside cannot defile him . . .?' whereas 'What comes out of a man is what defiles a man'. This contrast between what 'goes in' and what 'comes out' Jesus now explained to the disciples, which He had not done to the crowd. What 'goes in' is food. It cannot defile because (v. 19) 'it enters, not his heart but his stomach, and so passes on' – a dictum by which (Mark adds) Jesus 'declared all foods clean', effectively abrogating the Old Testament food regulations. What 'comes out', on the other hand, is sin. This is what defiles him, because it issues from his heart (vv. 20, 21).

There follows an ugly catalogue of thirteen vices. The first, which seems to be generic and to cover the rest, is 'evil thoughts'. Perhaps Christ was thinking of the hostile thoughts which the Pharisees were harbouring about Him at the very moment when they were professing their concern about proper purification. Next come six words in the plural, indicating repeated acts of sin, followed by six words in the singular, emphasizing the sinful state or act itself. 'All these', Jesus concluded, are 'evil things'. Further, they 'come from within, and they defile a man' (v. 23). This sentence contains an important twofold statement about the origin and outcome of sin, the cause and effect of all human misconduct. Its origin is the heart, and its outcome defilement in the sight of God.

Having looked briefly at Christ's answer to the disciples' question, we must pursue its implications. In general, the Pharisees were obsessed with external, ritual purification – clean hands, clean foods, clean vessels. Jesus, on the other hand,

stressed the essential inwardness of morality, that God's concern
is more with the heart than with the hands.

From these verses, and from other altercations which Jesus
had with the Pharisees over morality, four implications may be
drawn. They can be expressed in four assertions.

The new birth is indispensable

True, Jesus does not mention the new birth in this passage.
But the evangelical insistence upon regeneration arises directly
from His teaching here. Since the 'evil things' men do and say
originate in their heart, therefore a change of conduct depends
upon a change of heart.

It is difficult to understand those who cling to the doctrine
of the fundamental goodness of human nature, and do so in a
generation which has witnessed two devastating World Wars
and especially the horrors which occasioned and accompanied
the second. It is even harder to understand those who attribute
this belief to Jesus Christ. For He taught nothing of the kind.
This question is so important that we must pursue it awhile.
What did Jesus think and say about human nature?

The first thing to be said is that He taught the essential dignity
of man. Although He is never recorded as having used the
expression, there is no doubt that He accepted the Old Testament
assertion that God made man in His own image, endowing
him with capacities – rational, moral, social and spiritual –
which distinguish him from animals. And despite man's fallenness
and sinfulness (to which we shall come in a moment), Jesus
evidently thought of him as still retaining vestiges of his former
glory. So He spoke of man's value. Man is of more value than a
sheep, He said; of much more value than many sparrows.[1]
And the clearest evidence He gave of the value He placed on
man was His own mission, which was undertaken solely for man's
benefit. Like a shepherd who, having lost a single sheep, first
misses it and then braves hardship and danger to rescue it, so
God misses human beings who get lost and sent Jesus Christ
as the Good Shepherd to seek and to save them. Further, His
search for straying sheep would take Him to the cross. 'The good
shepherd lays down his life for the sheep.'[2] Nothing reveals
more clearly the preciousness of men to God and the love of

[1] Mt. 12:12; 10:31.   [2] Jn. 10:11.

God for men than the death of God's Son for their salvation. As William Temple put it, 'My worth is what I am worth to God, and that is a marvellous great deal, for Christ died for me.'[3]

Nevertheless, side by side with His teaching on the essential dignity of man Christ affirmed man's actual degradation. The Old Testament had taught that 'there is none that does good, no, not one';[4] Jesus took over this doctrine and endorsed it. Two or three times He referred to His contemporaries as an 'evil and adulterous generation'[5] – 'evil' because of their unbelief and disobedience, 'adulterous' because they had transferred their love and loyalty from the living God to idols of their own making.

Nor was He passing judgment on His own generation only; He was alluding to mankind as a whole. Thus in the Sermon on the Mount He said: 'If you then, who are evil, know how to give good gifts to your children, how much more will your Father who is in heaven give good things to those who ask him!'[6] This statement is particularly striking because it concedes that fallen men can give 'good' gifts. It is perfectly true that fathers (and mothers) love their children, make sacrifices on their behalf and give them good gifts; at the same time they do not escape the designation 'evil'. That is, even when we see people at their very best, following the noble instincts of parenthood, Jesus still calls them 'evil'.

Jesus confirmed His view of man's sin and corruption by all His teaching about man's lostness and sickness.[7] His vivid metaphors of the shepherd seeking the lost sheep and the physician healing the sick tell us as much about man's hopeless state as about his preciousness to the God who loves him.

It is specially plain in His controversy with the Pharisees over defilement. Let me draw your attention to what He says in this passage[8] about every human being, by giving a literal translation of the Greek: 'What comes out of *the man*, that defiles *the man*. For from inside, out of the heart of *the men* their evil thoughts come out. . . . All these evil things come out from

[3] In *Citizen and Churchman*, p. 74, quoted by F. D. Coggan in his 'The New Testament Basis for Evangelism', a paper contributed to *Evangelicals Affirm* (Church Book Room Press, 1948), p. 23.
[4] Ps. 14:3.   [5] *E.g.* Mt. 12:39; Mk. 8:38.
[6] Mt. 7:11.   [7] *E.g.* Lk. 15; Mt. 9:12.
[8] Mk. 7:20–23.

inside and defile *the man*.' The use of the definite article in each case must not be missed. Jesus Christ was not painting the portrait of some notorious evil-doer, but of every man. He was not giving us a description of some primitive tribe sunk in the darkness and degradation of heathenism. On the contrary, He was actually speaking about people who in varying degrees were cultured, refined, moral and religious – the Pharisees on the one hand and His own disciples on the other!

Jesus taught that within the soil of every man's heart there lie buried the ugly seeds of every conceivable sin – 'evil thoughts, acts of fornication, of theft, murder, adultery, ruthless greed, and malice; fraud, indecency, envy, slander, arrogance, and folly.'[9] All thirteen are 'evil things', and they come out of the heart of 'the man' or 'the men', every man. This is Jesus Christ's estimate of fallen human nature.

So then, according to Jesus, the 'evil things' which we think, say and do are not due primarily to our environment, nor are they bad habits picked up from bad teaching, bad company or bad example; they are due to the inward corruption of our heart. This is not to say that environment, education and example are unimportant, for their influence for good or bad is very strong, and Christians should set themselves in these spheres to promote the good and eliminate the bad. What we are saying (because Jesus said it long ago) is that the dominant force in a person's life is his heredity, and that the ultimate origin of his evil thoughts and deeds is his evil heart, his nature which is twisted with self-centredness. As God had said through the prophet Jeremiah centuries previously: 'The heart is deceitful above all things, and desperately corrupt; who can understand it?'[1]

Our Lord's favourite metaphor for illustrating that our words and deeds are governed by our heart was that of the tree and its fruit. 'You will know them by their fruits,' He said of false prophets. And more elaborately: 'So, every sound tree bears good fruit, but the bad tree bears evil fruit. A sound tree cannot bear evil fruit, nor can a bad tree bear good fruit. . . . Thus you will know them by their fruits.'[2] We are not left to guess what He meant by this, because elsewhere He made it explicit. The tree is man's heart or nature, and the fruit his

[9] Mk. 7:21, 22, NEB.   [1] Je. 17:9.   [2] Mt. 7:16–20.

words and deeds. As the condition of a tree determines the fruit it bears, so a man's heart determines his behaviour. Thus, 'how can you *speak* good, when you *are* evil? For out of the abundance of the heart the mouth speaks.'[3] We say and do evil things because we have an evil heart or nature; it is from inside, out of our heart, that evil things and evil thoughts arise.

Modern psycho-analysis has tended only to confirm this teaching of the Old Testament which Jesus endorsed, because it has further uncovered the horrid secrets of the human heart. Psychology and experience tell us that the subconscious mind (which is roughly equivalent to what the Bible means by 'heart', namely the centre of our personality, the source of our thoughts and emotions) is like a deep well with a thick deposit of mud at the bottom. Normally, being at the bottom, the mud is safely out of sight. But when the well-waters are stirred, especially by the winds of violent emotion, the most evil-looking and evil-smelling filth breaks the surface – rage, spite, greed, lust, jealousy, malice, cruelty and revenge. These base passions keep bubbling up, raw and sinister, from the secret springs of the heart. And if we have any moral sensitivity, we must at times be appalled, shocked and disgusted by the foul things which lurk in the hidden depths of our personality.

The deduction which Christ draws from this principle (the principle that our heart controls our hands, or our nature governs our behaviour) is that only a 'radical' solution will do – a solution which goes to the root (*radix*) of the problem. In fact, the heart of the problem is the heart. So good moral conduct depends on our being given a new heart. And Jesus said this was possible: 'Make the tree good, and its fruit good.' Then this will come to pass: 'The good man out of the good treasure of his heart produces good.'[4]

Jesus spelled this out further in His conversation with Nicodemus.[5] It is important to note that Nicodemus was a Pharisee. At the same time, he represents the very best that Pharisaism could produce. He does not seem to have suffered from the hypocrisy which vitiated so much of the Pharisees' religion. On the contrary he appears to have been a sincere and humble seeker after the truth. Yet it was to him that Jesus said: 'Truly, truly, I say to you, unless one is born anew, he cannot see the

[3] Mt. 12:34.   [4] Mt. 12:33; Lk. 6:45.   [5] Jn. 3:1ff.

kingdom of God. . . . That which is born of the flesh is flesh,
and that which is born of the Spirit is spirit. Do not marvel
that I said to you, "You must be born anew" ' (vv. 3, 6, 7).
This new birth, He explained, is a birth *anōthen*, an adverb
which could equally well mean 'from the beginning, again,
anew' or 'from above' (like the Temple veil which was torn
in half 'from top' to bottom, Mk. 15 : 38). Probably Jesus
deliberately chose a word with two meanings, as several commentators have suggested, because the new birth is both a second
birth and a divine birth, both a fresh beginning and a miracle
of God. To be 'born anew' (vv. 3, 7) is to be 'born of the Spirit'
(vv. 5, 8). So the new birth is a profound inward change, the
implantation by God of a new life, the bestowal of a new nature,
the gift of a new heart. Though apparently it could be and was
experienced in Old Testament days, yet the Old Testament
describes it as one of the greatest blessings which the New
Covenant will bring: 'A new heart I will give you, and a new
spirit I will put within you . . . I will put my spirit within you,
and cause you to walk in my statutes. . . .' Again, 'I will put
my law within them, and I will write it upon their hearts.'[6]

In this new birth, and in the new life to which it introduces us,
the work of the Holy Spirit is paramount. It is the Spirit who
regenerates. It is the Spirit also who indwells every regenerate
believer[7] and sanctifies him. This is why Paul refers to holiness
as 'the fruit of the Spirit'.[8] Perhaps he is echoing Christ's own
teaching about trees and their fruit. At all events, the nine
beautiful graces he lists – 'love, joy, peace, patience, kindness,
goodness, fidelity, gentleness, and self-control' (NEB) – are
qualities which the Holy Spirit Himself produces, cultivating
them in a Christian's character as in an orchard.

So the Christian should resemble a fruit-tree, not a Christmas
tree! For the gaudy decorations of a Christmas tree are only
tied on, whereas fruit *grows* on a fruit-tree. In other words,
Christian holiness is not an artificial human accretion, but a
natural process of fruit-bearing by the power of the Holy Spirit.
As Jesus was later to promise His apostles in the Upper Room:
'I am the vine, you are the branches. He who abides in me, and
I in him, he it is that bears much fruit, for apart from me you

[6] Ezk. 36:26, 27; Je. 31:33. [7] See, *e.g.*, 1 Cor. 6:19; Rom. 8:9.
[8] Gal. 5:22, 23.

can do nothing.'⁹ Dr J. W. C. Wand, formerly Bishop of London, has put this truth succinctly in writing that holiness is 'not the laborious acquisition of virtue from without, but the expression of the Christ-life from within'.

These great doctrines – the indispensable necessity of the new birth for a new life, or the work of the Holy Spirit in both regeneration and sanctification – are true evangelical emphases. They are part and parcel of Christ's teaching about the essential inwardness of evil and therefore the essential inwardness of morality also. As Bishop Ryle expressed it: 'We hold that a mighty spiritual disease like this requires a mighty spiritual medicine for its cure. . . . We dread fostering man's favourite notion that a little church-going and sacrament-receiving – a little patching, and mending, and whitewashing, and gilding, and polishing, and varnishing, and painting the outside – is all that his case requires. . . . It requires nothing less than . . . the grace of God the Holy Ghost entirely renewing the heart. . . . I believe that ignorance of the extent of the fall, and of the whole doctrine of original sin, is one grand reason why many can neither understand, appreciate nor receive Evangelical Religion. Next to the Bible, as its foundation, it is based on a clear view of original sin.'¹

At this point it seems right to add a word of caution, even of evangelical self-criticism and penitence. Our right emphasis on the necessity of the new birth and on the impossibility of true holiness without it has sometimes led evangelicals to a wrong consequence. This is best described as 'pietism'. Historically, the word has been used to denote various tendencies, good and bad. I am using it here, for want of a better term, to refer to that kind of personal devotion which results in a withdrawal from social and even moral responsibility. The kind of 'pietistic' position I have in mind might be argued thus: 'If goodness is the fruit of the Spirit, the natural produce of a heart renewed and indwelt by the Spirit, then this and nothing else really matters. There is no need to teach ethical conduct to Christian people, for it will come to them naturally. Further, there is no sense in seeking to promote morality in unrenewed people or to secure better social structures, since moral and social

⁹ Jn. 15:5.
¹ *Knots Untied* by Bishop J. C. Ryle (Thynne, 1871), pp. 4, 5.

renewal are the automatic consequence of personal renewal and cannot take place without it.'

I do not think this overstates the case. Evangelical Christians have undoubtedly thought and spoken like this from time to time. Indeed, I have done so myself. But this point of view is a false deduction from a true doctrine. Vital, indeed indispensable, as the new birth is for entry into God's kingdom and for Christ-likeness, it is not the be-all and end-all of Christian life and responsibility. We have other duties to both the renewed and the unrenewed, that is, to both Christians and non-Christians.

Take the renewed first. To say that sanctification is a *natural* consequence of regeneration, is not to say that it is an *automatic* consequence. The truly regenerate Christian can still behave badly and thoughtlessly, sin grievously, fail in personal relationships and get into marriage problems. This is evident in the New Testament and in the lives of our fellow-Christians, yes, and we know it in our own lives also. Hence the detailed moral instructions which are given in the Epistles – about controlling the tongue, about the duty of working hard to earn our living, about being honest, just, hospitable, forgiving and kind, about sexual purity, and about the reciprocal duties between husbands and wives, parents and children, masters and servants. But were these not Christian people, regenerate people, to whom the apostles addressed these admonitions? Yes, they were! But the apostles did not take the holiness of the regenerate for granted; they worked for it by detailed instruction, by exhortation, example and prayer.

What about the unrenewed, however? Here too we have a Christian responsibility. It would be wrong to argue that, since the key to morality and justice is the new birth, and since social renewal depends on personal renewal, it is useless either to teach righteousness to the unrenewed or to concern ourselves with the structures of society. We have no liberty to say that our sole responsibility as Christians is to preach the gospel of salvation, since moral and social righteousness will then follow naturally.

I say we do not have this liberty, because the Scripture itself does not grant it to us. If, therefore, evangelicals concentrate exclusively on personal conversion and personal morality, we are not being true to our claim to be biblical Christians. How is this? We need to remember that the living God of the biblical revelation is not only the Saviour and Father of His covenant people; He is also the Creator, Lord and Judge of all mankind. And He is a righteous God who loves righteousness, who is concerned (as Amos showed[2]) for the practice of righteousness and for the punishment of unrighteousness in every human community, in heathen nations as well as in Israel and Judah. Similarly, Christian parents are to bring up their children 'in the discipline and instruction of the Lord'[3] from their earliest days, and not wait until their children profess conversion before they teach them morality. Again, the God-given function of every state, however secular and godless it may be, is to punish the evil-doer and reward the law-abiding citizen, and so restrain evil and promote good in the whole community, whether Christian or not.[4] Further, although the individual has – or can have – more influence on his environment than his environment has on him, and although it is more his heredity than his environment which makes every man what he is, this is no excuse for being callously indifferent to his environment. For people are profoundly affected by their environment (whether by 'environment' we are thinking of political tyranny, social injustice, racial discrimination, unemployment, poverty, bad housing, undernourishment or an inadequate health service). Besides, even if people were not adversely affected by a bad environment, it would still be right to play our part in the attempt to improve it. It is not a matter of expediency only, but of simple justice and love. So the Christian should seek to be a good citizen as well as a good witness. If he tries to spread the good news of salvation through Jesus Christ, of a new birth and a new life, he should also join in the fight against social injustice and political oppression, and so contribute, however little, to the search for a social order which guarantees freedom, justice, dignity and welfare for all men.

God looks on the heart

A second deduction which may be drawn from Christ's controversy with the Pharisees over morality is that God's primary concern is with the condition of a man's heart. 'For from within,'

[2] See Am. 1:3 – 2:5.   [3] Eph. 6:4.
[4] See Rom. 13:1ff.; 1 Pet. 2:13, 14.

He insisted, 'out of the heart of man, come evil thoughts. . . .
All these evil things come from within.'[5] Again, 'God knows
your hearts.'[6]

As a matter of fact, several of the 'evil things' Christ listed
not only come out of the heart, but remain in the heart as inward
and secret offences. Thus, 'evil thoughts' may break out in evil
words or deeds, but they are still evil even if they never visibly
erupt. 'Covetousness' may lead to theft, and 'envy' to many
sins, but they too are evil when they never get further than our
thoughts and desires. Similarly, 'pride' usually betrays its
presence in haughty looks and vain practices, but even if the
proud man succeeds in preserving a humble appearance, his
secret pride is still an abomination to the Lord. So the heart's
desires, in Paul's language 'the lusts of the flesh', are themselves
evil in God's sight, quite apart from the sins of speech and action
to which they frequently give birth.

This leads us to the astonishing statement which Jesus made
to His disciples in the Sermon on the Mount, namely that 'unless
your righteousness exceeds that of the scribes and Pharisees,
you will never enter the kingdom of heaven'.[7] Now the Pharisees
were, in their own way, very righteous indeed. They calculated
that the law contained 248 commandments and 365 prohibitions, and they were meticulous in observing them all (at
least outwardly). They could say, as did Saul the Pharisee,
that they were 'in legal rectitude, faultless'.[8]

How then could Jesus insist that the righteousness of His
disciples must exceed the righteousness of the Pharisees, and
warn them that, if it did not, they would never enter God's
kingdom? The answer is not difficult to find. Despite the
Pharisees' zeal for righteousness, their view of it was superficial.
They concentrated their attention on a wooden, external
conformity to the law (as they understood it) and imagined that
this was enough. They also overlarded it with their traditional
interpretations.

But Jesus taught in the Sermon on the Mount that God's
standards were much higher and His scrutiny much deeper
than the Pharisees ever realized. He went on immediately
(Mt. 5 : 21–48) to utter six parallel instructions, each introduced

[5] Mk. 7:21, 23.   [6] Lk. 16:15.   [7] Mt. 5:20.
[8] Phil. 3:6, NEB.

by the same formula, 'You have heard that it was said. . . . But
I say to you . . .' It is widely supposed that Jesus was now in-
augurating a new law, and that in doing so He was contradicting
and repudiating the old. Nothing could be further from the
truth. Indeed, the suggestion that He should do this is ante-
cedently so improbable as to be impossible. Not only would
this run counter to His lifelong attitude of reverent assent to
Scripture, but He had just asserted that He had not 'come to
abolish the law and the prophets . . . but to fulfil them' (v. 17).
He then solemnly added that 'till heaven and earth pass away,
not an iota, not a dot, will pass from the law until all is accomplished' (v. 18), and warned His hearers that anybody who
'relaxes one of the least of these commandments and teaches
men so, shall be called least in the kingdom of heaven' (v. 19).
In the light of these statements it is absurd to argue that Jesus
was disagreeing with the law.

No. What Jesus was contradicting here was not Scripture
but tradition, not what 'is written' but what 'was said', not
God's Word but the false interpretations of it of which the
scribes and Pharisees were guilty. In each case they were attempting to reduce the challenge of the divine law in order to suit
their convenience, either by restricting what it commanded or
by extending what it permitted. A quotation by Professor C. E. B.
Cranfield from H. Roux is appropriate here:[9] 'It is characteristic
of all those who would find their justification in the Law, that
they always end by modifying it or perverting it, in order to
escape from it and to make void its authority.' This is why
Jesus said that the righteousness of Christian disciples must
exceed the righteousness of Pharisees. The Pharisees were tamper-
ing with the law to make it less exacting; the disciple must accept
its full force and all its implications.

Take the permissions of the law, which the traditions of the
elders sought to extend. The law permitted divorce when the
husband found 'some indecency' in his wife;[1] but tradition was
increasingly extending this permission to include any arbitrary
whim of a husband.[2] In His answer Jesus referred them back
to the lifelong purpose of marriage according to its institution

---

[9] Cranfield, p. 244.   [1] Dt. 24:1ff.
[2] *Cf.* Mt. 19:3, where the Pharisees asked: 'Is it lawful to divorce one's wife
for any cause?'

in Genesis, and then seems to have restricted the ground of divorce to sexual unfaithfulness.[3] Again, the law permitted retribution in the lawcourts, in order to guide the magistrate and to restrict penalties to this maximum or to some equivalent restitution ('an eye for an eye and a tooth for a tooth'). Traditional interpretation, however, seems to have extended this permission to the realm of personal relationships and to have used it to justify personal revenge. Jesus insisted that such teaching was a perverse manipulation of the law, and that in personal ethics the Christian way was to accept an injustice without resistance or redress.[4]

The scribes did not only attempt to extend the law's permissions; they also tried to restrict the law's uncomfortable commands. Thus, God's law said 'you shall love your neighbour'. Tradition interpreted the word 'neighbour' narrowly, applying it only to a fellow-Israelite, even only to a friend. In so doing the scribes were effectively perverting the command 'you shall love your neighbour' into 'you shall love your neighbour *and hate your enemy*' (which, of course, the law nowhere says). As H. M. Scott writes: 'Pharisaic ethics taught to hate Gentiles as enemies.'[5] Jesus contradicted this tradition and taught instead that, properly understood, our neighbour includes our enemy: 'I say unto you, Love your enemies. . . .'[6] Similarly, the scribes restricted the command, 'You shall not swear falsely, but shall perform to the Lord what you have sworn' as if it only prohibited some oaths and permitted others. But Jesus accepted no such restriction. On the contrary, the true implication of the command, He said, was 'Do not swear at all'. All promises must be kept, and the Christian disciple should be so truthful that he has no need to confirm any promise with an oath. 'Let what you say be simply "Yes" or "No"; anything more than this comes from evil.'[7]

It is the same in principle with the remaining two commandments Jesus mentions, those relating to murder and adultery. As with the superficial morality of today, so with the traditions of the Jewish elders, these prohibitions were restricted to the act alone. But Jesus emphasized that they had a much more searching application. The angry thought and the insulting

[3] Mt. 5:31, 32. [4] Mt. 5:38–42. [5] Scott, p. 354.
[6] Mt. 5:43–48. [7] Mt. 5:33–37.

word are also breaches of the prohibition of murder, He said, and expose us to the danger of judgment. Similarly, the lustful look is equivalent to adultery, for 'every one who looks at a woman lustfully has already committed adultery with her *in his heart*'.[8]

These six illustrations leave us in no doubt what Jesus meant when He said that Christian righteousness must exceed Pharisaic righteousness. Christian righteousness accepts the full implications of the law without trying to dodge them. It recognizes that the law's domain extends beyond the actual deed to the word, and beyond the word to the thoughts and motives of the heart. Pharisaic righteousness was an outward conformity to human traditions; Christian righteousness is an inward conformity of mind and heart to the revealed will of God.

It is necessary now to add that the 'new morality' has a similar (though not identical) tendency to that of Pharisaic morality. True, the advocates of the new morality think that the opposite is the case. They maintain that Jesus had a much more liberal attitude to the law than the Pharisees (witness His 'sabbath-breaking' and their horrified reaction), and they go on to claim that what they are saying to the defenders of the old morality is no different from what Jesus was saying to the Pharisees. We do not believe, however, that Jesus either broke the sabbath law or would even have dreamed of doing so (since He accepted its divine origin). What He did was to infringe some of the traditions of the elders about the sabbath, and in so doing to show the true intention of God's command. We shall come back to this later.

Of course there is a radical difference between Pharisaic morality and the new morality, in that the former was absolutist and prescriptive, while the latter is relativistic and situational. Nevertheless, there is one point at which a comparison may fairly be drawn between the two. It is that both have the effect of diminishing the law's demands. The Pharisees were guilty of misinterpreting the law, Jesus said, and so of reducing its challenge. The teaching of the new morality goes further and insists that the category of 'law' has been altogether abolished for the Christian. He is not 'under law', they say, in any sense. Only one law has not been abrogated, namely the compre-

[8] Mt. 5:21-26 and 27-30.

hensive law of love. This is an absolute; there are no others. 'Nothing prescribed except love' is the new morality's slogan. All morality is relative to this one and only absolute. 'Nothing else makes a thing right or wrong.'[9]

It is essential to be fair to the new moralists. They are not – at least the best of them are not – encouraging moral licence. Some of them even maintain that the demands of love are *more* rather than less exacting than those of law. Thus, Dr Robinson urges that 'love's casuistry must cut deeper and must be more searching, more demanding, than anything required by the law'.[1] This is a doubtful claim, however, because the new morality repudiates all absolutes but love, whereas the old morality seeks to meet the demands of both law and love together. Further, there can be no doubt that the popular understanding of the new morality, whoever is to blame for this state of affairs, is that it is a lot less demanding than the old and that even the ancient prohibition of adultery may be disregarded if the adulterer sincerely believes that his action is consistent with love.

What the biblical Christian would wish to affirm is that, in the Christian morality of the New Testament (never mind whether we call it 'new' or 'old'), love and law are not incompatible, still less mutually exclusive. For love needs law to guide it. It is rather naïve to claim that love has no need of any direction outside itself because 'it has a built-in moral compass, enabling it to "home" intuitively upon the deepest need of the other'.[2] Do the new moralists forget that man is fallen? Love is not infallible. Indeed, it is sometimes blind. So God has given us commandments to chart the pathways of love. The five commandments of the second table of the law are all expressions of love. Hence Paul's statement: 'he who loves his neighbour has fulfilled the law. The commandments, "You shall not commit

---

[9] Quotations from J. A. T. Robinson's *Honest to God* (SCM Press, 1963), pp. 114–119.

[1] *Honest to God*, p. 118; cf. *Christian Morals Today*, p. 42.

[2] *Honest to God*, p. 115. Actually, as in the general relation between law and love, so more particularly in love's need of law, Dr Robinson has modified in *Christian Morals Today* (1964) the more rigorous position he adopted regarding the new morality in chapter 6 of *Honest to God*. He now writes: 'The Christian can never say that he is beyond or outside the sphere of law. He needs it . . .' (p. 21). Again, 'the deeper one's concern for persons, the more effectively one wants to see love buttressed by law' (p. 26).

adultery, You shall not kill, You shall not steal, You shall not covet," and any other commandment, are summed up in this sentence, "You shall love your neighbour as yourself." Love does no wrong to a neighbour; therefore love is the fulfilling of the law.'[3] Love is not the finish of the law (in the sense that it dispenses with it); love is the fulfilment of the law (in the sense that it obeys it). What the New Testament says about law and love is not 'if you love you can break the law', but 'if you love you will keep it'.

Why, then, does Paul say that Christians are 'not under law' (a kind of proof text of the new morality)? It is true that he uses this expression several times, but never as a suspended negative. He always supplies (or at least implies) a contrast. Indeed, you can never understand the meaning of a negative unless you know with what it is being contrasted. For example, if I simply wrote of someone that 'he does not behave like a man', you would not know if I was being extremely complimentary and implying that he was more like an angel, or if I was being rude and implying that he was more like a child, or a woman, or even a beast. I remember once, on my return from a trip to America and Australia, that I shocked my friends by saying, 'I haven't had a bath for seven weeks.' Before they had time to take me to task for my unhygienic habits, however, I was able to add, 'But I've had a shower every day!' Thus, every negative is misleading unless it is read in the light of the positive with which it is being contrasted.

Now Paul never expressed his negatives in isolation. His statements that the Christian is 'not under law' never meant that the category of law has been altogether abolished for him, but rather that he does not look to the law for either his justification or his sanctification. It would in any case be useless for him to do so, because of the law's 'weakness'. Paul writes: 'God has done what the law, *weakened by the flesh*, could not do.'[4] It will be seen from this that the weakness of the law is not in itself but in us. Because of our fallen nature, we cannot by ourselves keep the law. And because we cannot keep the law, it can neither justify nor sanctify us. Instead, God has done for us and in us what the law could not have accomplished. And He

[3] Rom. 13:8-10; *cf.* Gal. 5:14; 6:2.   [4] Rom. 8:3.

has done it by the sending of both His Son and His Spirit. He justifies us through the death of His Son and sanctifies us through the indwelling of His Spirit.[5] That is, God's way of acceptance is not our striving to obey the law but the finished work of Christ. His way of holiness also is not our striving to obey the law, but the inward work of the Spirit.

It is in this double sense, then, that Paul declares we have been 'freed' from the law and urges us to stand fast in the freedom with which Christ has set us free.[6] It is in this sense too that he tells us we are 'not under the law'. We are now in a position to understand his negative from its positive counterparts. As for our justification: 'You are not under law but under grace.'[7] As for our sanctification: 'if you are led by the Spirit you are not under the law.'[8] That is, our justification depends not on law but on grace, and our sanctification not on law but on the Spirit. The Christian believer looks to the law for neither his justification nor his sanctification; instead he looks to grace for both. For 'law' means our own efforts at obedience; 'grace' means the saving initiative of God through His Son and His Spirit.[9]

But this repudiation of law both as the ground of our justification and as the means of our sanctification does not dispense with it as the standard of our conduct. The contrary is the case. Although we are not justified by law but by grace, yet God justifies us 'in order that the just requirement of the law might be fulfilled in us . . .'.[1] Again, although we are not sanctified by the law but by the Spirit, yet what the Spirit does in sanctifying us is precisely to write the law in our hearts![2] Thus the observance of the law, though not the ground of our justification, is the result of it, and though not the means of our sanctification is the essence of it. Samuel Bolton, the Puritan, summed up Paul's teaching about the law and the gospel in this epigram: 'The law sends us to the Gospel, that we may be justified, and the

---

[5] Rom. 8:3, 4.   [6] Rom. 8:2; Gal. 4:5; 5:1.
[7] Rom. 6:14, 15; cf. Gal. 5:3, 4.   [8] Gal. 5:18; cf. v. 23.
[9] Hence the contrast in Rom. 8:3 between 'law' and 'God'; 'God has done what the law . . . could not do.'
[1] Rom. 8:4.
[2] Je. 31:33; 2 Cor. 3:3. The contrast between the Old Covenant and the New is not between 'law' and 'no law', but between the law on tablets (an external code) and the law in our hearts (an inward work of the Spirit).

Gospel sends us to the law again to enquire what is our duty being justified.'[3]

So when in one place Paul writes 'neither circumcision counts for anything, nor uncircumcision, but a new creation'[4] and in another place 'neither circumcision counts for anything nor uncircumcision, but keeping the commandments of God',[5] he is not contradicting himself. For the new creation (or new birth) issues in a new carefulness to keep God's commandments. Indeed, John insists that 'sin is lawlessness', while one of the indispensable evidences of the new birth is that we do not persist in such sin but obey God's commandments instead.[6]

And when the Holy Spirit writes God's law in our hearts, He gives us both an inward apprehension of its meaning and an ardent desire to obey it. The language of the regenerate believer, with which the stance of the new morality cannot easily be reconciled, is 'Oh, how I love thy law! It is my meditation all the day'; 'I delight in the law of God, in my inmost self', and 'the precepts of the Lord are right, rejoicing the heart'.[7]

Thus we are back to the *heart* again, to the difference between Pharisaic righteousness and Christian righteousness, and to Christ's insistence on an observance of God's law which is not a reluctant, external conformity, but a willing, inward conformity of mind and will and heart.

The moral takes precedence over the ceremonial

The third implication which may be drawn from Christ's controversy with the Pharisees over morality concerns the comparative importance of moral and ceremonial duties. The Pharisaic concept of both defilement and purification was largely a ritual one. They were scrupulous in regard to what they were allowed and not allowed to eat. In addition, the vessels in which the food was prepared, and from which it was later eaten, had first to be cleansed with flawless ceremonial exactitude.

---

[3] *The True Bounds of Christian Freedom* (1645) quoted by E. F. Kevan in *Keep His Commandments* (Tyndale Press, 1964), pp. 28, 29. And see chapter XIX.5, 6 of the Westminster Confession for its clear statement of the permanent, binding authority of the moral law.
[4] Gal. 6:15.
[5] 1 Cor. 7:19.
[6] *E.g.* 1 Jn. 2:3–5; 3:4–10, 22–24; 5:1–5, 18.
[7] Ps. 119:97; Rom. 7:22; Ps. 19:8.

And they would never eat it with defiled (that is, unwashed) hands. Thus, foods, vessels and hands all had to be clean.

Now some of these laws were laws of God, and with their observance Jesus had no quarrel. Other regulations, though belonging to 'the traditions of the elders' rather than Scripture, nevertheless were not contradictory to Scripture, and their practice was therefore optional. Yet in their concentration on ceremonial matters the Pharisees came to think of morality as an external condition, indeed largely a matter of bodily purification. Hence Christ's emphasis that what defiles a man is what comes out from inside him, from his heart. In other words, the purity God requires first of all is not ceremonial (clean foods, hands and vessels) but moral (a holy life).

Some striking examples of this principle occur in Matthew 23, in which Jesus pronounced a number of 'woes' upon the scribes and Pharisees. 'Woe to you, scribes and Pharisees, hypocrites! for you cleanse the outside of the cup and of the plate, but inside they are full of extortion and rapacity. You blind Pharisee! first cleanse the inside of the cup and of the plate, that the outside also may be clean' (vv. 25, 26). The Lord's complaint was this: the Pharisees were intent on the ritual cleansing of their cups and plates, but did not bother if the food and drink contained in their ceremonially clean vessels were morally unclean because obtained by dishonesty and greed. They were blind to this anomaly.

Again, 'Woe to you, scribes and Pharisees, hypocrites! for you tithe mint and dill and cummin [i.e. you are meticulous in giving God a tenth of even the smallest herbs you grow in your back garden], and have neglected the weightier matters of the law, justice and mercy and faith; these you ought to have done, without neglecting the others' (v. 23). Jesus was not here inciting them to break the tithing law. He was reproaching them rather for their lack of a sense of proportion. God's law contains both ceremonial regulations and moral commandments. But the two, He implied, were not of equal importance; the moral is 'weightier' than the ceremonial. Yet it was this that the Pharisees were neglecting in their obsession with ceremonial obligations. So blind were they in their unbalance, Jesus added with a touch of humour, that they were like people who fuss over a foreign body in their drink. They carefully strain out a tiny midge and then go and swallow a camel by mistake! (v. 24).

Perhaps the most conspicuous examples of the Jewish leaders' false scrupulosity occurred at the end of Christ's life.[8] Anxious to eat the Passover, they refused to enter the praetorium (where Jesus was on trial before Pilate) '"so that they might not be defiled'. Anxious not to profane the sabbath (the high day of the festival) by permitting the three crucified men to remain on the cross, they asked Pilate's authority to have their legs broken to hasten their death and the removal of their bodies. They did not see the anomaly of avoiding these comparatively trivial defilements while they were committing the heinous crime of plotting and securing the death of God's Christ. As Bishop Ryle put it: 'The chief priests and their party made much ado about eating the passover lamb and keeping the feast, at the very time when they were about to slay the true Lamb of God, of whom this passover was a type!'[9]

It is easy to laugh at the Pharisees and to forget that the Pharisaic spirit is by no means dead. All those whose view of sin, morality and religion is superficial and external, and to whom the ceremonial is more important than the moral, are twentieth-century Pharisees. Some reduce their religion to a few neat and simple rules – for example, a brief perfunctory 'quiet time' every day and a church service every Sunday – and imagine that nothing more is required of them.

Others speak and act as if the really important question is whether a Christian refrains from such things as smoking, drinking and wearing make-up. There are some churches in the world which even excommunicate their members for practices like these. But these are the 'mint, dill and cummin' of our day, the herbs of the evangelical's back garden. Although every Christian should reach a conscientious decision about them, it is absurd to equate them with 'the weightier matters of the law'.

Yet others concentrate on social and cultural taboos like manners, speech or clothing. And if somebody is not dressed in what they regard as the correct fashion, or does not speak the Queen's English with an Oxford accent, or fails to hold his

[8] See Jn. 18:28; 19:31.
[9] *Expository Thoughts on the Gospels* (Hodder and Stoughton, 1856). Comment on Jn. 18:28.

knife and fork in the proper way and at the correct angle, he is immediately despised and dismissed.

Worst of all, perhaps, is the extraordinary way in which we (perhaps women especially) tend to judge others by outward appearances. After a lady has left the room, as soon as the door is closed behind her, the remarks begin to come: 'My dear, isn't she plain?' 'That bundle of rags she's wearing!' 'Those eyelashes!' 'That skin!' So whether we accept her or not depends on her complexion or clothing, or even on the length, number, colour and shape of her eyelashes!

All these are forms of modern Pharisaism. It is as if we come to Jesus and say: 'Lord, why does so-and-so eat with defiled hands?' It is to judge people by purely external criteria, instead of by their moral character. It is to overlook the fact that what defiles people in God's sight is not what is on their outside but on their inside – the evil thoughts of the heart.

People matter more than things

Christ's controversy with the Pharisees over morality stressed not only the precedence of the inward over the outward and the moral over the ceremonial, but also the personal over the impersonal. In brief, He taught that people matter more than things.

It is significant that all but the last two ('pride' and 'foolishness') of the thirteen 'evil things' which Jesus catalogued are social offences, sins against persons. He included breaches of the five commandments of the second table (murder, adultery, theft, slander and covetousness) and added malice, deceit and envy. Without doubt He chose His list of 'evil things' deliberately. He showed by it that our corrupt heart is not only in revolt against God but at enmity with our neighbour also. Further, in their concentration on the external and ceremonial, the Pharisees were as neglectful of love as they were of morality. Their punctilious concern for ritual niceties was accompanied by a bitter, scornful, critical attitude. So Jesus taught the importance of social righteousness, and particularly of true caring about people. Twice He quoted God's Word in Hosea 6:6: 'I desire mercy, and not sacrifice.' In other words, according to God's reckoning, compassion matters more than ceremonial rules and regulations, people more than things. Jesus applied this scriptural principle to two practices for which the Pharisees criticized Him.

The first was sabbath-breaking. The disciples were walking through the cornfields one sabbath day, and, as they did so, were evidently plucking, rubbing and eating the corn. The Pharisees strongly objected to this, no doubt on the ground that according to their tradition plucking was equivalent to reaping and rubbing to threshing and that these were prohibited works on the sabbath.[1] A little later, in a synagogue, Jesus healed a man with a withered hand.[2] In these two instances, as always, Jesus was motivated by love. He was concerned that hungry people should be fed and sick people healed. Indeed He cared enough about their need to break the scribal rules in order to meet it. 'If you had known what this means, "I desire mercy, and not sacrifice," ' He said to the Pharisees, 'you would not have condemned the guiltless.'[3] After all, they themselves took their farmstock to water on the sabbath,[4] and would go to the rescue of one of their sheep if it fell into a pit on the sabbath; had they then more pity for animals than for humans? Besides this, though they would not let Jesus do good and heal on a sabbath, they were themselves prepared to do harm and plot to kill Him. Hence His barbed question to them, which Mark records: 'Is it lawful on the sabbath to do good or to do harm, to save life or to kill?'[5] He thus exposed their hypocrisy.

The second issue on which He used the Hosea quotation was the question of fraternizing with sinners. When Levi-Matthew was converted, he invited his friends and colleagues to a meal to meet Jesus. Seeing Jesus in such company, the Pharisees were appalled, for one of the vows they all took on entering the Pharisaic brotherhood was never to be a guest of one of the common people. Yet here was Jesus sitting in a sinner's house and eating with him! Jesus defended His action from the analogy of a doctor and his patients, and then quoted Hosea again: 'Go and learn what this means, "I desire mercy, and not sacrifice." '[6]

In both cases, regarding sabbath observance and fraternization, the Pharisees were shocked because Jesus had broken

[1] Mt. 12:1ff.   [2] Mt. 12:9ff.   [3] Mt. 12:7.
[4] Lk. 13:15.   [5] Mk. 3:4.   [6] Mt. 9:9-13.

their rules. He did it because for Him love was the pre-eminent virtue. He cared deeply about the hungry, the sick and the sinful, and in order to serve their need He was prepared to infringe the scribal traditions. I do not myself believe that He broke the Mosaic law itself. But if it could be shown conclusively that He did, the new moralists are still not justified in taking this as evidence that He abrogated the law, or even disregarded it. The most that could be said is that when two divine laws are in conflict (as sometimes happens in our fallen world), then the law of love takes precedence. This was so in the matter of Corban, for the honour due to parents has priority over the keeping of a rash vow, since people matter more than things. Such was the implication of His favourite text, 'I desire mercy, and not sacrifice.'

We have seen that the Pharisaic view of morality was superficial because external. Therefore any attempt to externalize either religion or morality today, or to reduce it to a few shallow rules, is a form of modern Pharisaism. Evangelicals are by no means always free from this tendency. Yet it is a hallmark of true evangelical religion to emphasize that sin and morality are inward rather than outward, that what defiles us in God's sight is what emanates from the heart, that a new birth is indispensable to a new life, and that therefore what pleases God is heart-religion and heart-morality.

6 WORSHIP: LIPS OR HEART?

Christians believe that true worship is the highest and noblest activity of which man, by the grace of God, is capable. It is sad, therefore, that it should ever be a subject of controversy. But it is. Granted that God is seeking worshippers (as Jesus said He was), what kind of worshippers does He seek? Granted that man is under obligation to worship God (as the Bible everywhere says he is), what kind of worship should he offer? Not all worship is equally acceptable to God, irrespective of its nature. On the contrary, the same Bible which emphasizes man's duty to worship adds that some of his worship is actually such 'an abomination' to God, that He 'hates' and 'despises' it, 'cannot endure' it and therefore rejects it.[1]

Two basic assumptions

This repudiation of Israel's worship by God in the seventh and eighth centuries BC Jesus repeated to the Pharisees of His own day. Indeed, He quoted Isaiah 29 : 13 as a 'prophecy', meaning not just that this verse foretold the hypocrisy of the Pharisees, but that it expressed a divinely revealed principle which was equally applicable to them.

'And he said to them, "Well did Isaiah prophesy of you hypocrites, as it is written,
'This people honours me with their lips,
but their heart is far from me;
in vain do they worship me . . .'." '[2]

Two assumptions underly these words – assumptions shared by Christ and the Pharisees – which should still be common ground in the modern debate about worship.

[1] E.g. Is. 1:12-14; Am. 5:21-24.   [2] Mk. 7:6, 7a.

The first is that worship is a *proper* activity. Quoting Isaiah, Jesus said 'This people honours me . . .'. God's quarrel with the inhabitants of Jerusalem, and Christ's quarrel with the Pharisees, was not that they honoured God but that they did so in the wrong way. All men should honour God, should ascribe to Him the honour and glory which are due to His name. Indeed, this is the meaning of worship. The very word 'worship' implies it. Being an abbreviation of 'worthship', it indicates that God is worthy to be praised, that worship is but a due recognition of His absolute worth. In worship we come to Him as creatures to honour Him as our Creator, as sinners to honour Him as our Saviour, as children to honour Him as our Father, as servants to honour Him as our Lord. Worship is, therefore, not an optional activity which may be added to life's curriculum by those who enjoy that sort of thing, and discarded by those who do not. It is rather an obligation because it is the acknowledgment of plain facts.

The second assumption which underlies the words of Isaiah and of Christ is that, if worship is a proper activity, it is also a public activity: '*This people* honours me. . . .' Of course there is a place for private worship, the adoration of God by an individual in his solitariness (*e.g.* 'when you pray, go into your room and shut the door and pray to your Father who is in secret', Mt. 6 : 6). But the worship referred to here is public, the worship of God by His people when they meet together. Jesus took it for granted that they would assemble for public worship. It is safe to say that He never envisaged a 'religionless Christianity'.

In this further controversy with the Pharisees, then, Jesus is finding fault neither with the practice of worship itself, nor with its public and corporate nature, but rather with its external quality, its formalism, its hypocrisy: 'Well did Isaiah prophesy of you *hypocrites*. . . .' They were not true worshippers at all, but play actors. The honour they gave to God was a pretence, not a reality. And the essential distinction here is between the worship of the lips and of the heart. Worship may (and at least in public will) be expressed through the lips. But worship does not consist of words. Just as the morality acceptable to God is an affair not of the hands but of the heart, so the worship acceptable to God is not the honour paid Him by the lips, but the humble adoring devotion of the heart. Pharisaic worship is lip-worship; Christian worship is heart-worship.

What, then, are the characteristics of true heart-worship?

Rational worship

The first characteristic of heart-worship is that it is rational; the mind is fully involved in it. For the 'heart' in Scripture is not simply equivalent to the emotions, as it usually is in common parlance today. In biblical thought the 'heart' is the centre of the human personality and is often so used that the intellect is more emphasized than the emotions. Thus, the exhortation in Proverbs 23 : 26, 'My son, give me your heart,' has often been interpreted as an entreaty for our love and devotion. It has served as a convenient text for many sermons on whole-hearted discipleship. But in reality it is a command to listen, to pay attention, to sit up and take notice, an appeal more for concentration than for consecration. This is particularly clear in the book of Proverbs, in which it is written that the heart should incline to 'understanding' and be 'wise'.[3] Indeed in the Wisdom Literature of the Old Testament the Revised Standard Version sometimes translates the word 'heart' as 'mind'.

But passages could be quoted from the New Testament also, in which the 'heart' means above all the 'mind'. One example must suffice. The conversion of Lydia, the Asian seller of purple goods who traded in Philippi, is described by Luke in these terms: 'The Lord opened her heart to give heed to what was said by Paul.'[4] In other words, He opened her understanding to grasp and receive the gospel.

Of course the heart includes more than the mind. But it does not include less. So heart-worship is rational worship. To love God with all our heart involves loving Him with all our mind.

This leads us to state the first fundamental principle of Christian worship, namely that we must know God before we can worship Him. It is true that Paul found an altar in Athens which was inscribed 'to an unknown God'. But he recognized it as a contradiction in terms. It is impossible to worship an unknown god, since, if he is himself unknown, the kind of worship he desires will be equally unknown. That is why Paul

[3] *E.g.* Pr. 2:2; 23:15.   [4] Acts 16:14.

said to the philosophers: 'What therefore you worship as unknown, this I proclaim to you.'[5]

The same principle emerges clearly in Christ's conversation
with the Samaritan woman at Jacob's well. For more than 700
years the Samaritans and the Jews had developed their religious
life independently. Their separate development had a political
origin, in that the Samaritans were a mixed race descended
partly from Israelites and partly from Mesopotamian foreigners
who had been settled there in the eighth century BC.[6] But
spiritually it was due to their reliance on different Scriptures.
The Samaritans accepted the Pentateuch, but rejected the
subsequent revelation which God had given of Himself through
the prophets. Having the law without the prophets, the Samaritans' knowledge of God was necessarily incomplete. It is to this
that Jesus referred in His talk with the woman by the well:
'You [i.e. the Samaritans] worship what you do not know; we
[i.e. the Jews] worship what we know, for salvation [i.e. the
promised Messiah] is from the Jews.' Jesus continued: 'But
the hour is coming, and now is, when the true worshippers will
worship the Father in . . . truth.'[7] So 'true worship' is 'worship
in truth'; it is worship of God the Father as He has been fully
and finally revealed in Jesus Christ, His Son.

If Samaritan worship was (to say the least) impoverished
because of their rejection of prophetic teaching, much Jewish
worship was spoiled by ritualism. It was lip-worship (the mouth-
ing of meaningless words), not heart-worship (the intelligent
adoration of the mind). In Isaiah's day the people whose lips
made an approach to God, while their heart kept its distance,
are likened to blind men and drunkards; they neither knew nor
understood what they were saying. How could their worship
be acceptable to God when they turned a deaf ear to His word
spoken through His prophets? Similarly, the Pharisees were
rejecting Christ's testimony to the Father; so their worship
could not be heart-worship.

It is because of this fundamental principle that our English
Reformers gave us a Book of Common Prayer in the vulgar
tongue (as they expressed it), i.e. not in Latin but in English
which could be 'understanded of the people'. They also saturated
the Prayer Book services in Scripture. No man or woman can

[5] Acts 17:22ff.   [6] See 2 Ki. 17:24ff.   [7] Jn. 4:22, 23.

come to public worship in the Church of England without
hearing the Word of God. In the Old and New Testament
lessons, in the psalms and canticles, in the biblical quotations
and allusions which abound in the prayers, as well as in the
sermon, the Word of God is brought to the people. All this
was deliberate, for the Reformers knew that it is the Word of
God which evokes the worship of God. So, for example, throughout Morning and Evening Prayer, the worshippers are caught
up in the rhythmic swing of the pendulum from God's Word
to man's response. God speaks through a scripture sentence
and a call to penitence; the congregation respond in the confession of sin. God speaks through the 'absolution' or declaration
of His pardon grounded upon biblical promises; the congregation
respond in psalms of praise. Again, God speaks through the
lessons; the congregation respond in canticle, creed and collect.
And this principle of rational, biblical worship, which guided
Cranmer in composing the Prayer Book services, applies equally
to every well-constructed Free Church service, in which the
worship is 'responsive' to the Word.

The sermon, too, far from being out of place in public worship, is indispensable – at least if it is a true sermon, namely an
exposition of Scripture. For Scripture is the revelation of God,
and worship is godliness. The two belong together, as the former
elicits and promotes the latter. The same is true of the sacraments.
Strictly speaking, the sacraments are not themselves worship,
any more than the sermon is worship. Sermon and sacrament
are both manward rather than Godward in their direction.
They set forth, the one audibly and the other visibly, the glory
of God's grace in the salvation of sinners. Therefore, though
not themselves acts of worship, they lead to worship – the
adoration of the God who once gave Himself for His people
and now gives Himself to them today.

If the worshippers whom God is seeking are those who draw
near to Him with their heart and worship Him in truth, we
must be careful, when we go to church, not to leave our minds
behind. The late Dr Rufus M. Jones once received a letter
from someone who objected to his emphasis on intelligence in
Christianity. The critic wrote: 'Whenever I go to church, I
feel like unscrewing my head and placing it under the seat
because in a religious meeting I have never had any use for

anything above my collar button.'[8] Dr Jones's correspondent had little understanding of the kind of worship which is acceptable to God.

We must therefore beware of all forms of emotional, aesthetic or ecstatic worship in which the mind is not fully engaged, and especially of those which even claim that they are superior forms of worship. No, no. The only worship pleasing to God is heart-worship, and heart-worship is rational worship. It is the worship of a rational God who has made us rational beings and given us a rational revelation so that we may worship Him rationally, even 'with all our mind'.

Hence, too, the only perfect worship which is offered to God is in heaven, not on earth, because it is in heaven that God is clearly seen and fully known: 'his servants shall worship him; they shall see his face, and his name shall be on their foreheads.'[9] Because on earth we 'see through a mirror dimly', our best worship is bound to be imperfect. Because in heaven we shall see Him face to face, we shall be able to worship Him as He is.

> Weak is the effort of my heart,
> And cold my warmest thought,
> But when I see Thee as Thou art,
> I'll praise Thee as I ought.

Meanwhile, as we remain on earth, our mind must be in our worship. We must listen humbly to the reading and the preaching of God's Word, in order that we may increase in the knowledge of God. And we must concentrate, giving our whole attention to what we are saying or singing, so that we may worship God for all we have so far come to know Him to be.

Spiritual worship

Heart-worship is spiritual as well as rational. If our mind is involved, our spirit is involved also. We can illustrate this best by referring again to Christ's conversation with the Samaritan woman. We have already seen that for seven centuries there had been rivalry, often fierce and bitter, between the Jews and the Samaritans. One of the chief points at issue, theologically

[8] Quoted by John S. Bonnell in *The Practice and Power of Prayer* (Westminster Press, Philadelphia, 1954), p. 85.
[9] Rev. 22:3, 4.

speaking, was the correct place at which to worship. As the woman said to Jesus by the well-side: 'Our fathers worshipped on this mountain [*i.e.* Gerizim]; and you say that in Jerusalem is the place where men ought to worship.' Jesus replied: 'Woman, believe me, the hour is coming when neither on this mountain nor in Jerusalem will you worship the Father . . . the true worshippers will worship the Father in spirit and truth, for such the Father seeks to worship him. God is spirit, and those who worship him must worship in spirit and truth.'[1]

With these words Jesus taught that the nature of our worship must accord with the nature of the God we are worshipping. If it is the rational worship of a rational God, it is also the spiritual worship of a spiritual God. In contrast to the Samaritans (who rejected three-quarters of the Old Testament), Christian worship is 'in truth'; in contrast to the Pharisees (who gloried in external rites), it is 'in spirit'. Because God is spirit, our worship of Him is not tied to, or dependent on, any particular place or form. In essence, the worship pleasing to God is inward not outward, the praise of the heart not the lips, spiritual not ceremonial. It is not the movement of our bodies in elaborate ritual (however graceful and elegant); it is the movement of our spirit towards Him in love and obedience.

This is not to say that church buildings are unnecessary. At least in countries where the climate is intemperate, they are convenient, not to say essential. But God is not restricted to buildings, still less to particular parts of buildings. Even in Old Testament days, in which He condescended to man's weakness by causing the 'shekinah glory' to rest visibly on the mercy seat in the Holy of Holies, spiritually-minded Israelites knew that this was but an emblem of God's presence, and not God Himself. As Solomon put it at the dedication of his Temple: 'Will God indeed dwell on the earth? Behold, heaven and the highest heaven cannot contain thee; how much less this house which I have built!'[2]

However, if God is not tied to buildings, He is tied to His people. To them He has tied Himself by the most solemn covenant: 'I will be their God, and they shall be my people.' With this covenant went the further promise that He would never 'fail nor forsake' them. And Jesus Christ confirmed this promise

[1] Jn. 4:20–24.   [2] 1 Ki. 8:27.

WORSHIP: LIPS OR HEART?

of the presence of God with the new Israel: 'Where two or three are gathered in my name, there am I in the midst of them.' '. . . and lo, I am with you always, to the close of the age.'[3]

If, then, we want to inherit these promises and enjoy the presence of God in our worship, it is not the place that matters, but the company, not a church but *the* church, not a building but God's people. Whenever the people of God have come together, indoors or in the open air, in church or shack, in majestic cathedral or dingy catacomb, these words have come true: 'you have come to Mount Zion and to the city of the living God, the heavenly Jerusalem, and to innumerable angels in festal gathering, and to the assembly of the first-born who are enrolled in heaven, and to a judge who is God of all, and to the spirits of just men made perfect, and to Jesus, the mediator of a new covenant, and to the sprinkled blood that speaks more graciously than the blood of Abel.'[4]

What is true of buildings for worship is equally true of forms of worship. We do not say that outward forms are in themselves unnecessary or wrong, any more than are material buildings. To be sure, heart-worship can be silent worship, and we should probably have more periods of silence in our church services. But if it is to be truly congregational as well, that is, in words. These words may be set forms or extempore speech. Both can be the free and sincere utterance of the heart. Both can equally degenerate to the level of heathen incantation. External forms and ceremonies are harmless, even helpful, only if they exhibit true doctrine (and are not what Cranmer called 'dark and dumb', *i.e.* having an obscure meaning or no meaning), and only if they can be the proper expression of inward worship.

Let me give a simple example. In some churches the worshippers kneel to pray. It is not necessary to do so. Other Christians sit or stand for prayer. Yet those who kneel like to do so because kneeling seems to express for them the true doctrine of the greatness of God and of the littleness of men in His sight. It also helps them to humble themselves in reverence before Him. At the same time, it is perfectly possible to bow the knee physically without ever bowing our neck to Christ's yoke or our heart and will to His commandments.

[3] Mt. 18:20; 28:20.   [4] Heb. 12:22-24.

It is not only possible; it is all too common. No alert reader
of the Bible can miss its frequent warnings of the dangers of
religious externalism. We have already seen how Christ applied
to the Pharisees what Isaiah had spoken several centuries
previously to Judah. The worship of the Pharisees was nothing
but an outward religious display. The same alarm note is sounded
in many other places. 'Thou hast no delight in sacrifice; were I
to give a burnt offering, thou wouldst not be pleased. The sacrifice acceptable to God is a broken spirit; a broken and contrite
heart, O God, thou wilt not despise'.[5]

The contemporary church is far from having grown out of the
need for this warning. Colourful ceremonies, rich pageantry and
splendid music are neither pleasing to God nor profitable to
men, unless they are the vehicles of something else, namely
spiritual worship.

Evangelical Christians have not always been of one mind
about the place of beauty in worship. Some, in their anxiety
to heed the warnings of Scripture, have perhaps gone too far
in the direction of the austere and the drab, even the slovenly.
Others have found that beauty of sight and sound are not
necessarily incompatible with inward reality. The same applies
to other external accompaniments of worship. Some evangelicals
are uninhibited in clapping their hands, swaying their bodies
and shouting aloud their Hallelujahs. Others prefer their public
worship to be restrained and dignified, remembering that we
are to 'offer to God acceptable worship, with reverence and
awe; for our God is a consuming fire'.[6] Since God has made us
different people with different temperaments, we should respect
one another and give one another liberty in these matters.
What all of us must and do insist upon, since Scripture teaches
it and Jesus endorsed it, is this: what concerns God above
everything is our heart not our lips, our spirit not our body.

Spiritual worship means more than this, however. It indicates
not only that it is our spirit which worships, but that it is God's
Spirit who prompts our worship. 'We are the true circumcision,'
writes the apostle Paul, emphasizing a vital distinction between
Jewish and Christian worship, 'who worship by the Spirit of
God. . . .'[7] The Spirit's inspiration is as necessary as the Son's

[5] Ps. 51:16, 17.   [6] Heb. 12:28, 29.
[7] Phil. 3:3, RSV margin. Most of the best manuscripts support this reading,

mediation in our approach to the Father: 'for through him we . . . have access in [or by] one Spirit to the Father.'[8] All Christian prayer is through Christ and by the Spirit. The Holy Spirit 'helps us in our weakness' and enables us to cry 'Abba! Father!', making us conscious of our filial relationship to God.[9] Besides this, true worship is in a sense uncongenial to human nature, for human nature is self-centred, while worship is God-centred. Only the Holy Spirit can lift us out of ourselves, turn us inside out and focus our devotion upon God. If worship is evoked by the Word of God (as we have seen), it is the Spirit of God who uses the Word of God to evoke it. We need often to pray:

> Almighty God, unto whom all hearts be open, all desires known, and from whom no secrets are hid; Cleanse the thoughts of our hearts by the inspiration of thy Holy Spirit, that we may perfectly love thee, and worthily magnify thy holy Name; through Christ our Lord.

Spiritual worship is inward worship, inspired by the Spirit of God in the spirit of man.

Moral worship
True heart-worship is moral as well as rational and spiritual. In addition to the mind and the spirit, the conscience is involved.

It is significant that, before Jesus described to the Samaritan woman the kind of worshippers the Father was seeking, He said to her: 'Go, call your husband, and come here.' When she replied that she had no husband, Jesus went on: 'You are right in saying, "I have no husband"; for you have had five husbands, and he whom you now have is not your husband; this you said truly.'[1] Before she could offer the worship Jesus was about to portray, her sin must be exposed, confessed and forgiven.

This is why most forms of public worship are introduced by an act of penitence and confession. Certainly in the Church of England both Morning and Evening Prayer have a 'penitential

---

rather than 'who worship God in spirit'; it represents the difference of only one or two letters in the Greek original.
[8] Eph. 2:18. [9] Rom. 8:26, 27; 8:15, 16; Gal. 4:6.
[1] Jn. 4:16–18.

introduction', and before the Lord's Supper is administered the Ten Commandments are recited in full or in summary and sin is confessed. This is a clear recognition that before we are ready to worship we must engage in confession. Before we stand for praise, we must kneel in humble penitence. For, 'Who shall ascend the hill of the Lord? And who shall stand in his holy place?' The answer is: 'He who has clean hands and a pure heart. . . .'[2] We are not fit to tread the courts of heaven in the rags of our sin and guilt.

Again and again the biblical authors insist that worship without morality is positively displeasing to God: 'The sacrifice of the wicked is an abomination to the Lord.' 'Has the Lord as great delight in burnt offerings and sacrifices, as in obeying the voice of the Lord? Behold, to obey is better than sacrifice, and to hearken than the fat of rams.' 'I hate, I despise your feasts, and I take no delight in your solemn assemblies. . . . But let justice roll down like waters, and righteousness like an everflowing stream.' 'What to me is the multitude of your sacrifices? says the Lord; I have had enough of burnt offerings of rams and the fat of fed beasts. . . . Bring no more vain offerings; incense is an abomination to me. . . . When you spread forth your hands, I will hide my eyes from you; even though you make many prayers, I will not listen; your hands are full of blood. Wash yourselves; make yourselves clean; remove the evil of your doings from before my eyes; cease to do evil, learn to do good; seek justice, correct oppression; defend the fatherless, plead for the widow.'[3]

There can be no doubt that this reiterated emphasis is necessary. The history of the world has been soiled by the pursuit of religion without morality, of piety without love. Sometimes the conscience of worshippers has been so blind or hard that they have actually introduced evil into their acts of worship, and even identified the two. Perhaps the worst example of this has been the degrading practice of ritual prostitution. But the mingling of devotion to God and injustice to man is equally perverted. During Israel's religious boom in the eighth century BC Amos castigated those frequenting the local sanctuaries because he said they 'lay themselves down beside every altar

[2] Ps. 24:3, 4; cf. Ps. 15.
[3] Pr. 15:8; 1 Sa. 15:22; Am. 5:21, 24; Is. 1:11–17.

upon garments taken in pledge; and in the house of their God they drink the wine of those who have been fined [*i.e.* unjustly so]'.[4]

It was the same with the Pharisees of our Lord's day. They attended both synagogue and Temple. They searched the Scriptures. They fasted, prayed and gave alms. Their dress, speech and manner were egregiously religious. Yet their hearts were full of sin, greed and pride. Jesus described them as those who 'devour widows' houses and for a pretence make long prayers'.[5] Similarly, some church-goers today will come to public worship while at the same time negotiating a dishonest business deal, cultivating an immoral relationship, harbouring resentment against someone who has wronged them or plotting their revenge.

We must repudiate every pretension to religion which is not accompanied by righteousness. The claim to mystical experience without moral obedience is a lie and a delusion. The reason for this should be plain. It concerns the very nature of God. 'God is light and in him is no darkness at all. If we say we have fellowship with him while we walk in darkness, we lie and do not live according to the truth. . . . He who says "I know him" but disobeys his commandments is a liar, and the truth is not in him. . . . He who says he is in the light and hates his brother is in the darkness still.'[6] The contrast which John repeatedly draws is between verbal profession and moral reality, between what we say and what we are. Religion without righteousness is vain. Faith without works is dead.

The principle which lies behind the indissoluble marriage of worship and morality is that worship is much more than a matter of singing hymns and saying prayers. These things, if they exist in isolation, are merely lip-worship. If they are heart-worship, they express more even than the praise of the mind and of the spirit; they set forth in concentrated form the devotion of our whole life. Into one hour's public worship on Sunday is condensed the dedication of the week. Our sacrifice of praise is a token of the sacrifice of ourselves, our souls and our bodies.

Christ's controversy with the Pharisees about worship was that their religion was formal and external. He called it 'hypocrisy' or play-acting. It was a worship of the lips alone, and therefore empty, lacking all inward reality. 'In vain do they worship me,' He said, quoting Isaiah.

In contrast to Pharisaic worship, Christian worship is heart-worship. In whatever outward forms it is expressed, it is in essence rational (involving the mind), spiritual (involving both man's spirit and God's) and moral (involving the conscience and the whole life). Such are the worshippers whom the Father is seeking, Jesus said.

7 RESPONSIBILITY: WITHDRAWAL OR INVOLVEMENT?

What should be the attitude of the followers of Jesus towards those who do not follow Him? There is a wide variety of possible attitudes, all of which have been adopted by Christian people at different times. Do we despise them, fear them, shun them, tolerate them, condemn them, or seek to serve them? What is the true responsibility of the church to the world?

Once again we discover that there was a fundamental difference of attitude in this matter between the Pharisees and Jesus Christ. And once again we have to ask ourselves whether our attitude is Christian (because Christ's) or Pharisaic (because in reality a modern version of that adopted by the Pharisees in our Lord's day).

Luke sums up the difference in his editorial introduction to the parables of the lost sheep, lost coin, and lost son: 'Now the tax collectors and sinners were all drawing near to hear him. And the Pharisees and the scribes murmured, saying, "This man receives sinners and eats with them." '[1]

At first sight the reaction of the Pharisees to Christ's reception of the publicans and sinners may seem surprising, for the Pharisees were keen on winning adherents. Jesus Himself referred to their zeal in doing so: 'You traverse sea and land to make a single proselyte,' He said.[2]

But proselytism and evangelism are not the same thing. To proselytize is to convert somebody else to our opinions and culture, and to squeeze him into our mould; to evangelize is to proclaim God's good news about Jesus Christ to the end that people will believe in Him, find life in Him and ultimately be conformed to His image, not ours. The motive behind prose-

[1] Lk. 15:1, 2.　　　　　　　　[2] Mt. 23:15.

lytism is concern for the spread of our own little empire; the motive behind evangelism is concern for the true welfare of men and thereby for the name, kingdom, will and glory of God.

Now the Pharisees were great proselytizers. They loved to draw another person into their orbit and subdue him to their influence. By doing so, Jesus said, they ruined him: 'when he becomes a proselyte, you make him twice as much a child of hell as yourselves.' But if the Pharisees were good at proselytism, they were no good at evangelism, for they had no evangel, and no pity either. So, when the publicans and sinners were all drawing near to Jesus, instead of rejoicing, they complained.

It is important to understand what lay behind the radically different attitude to sinners adopted by Christ and by the Pharisees.

The attitude of the Pharisees

The seed from which Pharisaism sprang was good seed. It was the Old Testament doctrine of the church as the holy people of God.

The Pharisees knew, as every Jew knew, the history of the distinctness of Israel from all the nations under heaven. God had chosen Abraham and his posterity, and had covenanted to be their God. He confirmed His covenant to Isaac and to Jacob and to Jacob's descendants, the so-called 'children of Israel'. He renewed His covenant with them at Mount Sinai after delivering them from their Egyptian bondage. 'You shall be my people,' He said, 'and I will be your God.' More fully: 'if you will obey my voice and keep my covenant, you shall be my own possession among all peoples; for all the earth is mine, and you shall be to me a kingdom of priests and a holy nation.'[3]

But Israel disobeyed God's voice and broke His covenant 'till the wrath of the Lord rose against his people, till there was no remedy',[4] and the second – the Babylonian – captivity began. Then, yet again, God remembered and renewed His covenant with His chosen people, redeemed them from their exile and restored them to the promised land. And when they returned, they were determined as never before to be a separate people, holy unto the Lord their God. They 'separated themselves from the peoples of the lands to the law of God'. They

[3] Ex. 19:5, 6.   [4] 2 Ch. 36:16.

undertook not to intermarry with them, nor to break the sabbath through trading with them.[5]

The repatriated exiles went further than this, however. Misunderstanding the nature of the holiness God required of them, they began to cultivate a false separatism. They forgot the prophetic description of their destiny to be 'a light to the nations'.[6] Instead, they withdrew from all contact with the heathen. And so Pharisaism was born. The real parting of the ways arrived when Palestine became absorbed into the far-flung empire of Alexander the Great, and Greek influence started to infiltrate into Judaism. Some Jews surrendered to it (the Hellenists); others resisted it (the Hasidaeans, from *Hasidim* or 'pious ones'). Out of the Hellenists came the Sadducees, out of the Hasidaeans the Pharisees.

The very word 'Pharisees' accurately describes them, for it is in fact an Aramaic term for 'separatists'. The Pharisees were the religious exclusives of their day. In their determination to conform strictly to the law they held aloof from any and every contact which (in their view) might 'defile' them. This entailed an avoidance not only of Gentiles, not only of hellenized Jews, but of the 'common people' as well, who through ignorance of the law no doubt broke it and as law-breakers were unclean.

The superior and scornful attitude which the Pharisees adopted towards the common people appears several times in the Gospels. Thus, disturbed by the early popularity of Jesus, they attributed it to the people's ignorance. They asked sarcastically: 'Have any of the authorities or of the Pharisees believed in him? But this crowd, who do not know the law, are accursed.'[7] So well known was this Pharisaic ostracism of the unclean common herd that Jesus used it to explain what the local church's excommunication of a stubbornly impenitent sinner would mean. We should treat him like 'a Gentile and a tax collector', He said,[8] that is, as the Pharisees treat such. Indeed, the very couplet 'tax collectors and sinners', so familiar to every reader of the Gospels, was borrowed from the vocabulary of the Pharisees. 'Sinners' was their scornful epithet not for a particularly disreputable section of the community but

[5] Ne. 10:28–31. For the intermarriages in Ezra's day by which 'the holy race . . . mixed itself with the peoples of the lands', see Ezra 9 and 10.
[6] Is. 42:6; 49:6; *cf.* Lk. 2:32. [7] Jn. 7:48, 49. [8] Mt. 18:17.

for all the common people who failed to observe the traditions of the elders, the ceremonial rules which the Pharisees and their predecessors had laid down. 'Tax collectors' were added as a specific example of the genus 'sinner'. Being in the employment of the heathen Romans, they were *ipso facto* defiled. Thus 'publicans and sinners' in the estimation of the Pharisees were beyond the pale, the outcasts of spiritual society. Hence their horror when Jesus ate and drank with them, and actually welcomed them into His company.[9]

The Pharisees would never have dreamed of fraternizing with 'sinners' themselves. Instead, they took active steps to avoid the very possibility. They banded themselves together in a closed brotherhood. Calling themselves the *Haberim*, the 'associates', they pledged themselves to observe all the ordinances of the ceremonial law and the traditions of the elders. In particular, as we saw in an earlier chapter,[1] they undertook by a solemn vow to tithe everything they ate, bought and sold, and not to be guest of the '*am-hā'āres*, nor to entertain one as a guest in his own clothes, nor to trade with him in any food.[2]

So the Pharisaic doctrine of holiness, of separation from the world, was a perverted doctrine. Instead of seeking to be holy in thought, word and deed, while retaining relationships of love and care with all men, they withdrew from social contact with 'sinners' and despised those who did not follow suit. They became a 'holy club' – as the early Methodists were called – a pietistic enclave which had virtually contracted out of the world. They also became harsh and censorious; they had no pity for people in ignorance, sin or need.

The attitude of Jesus
That 'the tax collectors and sinners were all drawing near to him' shows immediately that Jesus' attitude to them was totally at variance with that of the Pharisees. Indeed, the Pharisees

[9] *E.g.* Lk. 5:29–32; 15:1, 2.
[1] See above, p. 112.
[2] For the full details see Edersheim, vol. I, pp. 311, 312. *Cf.* also an early description of a Pharisee as 'one who separates himself from all uncleanness and from unclean food and from the people of the land who are not scrupulous in the matter of food' (article 'Pharisees' by D. Eaton in Hastings' *Dictionary of the Bible*, Clark, 1898–1904, vol. III, p. 826).

were scandalized by His free and easy fraternization with people with whom they would never associate. Even His own disciples at first displayed a Pharisaic spirit.

The Evangelists supply us with numerous illustrations of the difference between the Pharisaic and the Christian attitudes to the needy. They emphasize that Jesus Christ showed compassion for all sorts and conditions of men, however much they were despised and rejected by society.

Thus, when the parents tried to bring their children to Jesus, wanting Him to touch them, the disciples 'rebuked' them. They supposed that Jesus would take no interest in children, for children were 'not . . . loved in antiquity as now they are; no halo of romance and tenderness encircled them; too often they were subjected to shameful cruelties and hard neglect'.[3] But 'when Jesus saw it he was indignant, and said to them, "Let the children come to me, do not hinder them; for to such belongs the kingdom of God. . . ." And he took them in his arms and blessed them, laying his hands upon them.'[4]

It was much the same with Bartimaeus, a blind and ragged beggar, who was sitting by the roadside outside the gates of Jericho. Hearing that Jesus of Nazareth was passing by, he began to cry out, 'Jesus, Son of David, have mercy on me!' But many people in the crowd (including some of the disciples?) 'rebuked him'. They told him to be quiet, implying that Jesus had no time for blind beggars like him. He refused to be silenced, however, and cried out all the more, 'Son of David, have mercy on me!' Then Jesus stopped, commanded him to be brought to Him, asked him what he was wanting and restored to him his sight.[5]

One of six things which Rabbis were not permitted to do was to converse with a woman in public, even (according to one Rabbi) with his own wife. Jesus ignored this convention. He spoke freely with a woman of Samaria at Jacob's well, so that, when His disciples returned from the village and found them together, 'they marvelled that he was talking with a woman'.[6]

The Pharisees would gather up their robes and recoil in self-righteous horror from a prostitute. Jesus allowed one not only to approach Him, but to bathe His feet with her tears, wipe them

---

[3] *The Life of Christ* by F. W. Farrar (Cassell, 1874), p. 448.
[4] Mk. 10:13-16.   [5] Lk. 18:35-43.   [6] Jn. 4:27.

with her hair, kiss them and anoint them with ointment. Simon the Pharisee, His host on that occasion, was appalled.[7]

In those days it could be said that 'Jews have no dealings with Samaritans'. But Jesus was an exception to the rule and refused to be bound by this tradition. The one He engaged in conversation at Jacob's well was despised three times over, being a Samaritan, a woman and a sinner. But Jesus did not despise her.[8]

The law of Moses contained some careful regulations about lepers and leprosy, no doubt for hygienic reasons. The Rabbis went far beyond these precautionary measures. Supposing lepers to be under the judgment of God, they regarded them 'with loathing, and even flung stones at them to drive them away'.[9] In contrast to this cruelty, Jesus had compassion on them. When one came to Him, kneeling before Him and begging Him for help, Jesus did something unheard of. He actually 'stretched out his hand and touched him' and healed him.[1]

Similarly, He touched the sick. When many people afflicted with various diseases were brought to Him, 'he laid his hands on every one of them and healed them'.[2] Specially striking was His concern for the woman 'who had had a flow of blood for twelve years'. The contemporary Jewish view of her condition went well beyond the Mosaic rules of hygiene. But when she came behind Jesus in the crowd and touched His garment, though He asked her to declare herself, He did not reprove her for her action. Instead, He spoke words of tenderness to her and sent her away in health and peace.[3] He did not stop at physical contact with the sick; He even took the hand of a dead girl – which no Pharisee would have dreamed of doing – and restored her to life.[4]

Finally, in this list of people the Pharisees despised and shunned, we come back to 'publicans and sinners'. The Pharisee's prayer in the parable accurately expressed his (and their) attitude: 'God, I thank thee that I am not like other men, extortioners, unjust, adulterers, or even like this tax collector.'[5] In their view, the tax collectors belonged to the same category as the dishonest and the immoral, and they would not think

[7] Lk. 7:36–50.   [8] Jn. 4:4–42.
[9] Farrar, p. 196.   [1] Mk. 1:40–45.
[2] Lk. 4:40.   [3] Mk. 5:25–34.
[4] Mk. 5:21–24, 35–43.   [5] Lk. 18:11.

of accepting an invitation into the home of such disreputable folk. Jesus, on the other hand, invited Himself into the home of Zacchaeus, the notorious tax collector of Jericho, which provoked the reaction, 'He has gone in to be the guest of a man who is a sinner' (in breach of one of the Pharisees' initiatory vows).[6] When another tax collector named Levi-Matthew responded to the call of Christ, he made Him 'a great feast in his house' to celebrate his conversion; 'and there was a large company of tax collectors and others sitting at table with them'. Once again, and predictably, the Pharisees and scribes murmured saying: 'Why do you eat and drink with tax collectors and sinners?'[7] But Jesus went further than attending a party in Levi-Matthew's home; He was audacious enough to include him in His team of apostles.[8] He did not regard him as in any way unclean or shrink from this close association with him.

In all these Gospel incidents, which the Evangelists record, we see the distance which separated Jesus from the Pharisees. The Pharisees withdrew from contact with all outcasts. Jesus, however, welcomed them into His friendship; He touched untouchables.

Why was this? What was the cause of this disagreement between them? A simple answer may be given to these questions: the Pharisees' first concern was *themselves*, how to preserve their own purity, whereas Jesus Christ's first concern was *others*, how 'to seek and to save the lost'.[9]

In order to explain and defend His policy of fraternization, Jesus resorted to a number of telling metaphors or parables.

To begin with, He likened Himself to a doctor who spends himself in his care for the sick and risks catching their infection in order to do so. It was thus that He answered the Pharisees' indignant question why He ate with tax collectors and sinners. 'Those who are well have no need of a physician,' He said, 'but those who are sick; I came not to call the righteous, but sinners.'[1]

Again, when the Pharisees murmured, saying, 'This man receives sinners and eats with them,' He replied by likening

---

[6] Lk. 19:1–10.   [7] Lk. 5:27–30.
[8] Lk. 6:12–16. In Mt. 9:9 Levi is identified as Matthew, and in 10:3 he is called 'Matthew the tax collector'.
[9] Lk. 19:10.   [1] Mk. 2:15–17.

Himself to a shepherd who had lost one of his hundred sheep.
He would not abandon the missing one, nor wait hopefully
for it to bleat its way home. He would rather abandon the
ninety-nine that were safe in order to go out after the one that
was lost and in danger. He would go on searching until he found
it. And the discovery would lead to rejoicing, in which he would
want his friends and neighbours to share.[2] What distinguished
Jesus from the Pharisees was, in a word, 'grace', the divine
initiative which first seeks and then saves the lost sinner. Bishop
Stephen Neill has commented: 'the great and magnificently
honest Jewish scholar, C. G. Montefiore, asking himself at what
point, if any, the teaching of Jesus is completely new and original,
finds the point of originality here. The Rabbis had said that if
the sinner returns to God, God will receive him: they had not
said that the love of God goes out to seek the sinner where he is.
But in the Gospels it is so.'[3]

What one lost sheep was to a shepherd with a hundred, one
lost coin was to a woman with ten. Perhaps the *drachma*, the
silver coin she had mislaid, had sentimental as well as monetary
value. It may have been an ornament, or one of the ten silver
coins which Palestinian women wore in those days to show they
were married, approximating to the modern wedding ring.
At all events, when she lost it, she missed it. It did not occur to
her to resign herself to her loss. Instead, she lit a lamp and swept
the whole house, looking diligently for it until she found it.
And again, with the recovered coin as with the recovered sheep,
the finding led to rejoicing and the rejoicing to a celebration
in which friends and neighbours were invited to join. Even so,
Jesus said, there is 'joy in heaven', 'joy before the angels of God'
over just one, single, repentant sinner. It was this that the
Pharisees lacked. They did not rejoice; they murmured.[4]

The longest of the three parables about lostness (the Prodigal
Son) illustrates the same fundamental truth of the divine compassion, but elaborates it further and adds the subordinate
theme of the elder brother. The grace of God in the ministry

---

[2] Lk. 15:1-7.
[3] *The Synoptic Gospels* by C. G. Montefiore (London, 1927), vol. I, p. cxviii
and vol. II, p. 520. Quoted by S. C. Neill in *Christian Faith Today* (Pelican,
1955), p. 165.
[4] Lk. 15:8-10.

of Christ, already exhibited in the doctor, the shepherd and the woman, is now seen in the father. And it is not difficult to recognize the publicans in the prodigal son or in the elder brother the Pharisees.[5]

We should not minimize the waywardness of the younger son. When he later confessed 'I have sinned', he was telling the truth. He had lost both his fortune through folly and his honour through sin. He could scarcely have sunk any lower. Not only had he lost everything he possessed; he was himself lost.

But all the time his father remained on the look-out for him and never gave up hope. His patience did not waver. His love did not wane. He persevered. And when at last he caught sight of the returning boy, while he was still some distance away, immediately he 'had compassion, and ran and embraced him and kissed him'.

Once more the emphasis is on the initiative of grace. The father did not wait for his son to reach home; he ran out to meet and welcome him. He did not wait for him to make amends, or demote him to the servitude he knew he deserved; he instantly reinstated him as a son in the family and honoured him with a ring, with shoes and with the best robe. He did not even wait until the boy had finished his confession; he interrupted him to order a feast.

But as father and household began to make merry, a shadow was cast on their celebrations by the morose detachment of the elder brother. Learning the cause of the music and dancing, he was angry and refused to join in, despite the personal entreaties of the father. He resented the welcome accorded to his wastrel brother, especially as his own filial loyalty appeared to him to have been inadequately recognized. He represents those to whom religion is a matter of merit and its just reward, and to whom the concept of grace is unjust, even immoral. He knew nothing of the guilt which no human merit can expunge, nothing of the divine offer of an unmerited forgiveness, nothing of heavenly joy over penitent sinners. He was harsh, sour, self-righteous and pitiless. While others made merry, he stayed away and sulked. In brief, he was a Pharisee. And of the Pharisees Edersheim could write: 'theirs was not a Gospel to the lost: they had nothing to say to sinners.'[6]

[5] Lk. 15:11–32.   [6] Edersheim, vol. II, p. 253.

Christ's fraternization with outcasts was interpreted by the
Pharisees as an inexcusable compromise with sin; they did not
see it for what it really was, an expression of the divine compassion towards sinners.

The attitude of the Christian church

Leaving the first century and entering the middle of the twentieth,
it is necessary to ask what the attitude of the contemporary
church is towards outsiders, outcasts. Is it Pharisaic, or is it
Christian? I fear that it is often Pharisaic. That is, the church
tends (has always tended) to withdraw from the world and leave
it to its own devices. Evangelical churchmen have by no means
been free of this tendency, although indeed it is a denial of their
true character. Many examples could be given, illustrating
different causes of the same general attitude. Let me try to
enlarge on what I think are the four commonest.

1. The first is plain, unvarnished, Pharisaic *self-righteousness*.
It is the attitude of the elder brother who, whether he articulates
it in speech or not, thinks in his heart, 'Let the sinner stew in
his own juice. He is getting what he deserves; it simply serves
him right.' We do not use this outspoken language, but this
is the image which we often present to the world. To the out-
sider the church is often not inviting but forbidding, smugly
satisfied with itself and harshly condemning of others. Non-
Christians sometimes say that they find more acceptance, more
compassionate understanding of human foibles in the world
than in the church. To them the church is lacking in warmth,
even positively inhuman.

In saying this, I am not wanting the church either to condone
sin or to dispense with repentance, but only to offer people
what David Sheppard during his years at the Mayflower Family
Centre called an 'unjudging friendship'. Otherwise we give the
impression that the church is for saints, not sinners. True, it is
composed of 'saints' in the New Testament sense that every
Christian belongs to God and to the 'holy' ('separate') people
of God. But if we are saints, we are also still sinners. Our nature
is corrupt and our feet fall. We have not yet attained or become
perfect. It is rather that God's sheer grace has put us on the

road to becoming in character and conduct what in our standing before Him we already are, namely His.

So the 'holiness' of the church is more in its position as belonging to God, in its continuous aspiration and in its final destiny, than in its present actuality. Pharisaism is a false claim to holiness, a false view of the church. It turns the church into a preserve for the impeccably respectable, a museum of rare spiritual exhibits, instead of a convalescent home for the sin-sick, a refuge for the helpless, and a common lodging-house for wayfarers.

Abbé Michonneau asks what would happen in the average local church if a militant anti-clerical Communist or a street-walker were converted. Would they be welcomed? he asks: 'Oh, we accept Mary Magdalene because she is in the Gospel, but I should like to see her walk into one of our meetings! We read about the reluctance with which the Christian Jews of Jerusalem received Saul the persecutor, when he appeared before them as a neophyte – and we find their attitude astonishing; I should like to see him drop into one of our men's groups!'[7]

There is another aspect of this false view of the church. It is not only in moral terms that Pharisaism appears; it can take racial and social forms as well. And it often does. Whenever the church is more exclusive in its membership than Scripture enjoins, it has become Pharisaic. What unites the church is a common faith in Christ and a common share in the Spirit. Apart from this essential, Christians may have nothing at all in common. We differ from one another in temperament, personality, education, colour, culture, citizenship, language and in a host of other ways. Thank God we do. The church is a wonderfully inclusive fellowship, in which 'there is neither Jew nor Greek, there is neither slave nor free, there is neither male nor female'.[8] In other words, in Christ we have equality. Distinction of race and rank, which are divisive influences in other communities, have no place in the Christian community. To import class distinctions or the colour bar into the Christian brotherhood is to destroy it. 'Birds of a feather flock together' may be true in nature; it is not a Christian proverb. The glory of the church is not our likeness to one another, but

7 *Revolution in a City Parish* by Abbé G. Michonneau (Blackfriars, 1949), p. 21.
8 Gal. 3:28.

our unlikeness. Therefore to rebuff or cold-shoulder a brother because of the colour of his skin or the length of his hair or the accent of his speech is to betray Christ and join the Pharisees.

2. The second cause of the withdrawal of the church from the world is a genuine if mistaken *fear of contamination*. This is the spirit of monasticism. We should not condemn it outright, for it is the perversion of a noble ideal. It begins with a true biblical recognition that 'the world', human society which repudiates the rule of God, or simply godless secularism, is evil. It goes on to hear, and to desire to obey, the biblical injunctions not to love the world, nor to be conformed to it, but rather to keep oneself unstained from the world.[9] But then it takes a wrong turning. It assumes that the only effective way to avoid conformity to worldly standards is to avoid the company of worldly people, that the way to renounce worldliness is to go out of the world. The desire is right; it is the deduction which is a grievous mistake.

In saying this we are not questioning the sincerity of all monks and hermits. Nor are we denying Christendom's debt to the monastic orders. Though some monasteries were hotbeds of sin and avarice, others in former centuries were islands of Christian culture in a turbulent sea of barbarism.

As a matter of fact evangelicals, who have always been opposed to monasticism, have themselves been accused of it. And to some extent justly, I think. Thus Dr Eugene L. Smith, Executive Secretary of the New York office of the World Council of Churches, has written: 'I began to see them as the true monastics of this age, primarily concerned with the preservation of the faith in its purity in the midst of a collapsing and decadent world – and willing to accept, sometimes without question, the discipline that this requires.'[1]

Nevertheless, we must insist that monasticism in whatever form is not a truly Christian ideal. Because it is a withdrawal from the world it is an expression of Pharisaism, whose danger Jesus seems to have envisaged when He uttered His petition: 'I

---

[9] 1 Jn. 2:15-17; Rom. 12:2; Jas. 1:27.
[1] Quoted by R. Kenneth Strachan in *The Inescapable Calling* (Eerdmans, 1968), pp. 97, 98.

do not pray that thou shouldst take them out of the world, but that thou shouldst keep them from the evil one.'[2]

It needs to be added that many contemporary churches and Christians which have never seen the inside of a monastery are yet 'monastic' in outlook. That is, they live a life of religious seclusion, insulated from the world. They betray little if any concern for others outside their own fellowship, being pre-occupied rather with the business of self-preservation. It is this distortion which, more than anything else, has provoked the current fashion of 'religionless Christianity'. And indeed if by 'religion' is meant empty formalism and ecclesiastical self-absorption, it would be better for Christianity to be 'religion-less'. Seen as a protest against these things, we have much sympathy with this movement. Although we would insist that 'religion' in the sense of public worship will always be a proper expression of Christianity, yet such worship is not acceptable worship if it exists on its own and the worshippers have no comparable concern to live in the world as both witnesses and servants. A church which lives for itself alone must die. It is Pharisaic, not Christian. A truly Christian church exists for God and for others.

3. A third modern form of Pharisaism – fairly so-called because its contact with the world is unbalanced – has to do with the relation between *evangelism and social concern*. What is God's purpose (and therefore the church's responsibility) for the world? The question was posed when the Commission on World Mission and Evangelism met in Mexico City in December 1963: 'The discussion raised a theological issue which remained unresolved. Debate returned again and again to the relationship between God's action in and through the church and everything God is doing in the world apparently independently of the Christian community. Can a distinction be drawn between God's providential action and God's redeeming action? If the restoration and reconciliation of human life is being achieved by the action of God through secular agencies, what is the place and significance of faith? If the church is to be wholly involved in the world and its history, what is the true nature of its separate-ness? We were able to state thesis and antithesis in this debate,

[2] Jn. 17:15.

but we could not see our way through to the truth we feel lies beyond this dialectic, ... to a truer understanding of the relation between the world and the church in the purpose of God.'[3] Before attempting any kind of synthesis, we shall need to understand clearly both the evangelical thesis and the ecumenical antithesis.

The 'evangelical' thesis in its extremest form is that God's chief concern is the salvation of individual souls; that the church's sole responsibility is the proclamation of the gospel; and that therefore social action being the first cousin of the 'social gospel' must be firmly eschewed. When this view is caricatured, the missionary is pictured standing under a palm tree, wearing a *sola topi*, and declaiming the gospel to a group of ill-clad natives who sit respectfully round him on the floor. He sees his mission as essentially a preaching mission, he fulfils it in a rather paternalistic way, and he refuses to be distracted from it even by Christian medical and educational work. I think this exclusive emphasis on personal salvation is a good deal less common among evangelicals than our critics allow. Nevertheless, as an example of it, Philip Crowe quotes a certain R. N. Cust who argued in 1888 that missionary money 'was collected for the purpose of converting a soul, not sharpening an intellect'.[4]

The 'ecumenical' antithesis in its extremest form is that God's chief concern is not with the church but with the world. And His action in the world, we are told, is the establishing of *shalom*, 'peace'. This *shalom* is not an individual's peace of mind or conscience, however. Professor J. G. Davies describes it as 'a social happening', which expresses the 'totality', the harmonious community, which God means society to enjoy.[5] According to this kind of ecumenical thinking, *shalom* is almost equivalent to the kingdom of God and the new humanity. Indeed, the revolutionary movements of today's world, in which the old order is giving way to the new, are regarded as God's own renewing action by which *shalom*, the divine rule and the new humanity are being extended.

[3] From *The Witness of the Congregation in its Neighbourhood*, being the report of Section III of the meeting of the Commission on World Mission and Evangelism at Mexico, published in *Witness in Six Continents* edited by R. K. Orchard (Edinburgh House Press, 1964), p. 157.
[4] *Mission in the Modern World* (Patmos Press, 1968), pp. 12, 13.
[5] *Dialogue with the World* by J. G. Davies (SCM Press, 1967), pp. 13, 14.

Once these ecumenical spokesmen have asserted that God is thus primarily related to the world, not the church, they go on to define the church's mission in terms of discovering what God is doing in the world and catching up with it. 'If the goal of mission is the establishment of *shalom*, we are required to enter into partnership with God in history to renew society' (p. 15). Again, 'the church's task is simply to join Christ in *his* power struggle' (p. 53), that is, against the structures of social injustice. This is what is meant by the phrase 'let the world provide the agenda for the church'.

Such a quest for better social structures replaces (in many ecumenical circles today) the quest for individual conversions, while proclamation is ousted by the kind of dialogue in which the Christian meets the non-Christian on equal terms so that they can pool their ideas. 'I would be glad', Dr Davies has written, 'if the term conversion could be dropped from the Christian vocabulary' (p. 54). And the dialogue he prefers to proclamation is both difficult and dangerous. 'If I engage in dialogue with a Buddhist,' he writes, 'and do so with openness, I must recognize that the outcome cannot be predetermined either for him or for me. The Buddhist may come to accept Jesus as Lord, but I may come to accept the authority of the Buddha, or even both of us may end up as agnostics' (p. 55).

Similarly, Dr Erik Routley, reviewing in the *British Weekly* in November 1967 John Pellow's description of his ministry in the East End of London entitled *The Concrete Village*, could write: 'Earlier books are all in the key of old-fashioned mission – of the church "giving" and "saving" and dispensing spiritual bounty. This one is in the key of modern mission – of the church being a network of real relations between Christians and the equally real people who live in Stepney. Not "we've got it, you come and get it", but "here's my gift; there's yours: let's put them together and see what happens".' More drastically still, Dr E. Edmund Perry, Professor of History and Religion at Northwestern University, could tell the American Methodist Council of Evangelism in November 1965: 'I abhor the notion of individual salvation; Christianity is a societary term.'[6]

These forms of thesis and antithesis, although at opposite

[6] Quoted by Carl Henry in *Evangelicals at the Brink of Crisis* (World Books, 1967), p. 74.

extremes, yet resemble each other in that both contain an element of Pharisaism. For each side's involvement with the world is limited, unbalanced, and less than fully Christian.

The kind of evangelicalism which concentrates exclusively on saving individual souls is not true evangelicalism. It is not evangelical because it is not biblical. It forgets that God did not create souls but body-souls called human beings, who are also social beings, and that He cares about their bodies and their society as well as about their relationship with Himself and their eternal destiny. So true Christian love will care for people as people, and will seek to serve them, neglecting neither the soul for the body nor the body for the soul. As a matter of fact, it has not been characteristic of evangelicals in the past to be shy of social action, or even, when necessary, of political action. Perhaps the two most notable examples in England, both of which belong to the last century, are William Wilberforce, whose indefatigable campaign led to the abolition of the slave trade and later of slavery itself, and Anthony Ashley Cooper, the seventh Earl of Shaftesbury, who introduced legislation to improve the working conditions in factories and mines, of colliers and chimney sweeps. We saw earlier how brightly Christ's compassion for outcasts shone against the dark background of the Pharisees' indifference. Still today there are neglected groups of our human society – for example drug addicts, alcoholics, the mentally sick, and the elderly – who need what might be termed 'total care'. They challenge evangelicals to bold experiments which would combine gospel truth and practical service in a balanced expression of love.

The kind of ecumenism which concentrates exclusively on questions of social justice, however, on eliminating racial discrimination, hunger, poverty and war, forgets the Christian saying which is 'sure and worthy of full acceptance, that Christ Jesus came into the world to save sinners',[7] and forgets also His plain commission to the church to proclaim repentance and forgiveness to all nations.[8] Much of its theological basis is also, to say the least, extremely questionable.

Dr W. A. Visser 't Hooft, former General Secretary of the World Council of Churches, made a fine statement at Uppsala in July 1968 about the relation between these two Christian

[7] 1 Tim. 1:15.   [8] Lk. 24:47.

concerns: 'I believe that, with regard to the great tension between the vertical interpretation of the Gospel as essentially concerned with God's saving action in the life of individuals, and the horizontal interpretation of it as mainly concerned with human relationships in the world, we must get out of that rather primitive oscillating movement of going from one extreme to the other. . . . A Christianity which has lost its vertical dimension has lost its salt and is not only insipid in itself, but useless for the world. But a Christianity which would use the vertical preoccupation as a means to escape from its responsibility for and in the common life of man is a denial of the Incarnation, of God's love for the world manifested in Christ.' Again, 'it must become clear that church members who deny in fact their responsibility for the needy in any part of the world are just as much guilty of heresy as those who deny this or that article of the faith.'[9]

4. In our endeavour to find examples in the contemporary church of Pharisaic withdrawal from the world, we have so far alluded to self-righteousness, a monastic type of self-absorbed isolationism and an unbalanced emphasis on evangelism or social concern, each at the expense of the other. But the fourth and perhaps the commonest reason why we tend to stand aloof from the world is plain *laziness and selfishness*. We do not want to get involved in its hurt or dirt. Only the compassion of Christ will overcome our reluctance.

Certainly the world itself has cultivated a high degree of irresponsible detachment. It continues to talk the language of Cain: 'Am I my brother's keeper?'[1] A frightening example happened in New York on 13 March 1964. A decent, pretty young woman of 28 called Kitty Genovese was returning home from her job as manager of a bar. It was 3.20 a.m. She had parked her car and was walking the remaining few yards to her apartment, when she was attacked by a man and stabbed. She screamed for help. Several lights went on in the apartment block, and somebody shouted from an upper window, 'Let that girl alone.' The assailant looked up, shrugged his shoulders

[9] *The Uppsala Report 1968* edited by Norman Goodall (World Council of Churches, 1968), pp. 317, 318 and 320.
[1] Gn. 4:9.

and walked off. But as the lights went out again and nobody
came to her rescue, he returned and stabbed her a second time.
At her renewed screams more lights went on, windows were
opened and heads looked out. So the man got into his car and
drove away. But again, as nobody came to help her, he returned
to stab her for the third time and kill her. Not until 3.50 a.m.
did the police receive their first telephone call. By then she was
dead.

When the police questioned local residents, they found that at
least thirty-eight respectable, middle-class, law-abiding citizens
had heard this woman's screams and had watched her being
stabbed, but not one had done anything about it. She had even
recognized one witness and called to him by name, but he did
not reply. Why, the police asked, had these folk not come to
her aid? Some confessed that they did not know. A housewife
said she 'thought it was a lovers' quarrel'. A man explained
without emotion, 'I was tired. I went back to bed.' But 'the
word we kept hearing from the witnesses', said Police Lieutenant
Bernard Jacobs, 'was "involved".' 'People told us they just
didn't want to get involved.'[2]

Self-righteousness and snobbery, fear of contamination, a
distorted perspective of soul and body, and apathy. Underlying
these four causes of withdrawal there lurks a false view of God.
The God revealed by Jesus Christ is a God who cares. He loves
people who do not deserve to be loved. He makes His sun rise
on the evil as well as the good, and sends rain on the unjust
as well as the just. He made us body-souls and cares for us as
body-souls. And He has taken action – sacrificial action – to
supply a remedy for our sin. He has got Himself deeply involved
in our predicament.

So Jesus Christ Himself did not remain aloof, or refuse to get
involved, or hide away in the safe immunity of heaven. He
entered our world. He assumed our nature. He identified
Himself with our humanity. He exposed Himself to our tempta-

[2] The details of this fearful incident are culled from articles in *The New York
Times* for 27 March 1964 and *Life Magazine* for 10 April 1964, which Dr
Kenneth M. Scott, Director of the Christian Medical College and Hospital,
Ludhiana, Punjab, kindly obtained for me. His own briefer account of the
incident appears in his booklet *The New Era in Medical Missions* (IVF, 1965),
p. 1.

tions, sorrows and pains. He made friends with outcasts and was nicknamed 'a friend of tax collectors and sinners'.[3] He humbled Himself to serve people in their need. He washed His disciples' feet. He never drew back from any demanding situation. He was willing finally to bear our sins and our curse in our place.

And now He says to the church: 'As the Father has sent me, even so I send you.'[4] The church's mission reflects the Son's mission, and both express the character of the Father. What is this? He is not the Judge only, but the Saviour. He is not a rewarder of merit, but a bestower of mercy. He is the shepherd of lost sheep, the physician of sick souls, a father of infinite patience. Now He sends us out into the world like Christ – not to run away and escape, but to enter the pain of distraught humanity, to think and feel our way into people's doubts, difficulties and distresses, to be channels of the love of God as both servants and witnesses, to bring what relief we can and the good news of salvation through Christ's death and resurrection. Such is our responsibility. Nothing but costly involvement is Christian; withdrawal, to whatever degree, is Pharisaic. 'As our Lord took on our flesh, so He calls His Church to take on the secular world.' Otherwise we do not 'take the Incarnation seriously'.[5]

The conclusion brings us to one of the great paradoxes of Christian living. The whole church is called (and every member of it) as much to involvement in the world as to separation from it, as much to 'worldliness' as to 'holiness'. Not to a worldliness which is unholy, nor to a holiness which is unworldly, but to 'holy worldliness', a true separation to God which is lived out in the world – the world which He made and sent His Son to redeem.

Only the power of God can deliver us from the grudging, judging attitude of the elder brother, from the false Pharisaic fear of contamination-by-contact and from the aloofness which refuses to get involved. In place of all this we need the compassion of Christ. Let the Pharisees of today's church murmur their disapproval if they will, if only they will also say of us (as their ancestors said of our Master): 'this man receives sinners and eats with them.'

[3] Lk. 7:34.   [4] Jn. 20:21; cf. 17:18.
[5] *Witness in Six Continents*, pp. 151, 158.

8 AMBITION: OUR GLORY OR GOD'S?

Hidden motives play a large part in our everyday behaviour. The important question to ask is not merely what a person is doing, but why he is doing it. Modern psychology is concerned to probe our basic motivation. Industry and commerce study the subject of incentives in order first to attract good staff and then to encourage good work.

Certainly no man can know himself until he has honestly asked himself about his motives. What is the driving-force of his life? What ambition dominates and directs him?

Ultimately there are only two controlling ambitions, to which all others may be reduced. One is our own glory, and the other God's. The fourth Evangelist set them in irreconcilable opposition to each other, and in doing so disclosed Christ's fundamental quarrel with the Pharisees: 'they loved the glory of men', he wrote, 'more than the glory of God.'[1]

But what is 'the glory of God' that we should 'love' it and so set our will to seek it? The expression itself (in English as in Greek) is ambiguous. Indeed, so are many such genitives which may be either subjective or objective. Take as an example the phrase 'the love of God'. If the genitive is subjective, God is the subject of the love and it means God's love for us. If, on the other hand, the genitive is objective, God is the object of the love and what is meant is rather our love for God. So too with 'the glory of God'. If a subjective genitive, it would refer to the glory or praise which comes from God; if an objective, to the glory and praise which are due to God. The Authorized Version and the Revised Standard Version take it in the former sense and translate John 12 : 43: 'they loved the praise of men

[1] Jn. 12:43, literally.

more than the praise of God.' Linguistically and contextually, this is no doubt correct. Nevertheless, it is possible to argue that the phrase contains a deliberate ambiguity and that John intended to comprehend both meanings. Certainly the Pharisees were guilty of this double sin. They desired that praise and honour should be both given *to* men instead of God and received *from* men instead of God. This was the height (and depth) of Pharisaic perversity. For the whole Scripture teaches that God, not man, is to be both the subject and the object of glory. He is Himself the only rightful giver and recipient of it. We must examine this twofold truth and see how far short of it the Pharisees fell.

Glory to God not man

To love the glory of God more than the glory of men is to seek to bring glory to Him rather than to men. It is to desire that all men will honour God (not us or others), and that we and they will give to Him the glory which is His due. It is to fulfil the aspirations of the Lord's Prayer, to be concerned for the hallowing of God's name, the coming of God's kingdom and the doing of God's will.

The man Christ Jesus was imbued with this desire. 'I do not seek my own glory,' He could say. Again, 'He who speaks on his own authority seeks his own glory; but he who seeks the glory of him who sent him is true, and in him there is no falsehood.'[2] 'Father,' He prayed, 'glorify thy name.' This was the supreme passion of His life and ministry, so that He could claim at the end, 'I glorified thee on earth.'[3]

In this same ambition lay what was perhaps the greatest single secret of the strength of the Protestant Reformation. One of the essential differences between pre-Reformation religion and Reformation religion is that the former was in many respects man-centred, while the Reformers were determined to be God-centred. In the matter of authority they repudiated the traditions of *men*, because they held the supremacy and the sufficiency of *God's* Word written. In the matter of salvation they repudiated the merits of *men*, because they held the sufficiency of *Christ's* finished work. This is why they emphasized the doctrine of justification by grace alone through faith

[2] Jn. 8:50; 7:18.   [3] Jn. 12:28; 17:4.

alone. Thus Cranmer wrote of it in his Homily *Of the Salvation of Mankind by only Christ our Saviour from Sin and Death everlasting*: 'this doctrine advanceth and setteth forth the true glory of Christ, and beateth down the vain glory of man.'[4] This, too, is why they rejected the Mass. The notion that the Mass was in any sense a sacrifice of Christ was utterly abhorrent to them because they saw it as derogatory to the glory of Christ's only and perfect sacrifice. Nicholas Ridley said it was 'to the great and intolerable contumely of Christ our Saviour'. Cranmer used even stronger language and called it 'the greatest blasphemy and injury that can be done against Christ'.[5] The Reformers' reasons for all this protest were plain and pure. In emphasizing *sola scriptura* for the church's authority, and *sola gratia* with *sola fides* for the sinner's salvation, their motive in both was *soli Deo gloria*, to God alone be glory!

Of no leading Reformer was this more true than of John Calvin himself. His whole theology was centred on the sovereignty of God and the glory of God. This is how one of his biographers ends the story of his life: 'Calvin breathed his last on May 27, 1564, at the setting of the sun. He was buried very simply in the cemetery of Plainpalais. No stone marks his grave. Thus died without glory the man who throughout his life had proclaimed that to God alone belongs all the glory.'[6]

In this godly ambition the Reformers turned their backs on Pharisaism. For the Pharisees were obsessed with vainglory. They were not concerned to bring glory to God; they wanted the glory themselves. 'They loved the glory of men [*i.e.* their own glory] more than the glory of God.' How this vitiated their whole lives we shall see later. At this point it seems right to pause and see how much Pharisaism lingers even in Christian hearts. Indeed, so proud is our corrupt nature, that even in our most sacred moments we may find ourselves motivated rather by vainglory than by God's glory. Examples may be found in our worship, our evangelism and our ministry.

[4] *Homilies and Canons* (SPCK, 1914), pp. 25, 26. The Homilies were first published in 1547.
[5] Ridley's *A Piteous Lamentation* in his *Works*, p. 52. Cranmer's *Defence of the True and Catholic Doctrine of the Lord's Supper*, 1550, in his *Works* (Thynne, 1907), Book V, ch. 1, p. 232.
[6] *The Man God Mastered* by Jean Cadier, translated by O. R. Johnston (IVF, 1960), p. 176.

True heart-worship is the most God-centred, God-honouring activity in which man either can or will ever participate. It is to ascribe to God the glory due to His name, to be occupied with God and with God alone. It has been truly said that nothing so disinfects us of egoism.

Yet into public worship how subtly and swiftly does selfish vanity begin to intrude! The minister becomes proud of the way he is leading the service, the preacher of his eloquence and learning, the choir and organist of their musical ability and the congregation of their piety in being in church at all! Thus, just when our attention should be absorbed exclusively with God in self-forgetful adoration, we become self-conscious, self-righteous, self-important and self-congratulatory again.

True evangelism is closely allied to true worship. Paul calls it a sacrificial service in which the evangelist turns priest by the offering of his converts to God.[7] Evangelism is also a proclamation of the gospel by which men are saved from self-centredness to God-centredness. Yet much of our evangelism is man-centred. Our publicity boosts the speaker or the sponsor more than the Saviour. We become proud of our organization or puffed up with vanity over our own evangelistic zeal.

Or take, as a third example, the exercise of ministry in the church. 'Ministry' means 'service' – lowly, menial service; it is, therefore, peculiarly perverse to turn it into an occasion for boasting. Jesus specifically distinguished between 'rule' and 'service', 'authority' and 'ministry', and added that though the former was characteristic of pagans, the latter was to characterize His followers: 'You know that those who are supposed to rule over the Gentiles lord it over them, and their great men exercise authority over them. But it shall not be so among you; but whoever would be great among you must be your servant, and whoever would be first among you must be slave of all. For the Son of man also came not to be served but to serve, and to give his life as a ransom for many.'[8] Thus the Christian minister is to take as his model, not the Gentiles (or the Pharisees) who preferred to be lords, but the Christ who came to serve.

This is not to deny that some authority attaches to the ministry,[9] but rather to define and circumscribe it. It is the

[7] Rom. 15:16.   [8] Mk. 10:42–45.
[9] See, e.g., 1 Thes. 5:12, 13; 1 Tim. 3:5; Heb. 13:7, 17.

authority which inheres in sound teaching and consistent
example. It is never authoritarian to the extent that one man
attempts to exercise lordship over another man's mind, conscience
or will. 'Not as domineering over those in your charge but being
examples to the flock.'[1] Yet domineering is exactly what the
Pharisees were, keeping the people in subjection under them.
So were the pre-Reformation clergy, their despotic power being
buttressed by the universal belief that the keys of heaven were
in their hands.

Jesus exposed the tyranny of the Pharisees by drawing attention
to the tell-tale titles which they loved. He insisted that in the
church He was founding these titles were neither to be assumed
nor accorded: 'But you are not to be called rabbi, for you have
one teacher, and you are all brethren. And call no man your
father on earth, for you have one Father, who is in heaven.
Neither be called masters, for you have one master, the Christ.'[2]
In other words, in the church laity are not to adopt towards
clergy, nor are clergy to require of laity, nor are any Christian
people to assume towards one another, either a child–father
relation of dependence or a servant–master relation of unquestioning obedience or a pupil–teacher relation of uncritical acceptance.
Each of these attitudes is doubly offensive. For one thing it is
disruptive of the Christian brotherhood: 'you are all brethren.'
For another it usurps prerogatives which belong to God: 'you
have one Father (on whom you depend), who is in heaven',
'you have one master (whom you are to obey), the Christ' and
(Jesus might have added) 'you have one teacher·(whose instruction you can believe), the Holy Spirit'. Thus clerical domination
is an offence to both God and man, to the three Persons of the
Trinity and to the brotherhood of believers.

Certainly the apostle Paul had learned this lesson well.
When the Corinthian church split into factions, affirming their
allegiance to Paul, Apollos and Cephas, he was horrified. It
may be that the further slogan 'I belong to Christ' was not a
fourth party-cry but the apostle's own retort. That is, if the
Corinthians will insist on giving their loyalty to men, let it at
least be clear that, as for Paul, he belonged to Christ. So indeed
did they, although their behaviour contradicted it. They had
believed and been baptized into the name of Christ, not Paul.

[1] 1 Pet. 5:3.   [2] Mt. 23:8–10.

And so far from their belonging to Paul, Paul and his fellow-apostles belonged to them: 'For all things are yours, whether Paul or Apollos or Cephas or the world or life or death or the present or the future, all are yours; and you are Christ's; and Christ is God's.'[3]

One could wish that the church of subsequent generations had remembered and obeyed its Lord's command as explicitly as did the apostle Paul. It is true that most of the Christian leaders God has raised up have been as disturbed as he that men should use their names (I have already[4] quoted Luther's 'Please do not use my name; do not call yourselves Lutherans, but Christians'). But their followers have not always been so judicious or modest. We must agree with the sentiments which John Venn, Rector of Clapham, expressed on this matter at the beginning of the last century: 'It was a wise precept delivered by our blessed Lord to call no man master. Would to God that the names of Calvin and Arminius, as leaders of a party, had, like the body of Moses, been buried in oblivion. It should be the peculiar glory of the Church of Christ that it has but one master, the best, the wisest and the highest. By ranging under the banners of a party, we in effect desert those of Christ, and imbibe a spirit which is far more opposite to Christianity than any deviation in non-essential points from the Christian faith. Love to the brethren was laid down by our great Master, as the characteristic of His disciples, but, wherever a party spirit is embraced, there the love, which like that of Christ should be universal, is narrowed and confined to a set; and Christian character degenerates into a mode of selfishness.'[5] Again, 'How has the Christian world been divided and its peace destroyed by the adoption of the names and tenets of particular ministers as the badges of different parties in the Church: I am of Calvin, and I of Arminius, and I of Luther. Would to God that it had been always remembered that Christians are of Christ alone.'[6]

Looking back now over these different examples of vainglory, we have seen that our worship, our evangelism and our

[3] 1 Cor. 1:10–13; 3:21–23.
[4] See above, p. 29.
[5] Letter to the Editor of the *Christian Observer* in 1803. This and the following quotation appear in *John Venn and the Clapham Sect* by Michael Hennell (Lutterworth, 1958), pp. 262, 263.
[6] *Sermons*, vol. III, p. 192.

ministry all become tainted whenever in and through them we seek to bring glory to men (*i.e.* ourselves) rather than to God.

Glory from God not man

To love the glory of God more than the glory of men is also to seek approval from God rather than men.

This too was the declared ambition of Jesus. 'I do not receive glory of men,' He said.[7] Indeed, we know that He was despised and rejected by men, even by His own nation, and died as an outcast on a Roman cross. Yet God approved Him, declaring Him at both the baptism and the transfiguration His beloved Son in whom He was well pleased,[8] and finally vindicating Him by the resurrection and the ascension.[9]

Very different, however, was the ambition of the Pharisees. Their supreme concern was to stand high in the favour of men, rather than God, and this had an evil effect upon every aspect of their lives.

First, it prevented their conversion. The reason why they did not believe in Jesus was their fear of public opinion. 'How can you believe,' Jesus asked, 'who receive glory from one another and do not seek the glory that comes from the only God?'[1] As Jesus presented Himself to them as Messiah, Son of God and Saviour, their whole thought was: 'What will the Sanhedrin think?' Their vainglory blinded them to Christ's glory. It is the same today. 'The fear of man lays a snare.'[2] Jesus Christ still says to His would-be followers: 'Whoever is ashamed of me and of my words in this adulterous and sinful generation, of him will the Son of man also be ashamed, when he comes in the glory of his Father, with the holy angels.'[3]

Secondly, it silenced their witness. That is, it was both the reason why most did not believe in Him and the reason why the few who did believe in Him remained secret disciples and did not confess Him openly. John writes that towards the end of His ministry 'many even of the authorities believed in him, but for fear of the Pharisees they did not confess it, lest they should be put out of the synagogue: for they loved the praise

[7] Jn. 5:41.
[9] *E.g.* Rom. 1:4; Phil. 2:9–11.
[2] Pr. 29:25.
[8] Mk. 1:11; 9:7.
[1] Jn. 5:44.
[3] Mk. 8:38.

of men more than the praise of God'.[4] Their eyes were on men.
They could not contemplate the ridicule and rejection which
would follow an open commitment to Christ. They were hungry
for popularity and praise. The same self-regarding anxiety to
stand high in the opinion of others keeps many Christians dumb
today when they should be vocal in testimony to their Lord.
It also ruins the ministry of every preacher who is more concerned
to please the congregation than the Master (theirs and his).
'Not with eye-service, as men-pleasers, but in singleness of
heart, fearing the Lord'[5] is an instruction just as applicable
to ministers of the gospel as it is to domestic servants or employees.
Our ministry will never be blessed by God until we can cry
with honest defiance: 'Am I now seeking the favour of men, or
of God? Or am I trying to please men? If I were still pleasing
men, I should not be a servant of Christ.'[6]

Thirdly, it spoiled their social behaviour. Their vainglory
permeated all their public conduct. This is how Jesus summed
it up: 'The scribes and the Pharisees . . . do all their deeds
to be seen by men; for they make their phylacteries broad[7]
and their fringes long, and they love the place of honour at
feasts and the best seats in the synagogues, and salutations in
the market places, and being called rabbi by men.'[8] So then
in the dress they wore, in the functions they attended, in the
seats they occupied, and in the deferential greetings and titles
they were given they enjoyed being conspicuous and receiving
honour from men. Indeed, they went out of their way to win
the admiration of men.

Fourthly, and most seriously of all, it ruined their religious
practice, their 'piety'. So Jesus warned His disciples in the Sermon
on the Mount against following their bad example.[9] 'Beware
of practising your piety before men in order to be seen by them,'
He said (v. 1). The Revised Standard Version is surely right
to make this verse a separate introductory paragraph. It is
a general reference to the practice of piety, of which Jesus

[4] Jn. 12:42, 43.   [5] Col. 3:22.   [6] Gal. 1:10.
[7] Phylacteries were two little boxes normally of about an inch cube, one of
which was worn on the forehead and the other on the left hand. Inside them
were kept four parchment pieces on which quotations from the law were
inscribed.
[8] Mt. 23:2, 5-7; cf. Mk. 12:38-40.
[9] Mt. 6:1-6, 16-18.

went on to give three particular examples – giving (vv. 2–4), praying (vv. 5, 6) and fasting (vv. 16–18). These three practices were much emphasized by the Pharisees, all of whom gave money to the poor, spent time in prayer and abstained from food for spiritual purposes. Jesus had no quarrel with the three practices themselves. On the contrary, since He began each paragraph with the words 'when you . . .' (not 'if you . . .'), He evidently expected His disciples to engage in the same practices. They express to some extent our threefold Christian duty – in almsgiving to our *neighbour* whom we love and serve, in prayer to *God* on whom we depend, and in fasting to *ourselves* in self-discipline and self-control.

The difference between Pharisaic piety and Christian piety was not, therefore, in what they practised, but rather in how and why they practised it, and in the consequences of their practice.

This is so important, and the distinctions Jesus made are so relevant to religious practice today, that these verses will repay careful study.

The pattern of each of the three paragraphs is the same. Jesus contrasts first two possible ways (Pharisaic and Christian) of practising the piety in question, next the two motives behind them and then the two resulting rewards.

Alternative forms of religion

He begins with the alternative forms of piety, namely the ostentatious and the secret. In graphic, even humorous, detail Jesus describes the religious display of the Pharisee. When he is about to give alms, he gives a loud trumpet blast to draw attention to his charity (v. 2). When he prays, he chooses a conspicuous place either in the synagogue or at a street corner (v. 5). When he fasts, he disfigures his face, making himself dirty and dishevelled, perhaps smearing himself with ashes so as to look pale through his austerity diet, and he looks dismal as well (v. 16).

It is easy to poke fun at those Jewish Pharisees; our Christian Pharisaism is not so funny. We may not blow trumpets, but we like to see our name on subscription lists. We may not pray on street corners, but we like to gain a reputation for our disciplined devotional life. We may not put on sackcloth and ashes, but, if we ever did fast, we would certainly want to make sure everybody knew about it.

Christian piety, on the other hand, is secret piety. 'Secret' is the emphatic word of the whole section, being repeated six times. Thus (vv. 3, 4), when we give alms, not only are we not to tell others about our Christian giving, we are not even to let our left hand know what our right hand is doing. That is, we are not to dwell on it in our own mind in a spirit of self-congratulation. Instead, our giving is to be, in every way, un-self-conscious.

When we pray (v. 6), we are to go into our room and shut the door, not only against distraction and interruption, but also against all human spectators. Then in privacy and secrecy we are to pray to our Father 'who is in that secret place'.[1]

Similarly, when we fast (vv. 17, 18), we are to anoint our head and wash our face. This does not mean that we are to do anything unusual to our head and face. Christian piety does not put hypocrisy into reverse and affect a grinning countenance instead of a dismal one. No. We are, as it were, to wash our face and brush our hair in the ordinary way. Then, seeing no abnormality in our appearance or routine, nobody will guess what is going on in secret.

In each case ostentation is the stock-in-trade of the Pharisee; Christian piety is practised in secret.

Alternative motives for religion

Behind this divergence in form and practice there lies a divergence in motive. The motive of the Pharisee in the public parade of his piety is to catch the attention and win the admiration of men. The Pharisees were essentially men-pleasers. They practised their piety 'before men' in order to be 'seen by men' (vv. 1, 5, 16) and gave their alms in order to be 'praised by men' (v. 2).

The word Jesus gave to this religious show was 'hypocrisy', and when He told His disciples to 'beware of the leaven of the Pharisees', it was to this as much as to their teaching that He referred.[2] The *hypokritēs* is the actor, the man who plays a part on the stage, pretending to be someone he is not. He is wearing a mask. His appearance is not the reality, but a disguise. And the

[1] Mt. 6:6, JB.
[2] Cf. Mt. 16:5-12 with Lk. 12:1-3.

hypocrite in religion is the same. He is playing a game of 'let's pretend', and he does it to be seen (Gk. *theathēnai*) by men. That is, he is giving a theatrical display before an audience. It is all done for show, for applause.

The tragedy of it is that giving and praying and fasting simply cannot be treated in this way. For they are *real* activities, involving *real* people. If we turn them into a pretence, we actually destroy them. The purpose of almsgiving is to alleviate the distress of the needy, of prayer to enjoy communion with God, and of fasting to discipline oneself for some spiritual good. But the hypocrite is not interested in the real purpose these practices serve; he exploits them to gratify his own vanity. He gives for the benefit not of others, but of himself. He prays in order to seek not God's face but his own glory. He fasts not to discipline himself but to display himself. He actually uses God and his fellow-men (or practices intended to honour God and serve them) to pander to his own conceit. He turns religion and charity into an exhibitionist parade to boost his own ego. It is hard to exaggerate the perversity of this.

If the motive behind Pharisaic piety is selfish (the advancement of his own glory), the motive behind Christian piety is godly (the advancement of the glory of God). To begin with, the Christian recognizes that giving, praying and fasting are important in their own right. They are intended to express a genuine desire to serve others, to seek God and to discipline self. In one sense we have no need or wish to look further than this. Nevertheless, there is something further to be said. For although, as we have seen, these three practices relate obviously to others, God and self, yet the Christian also relates them all to God. He knows that his duties to others and to self are part of his duty to God, since everything he does as a Christian is done to please, honour and glorify God. So, although he gives and prays and fasts in secret so far as *men* are concerned, he does not do these things in secret so far as *God* is concerned. On the contrary, 'the secret place' in which he gives and prays and fasts is the very place which God sees and in which God is.

The beautiful truth is this: whereas to practise our religion *before men* is certain to degrade it, to practise it *before God* is equally certain to ennoble it. It is the only way to ensure that it will be real, genuine and true. Why is this? Partly because of who and what God is, and partly because this God 'sees' – not the outward appearance which is all men see but the heart, not the deed itself only but the thoughts and the motives which lie behind the deed. So to live and act in the presence of God ensures reality, while to practise our piety before men is to put on a charade.

I think a short digression is necessary at this stage. Some people are puzzled by the seeming contradiction between this prohibition of practising our piety before men to be seen by men (Mt. 6 : 1) and the earlier command to let our light shine before men that they may see our good works (5 : 16). Are we to live our Christian lives before men to be seen by them, it is asked, or not? The contradiction is verbal and superficial only, however. Three points may be made in clarification.

First, the two verses refer to different aspects of our Christian life. Our 'piety' which is not to be done before men to be seen by them is the practice of giving, praying and fasting; these duties can and should be secret. Our 'light' which we are to allow to shine before men to be seen, on the other hand, is our 'good works'; these are works of mercy like feeding the hungry, clothing the naked and nursing the sick, which clearly cannot be hidden from those who benefit from them.

Secondly, the two verses are directed against different failures. It is the sin of cowardice which made Jesus say 'let your light shine before men', but the sin of vanity which made Him say 'do not practise your piety before men'. As A. B. Bruce puts it: we are to 'show when tempted to *hide*' and 'hide when tempted to *show*'.[3]

Thirdly, despite these differences, the ultimate end of both the prohibition and the command is the same, namely the greater glory of God. Our piety must be secret and our good works public, in order that men may glorify not us but our heavenly Father.

Returning from this digression, we are ready now to consider the alternative rewards for piety.

[3] *The Synoptic Gospels* (*The Expositor's Greek Testament*). Commentary by A. B. Bruce (Hodder and Stoughton, 1897). Comment on Mt. 6:1.

Alternative rewards for religion

What reward does the Pharisee get for his vain display? The obvious answer is 'none': 'you will have no reward from your Father who is in heaven' (v. 1). But this states that he will receive no reward from *God*; it does not say that he will get no reward at all. As a matter of fact, he will be rewarded. He will get the reward he wants – no more and no less – the praise of men. What reward does an actor want when the play is finished? The applause of the audience. What reward does the religious play-actor get? The same: applause! But once the applause has died down, there is no further reward to come. This is the thrust of the solemn words Jesus repeated three times: 'Truly, I say to you, they have their reward' (vv. 2, 5, 16). That is to say, 'they have their reward already' (NEB) or 'they have had all the reward they are going to get!' (JBP). The verb was commonly used at that time for giving a receipt.[4] It indicates, writes Professor Tasker, 'that payment has been made *in full*'.[5]

The Christian, on the other hand, since he gives and prays and fasts in secret, neither expects nor receives a reward from men. But our heavenly Father will reward him, Jesus said. Incidentally, the true reading is not 'shall reward thee *openly*' (AV). The contrast is not between a secret act and a public reward, but between men who neither see nor reward and God who does both. Three times Jesus affirmed it: 'your Father who sees in secret will reward you' (vv. 4, 6, 18). Some Christians recoil from this. They declare that they wish for no reward; they even dismiss the promise. But Christian disciples are not at liberty to treat the teaching of their Lord and Master in this high-handed way. If Jesus said it, we may be sure that He meant it. What did He mean?

The difficulty has arisen partly because of the familiar Authorized Version gloss of the adverb 'openly', which makes us think of prize-day at school or college, with everybody clapping, and partly because the word 'reward' suggests to us a pat on the back, a silver cup or a cheque, and we do not readily imagine any other kinds of reward. What is the nature of the reward?

---

[4] See examples of this use of *apecho* from the papyri and ostraca, given by Moulton and Milligan.
[5] *The Gospel According to St Matthew* (*Tyndale New Testament Commentaries*). Commentary by R. V. G. Tasker (Tyndale Press, 1961), p. 71.

There is nothing in the context to suggest that the promised reward will be presented at some future 'prize-giving'. Since the hypocrite's reward is given him then and there, I am inclined to think the Christian's is also. May it not be an immediate and spiritual reward? Rich indeed are the rewards which God gives to those who are sincere in the practice of their piety. They give secretly, and share with God the secret discovery that 'it is more blessed to give than to receive'.[6] They pray in the secret place, and they find God there, waiting to satisfy their hunger with good things, to refresh their spirit and renew their strength. They fast in secret, and are rewarded by an increasing self-control, and by the joy, peace and liberty which are the fruits of self-control.

Modern Pharisaism and its remedy

We have now seen the stark contrast which Jesus paints in the Sermon on the Mount between Pharisaic and Christian piety. They assume different forms (the ostentatious and the secret), are directed by different motives (self-glorification and the glory of God) and receive different rewards (the applause of men and the blessing of God). Nothing could indicate more clearly than this the far-reaching influence of the false, Pharisaic ambition, namely to love the praise of men more than the praise of God. If it prevented their conversion, silenced their witness and spoiled their social behaviour, it entirely ruined their practice of piety.

The same Pharisaic spirit still haunts every child of Adam today. It is easy to be critical of Christ's contemporaries and miss the repetition of their vainglory in ourselves. Yet deeply ingrained in our fallen nature is this thirst for the praise of men. It seems to be a devilish perversion of our basic psychological need to be wanted and to be loved. We hunger for applause, fish for compliments, thrive on flattery. It is the plaudits of men we want; we are not content with God's approval now or with His 'Well done, good and faithful servant' on the last day. Yet, as Calvin put it: 'What is more foolish, nay, what is more brutish, than to prefer the paltry approval of men to the judgment of God?'[7]

The remedy lies, Jesus seems to have suggested, in the recognition that vainglory is a form of idolatry. 'You . . . receive glory

[6] Acts 20:35.   [7] *The Gospel According to St John.* Comment on Jn. 12:43.

from one another', He said to His Jewish contemporaries, 'and do not seek the glory that comes from *the only God*.'[8] His designation of the Father in this context as 'the only God' was deliberate and significant. He was implying by it that the giving and the receiving of 'glory' are both alike divine prerogatives. Glory (or praise) is due to God alone and must be sought from God alone, precisely because He is God. Once we recognize this, that glory belongs to God both in giving and receiving, then to substitute man for God in either is self-evidently idolatrous. It is to divert from God to men the glory which belongs to Him alone to bestow and to receive. And this is effectively to deny that God is God alone.

But why is God the only proper subject and object, giver and recipient, of glory?

Glory is due to God alone because He is our Creator. The source of our being is God. Both the material and the spiritual creation owe their origin to His will and power. The statement 'it is he that made us, and not we ourselves'[9] applies to both creations equally. Our very life is in God's hand. Physically, He 'gives to all men life and breath and everything'. Spiritually also, through Christ, He 'gives life to whom he will'.[1] Thus the Christian, who is physically alive and has been spiritually quickened, acknowledges his utter dependence of body and soul on the Lord, the Life-giver. His language can never cease to be 'by the grace of God I am what I am'.[2] To him this is not pious pretence, but sober fact. Humility is nothing but the truth.

Glory also comes from God alone because He is our Judge. Jesus taught this too: 'I do not seek my own glory,' He said; 'there is One who seeks it and he will be the judge.'[3] It is to God alone that we are ultimately responsible and must give an account of ourselves. It is to Him alone, therefore, that we should look for commendation or vindication. Besides, He alone is capable of true judgment because He is just and merciful, wholly impartial and knows the secrets of all hearts. If, therefore, we either receive glory from men or take it upon ourselves to give glory to men we are usurping a divine prerogative and putting men on the judgment seat of God.

[8] Jn. 5:44.   [9] Ps. 100:3, RSV margin.
[1] Acts 17:25; Jn 5:21; *cf*. Jn. 10:28; 17:2, *etc*.
[2] 1 Cor. 15:10.   [3] Jn. 8:50.

The apostle Paul is a fine example of one who sought glory from God alone. He had learned to be impervious to human flattery and criticism, not because he was temperamentally insensitive (far from it), but because he knew he had a heavenly Master and Judge to whom he was responsible and before whom his heart was an open book. He lived in the presence of God. Again and again in his Epistles he called God to witness. As a servant of Christ and steward of God's revealed secrets, he knew he was required to discharge his trust faithfully. So he could add: 'with me it is a very small thing that I should be judged by you or by any human court. I do not even judge myself. I am not aware of anything against myself, but I am not thereby acquitted. It is the Lord who judges me. Therefore do not pronounce judgment before the time, before the Lord comes, who will bring to light the things now hidden in darkness and will disclose the purposes of the heart. Then every man will receive his commendation from God.'[4]

Every sin is a surrender to the primeval temptation to become like God. It is a revolt against the 'Godness' of God, man's proud unwillingness to remain himself man or to let God be God. As Emil Brunner has expressed it: 'Man wants to be on a level with God, and in so doing to become independent of Him. . . . Sin is the desire for the autonomy of man; therefore, in the last resort, it is the denial of God and self-deification: it is getting rid of the Lord God, and the proclamation of self-sovereignty.'[5] And vainglory is a particularly idolatrous form of sin because it denies Him His unique glory as both Creator and Judge.

Pharisaism will yield to Christianity within us only when we humble ourselves and acknowledge that God is God, our Creator and our Judge, our Beginning from whom we come, our End to whom we go. Then we shall no longer live horizontally like the Pharisees (seeking glory from men and giving glory to men) but vertically (recognizing God as the sole bestower and recipient of glory). We shall love the glory of God more than the glory of men. Delivered from the burden and bondage of self-centredness, we shall begin to experience heaven on earth, the life whose centre is God's eternal throne.

[4] 1 Cor. 4:1–5; cf. Rom. 14:1–12.
[5] *Dogmatics*, II (Lutterworth Press, 1952), pp. 92, 93.

POSTSCRIPT:
JESUS TEACHER AND LORD

George Ingle, late, Bishop of Willesden, once wrote about 'the sad situation of a divided Church' and about the even sadder spectacle of 'division . . . within the same church'. He continued: 'Allegiance to *a* Church, or even to a party in that Church, comes before allegiance to Christ.'[1]

If I thought that being an evangelical Christian involved a party loyalty which took precedence over allegiance to Christ, I would give up being an evangelical immediately. The very idea of subordinating Christ to a party is abhorrent to me. The evangelical's sincerely held belief is that his very loyalty to Christ requires him to hold evangelical views.[2]

This, at any rate, has been the theme of this book. We have studied the major controversies of Christ and have tried to isolate the issues which He championed when in dialogue with the Pharisees and Sadducees. He attributed the Sadducees' error to their ignorance of the power of God. In contrast to the Pharisees He insisted that our authority is to be found in God's Word alone without the addition of human traditions and our acceptance in God's mercy alone without the addition of human merits. He taught that the morality and the worship pleasing to God are those of the heart, inward rather than outward. He emphasized that our Christian responsibility is to be involved in the world, not to withdraw from it, and that our overriding Christian ambition should not be to seek our own glory, but the glory of God.

[1] *The Lord's Creed* (Collins, 1964), pp. 9, 10.
[2] Every evangelical could echo Charles Simeon's statement of his own position: 'As for names and parties in religion, he equally disclaims them all: he takes his religion from the Bible; and endeavours, as much as possible, to speak as that speaks' (Carus, p. 178).

These issues emerge plainly from the debates of Jesus with the religious leaders of His day. And each debate has continued into our own day. Not one of them is dead. The only question is whether we range ourselves with Him or with those He criticized, whether our Christianity is in fact Christian or a modern version of Pharisaism or Sadduceeism.

In this connection I have myself been helped by some words Jesus spoke in the Upper Room just after He had washed the apostles' feet. When He had resumed His place He said to them: 'You call me Teacher and Lord; and you are right, for so I am. If I then, your Lord and Teacher, have washed your feet, you also ought to wash one another's feet.'[3]

Now 'Teacher' and 'Lord' were polite forms of address used in conversation with Rabbis. And the apostles used them in addressing Jesus. What He was now saying is that in His case they were more than courtesy titles; they expressed a fundamental reality. As the New English Bible renders it: 'You call me Teacher and Lord, and rightly so, for that is what I am.' I am in fact, He declared, what you call me in title.

This verse tells us something of great importance both about Christ and about Christians.

What it tells us about Christ concerns His divine self-consciousness. Though but a peasant from Galilee, carpenter by trade and preacher by vocation, He claimed to be the teacher and the lord of men. He said He had authority over them to tell them what to believe and to do. It is an evident (if indirect) claim to deity, for no mere man can ever exercise lordship over other men's minds and wills. Moreover, in advancing His claim He showed no sign of mental unbalance. On the contrary, He had just risen from supper, girded Himself with a towel, poured water into a basin, got on His hands and knees, and washed their feet. He who said He was their teacher and lord humbled Himself to be their servant. And it is this paradoxical combination of lordship and service, authority and humility, lofty claims and lowly conduct, which constitutes the strongest evidence that (in John's words in this passage) 'he had come from God and was going to God' (v. 3).

Secondly, the same verse reveals the proper relationship of Christians to Christ. This is not only that of a sinner to his

[3] Jn. 13:13, 14.

Saviour, but also of a pupil to his Teacher and of a servant to his Lord. Indeed, these things belong indissolubly together. He is 'our Lord and Saviour Jesus Christ'.[4] What, then, are the implications of acknowledging Jesus as Teacher and Lord?

Of course everybody agrees that Jesus of Nazareth was a great teacher, and many are prepared to go at least as far as Nicodemus and call Him 'a teacher come from God'.[5] Further, it is clear that one of the most striking characteristics of His teaching was the authority with which He gave it. He did not hum and haw and hesitate. Nor did He ever speak tentatively, diffidently, apologetically. No. He knew what He wanted to say, and He said it with quiet, simple dogmatism. It is this that impressed people so much. As they listened to Him, we read, 'they were astonished at his teaching, for his word was with authority'.[6]

There is only one logical deduction from these things. If the Jesus who thus taught with authority was the Son of God made flesh, we must bow to His authority and accept His teaching. We must allow our opinions to be moulded by His opinions, our views to be conditioned by His views. And this includes His uncomfortable and unfashionable teaching, some of which we have been considering in this book, like His view of God as a supreme, spiritual, personal, powerful Being, the Creator, Controller, Father and King, and of man as a created being, made in the image of God but now fallen, with a heart so corrupt as to be the source of all the evil things he thinks, says and does. Again, as we have seen, He taught the divine origin, supreme authority and complete sufficiency of Scripture as God's Word written, whose primary purpose is to direct the sinner to his Saviour in order to find life. He also taught (although we have not considered this) the fact of divine judgment as a process of sifting which begins in this life and is settled at death. He confirmed that the final destinies of men are the awful alternatives of heaven and hell, adding that these destinies are irrevocable with a great gulf fixed between them.

Yet these traditional Christian truths are being called in

---

[4] This full title occurs several times in the New Testament. See, *e.g.*, 2 Pet. 1:11; 3:18.
[5] Jn. 3:2.
[6] Lk. 4:32; *cf.* Mt. 7:28, 29; 13:53, 54; Mk. 1:22.

question today. The independent, personal, transcendent being of God, the radical sinfulness of man, the inspiration and authority of Scripture, the solemn, eternal realities of heaven and hell – all this (and more) is being not only questioned but in many places actually abandoned. Our simple contention is that no man can jettison such plain gospel truths as these and still call Jesus 'Teacher'.

There have been other religious teachers, even if less authoritative than Jesus. But Jesus went further, claiming also to be Lord. A teacher will instruct his pupils. He may even plead with them to follow his teaching. He cannot command assent, however, still less obedience. Yet this prerogative was exercised by Jesus as Lord. 'If you love me,' He said, 'you will keep my commandments.' 'He who loves father or mother . . . son or daughter more than me is not worthy of me.'[7] He asked from His disciples nothing less than their supreme love and loyalty.

So Christians look to Jesus Christ as both their Teacher and their Lord, their Teacher to instruct them and their Lord to command them. We are proud to be more than His pupils; we are His servants as well. We recognize His right to lay upon us duties and obligations: 'If I then, your Lord and Teacher, have washed your feet, you also *ought* to wash one another's feet.' This 'ought' we accept from the authority of Jesus. We desire not only to submit our minds to His teaching but our wills to His obedience. And this is what He expected: 'Truly, truly, I say to you, a servant [literally 'slave'] is not greater than his master.'[8] He therefore calls us to adopt His standards, which are totally at variance with the world's, and to measure greatness in terms not of success but of service, not of self-aggrandisement but of self-sacrifice.

Because we are fallen and proud human beings, we find this part of Christian discipleship very difficult. We like to have our own opinions (especially if they are different from everybody else's) and to air them rather pompously in conversation. We also like to live our own lives, set our own standards and go our own way. In brief, we like to be our own master, our own teacher and lord. People sometimes defend this position by saying that it would be impossible, and if it were possible it would be wrong, to surrender our independence of thought.

[7] Jn. 14:15; Mt. 10:37.   [8] Jn. 13:16.

Charlie Watts of the Rolling Stones beat group expressed this view when he said: 'I'm against any form of organized thought. I'm against . . . organized religion like the Church. I don't see how you can organize 10,000,000 minds to believe one thing.'[9] This is the mood of the day, both in the world and in the church. It is a self-assertive and anti-authoritarian mood. It is not prepared either to believe or do anything simply because some 'authority' requires it. But what if that authority is Christ's and if Christ's authority is God's? What then? The only Christian answer is that we submit, humbly, gladly, and with the full consent of our mind and will.

But do we? Is this in fact our regular practice? It is quite easy to put ourselves to the test. What is our authority for believing what we believe and doing what we do? Is it in reality what we think and what we want? Or is it what Professor So-and-so has written, what Bishop Such-and-such has said? Or is it what Jesus Christ has made known, either Himself directly or through His apostles?

We may not particularly like what He taught about God and man, Scripture and salvation, worship and morality, duty and destiny, heaven and hell. But are we daring to prefer our own opinions and standards to His, *and still call ourselves Christian*? Or are we presuming to say that He did not know what He was talking about, that He was a weak and fallible teacher, or even accommodated Himself to the views of His contemporaries although He knew them to be mistaken? Such suggestions are dreadfully derogatory to the honour of the Son of God.

Of course we have a responsibility to grapple with Christ's teaching, its perplexities and problems, endeavouring to understand it and to relate it to our own situation. But ultimately the question before the church can be simply stated: is Jesus Christ Lord or not? And if He is Lord, is He Lord of all? The Lordship of Jesus must be allowed to extend over every part of those who have confessed that 'Jesus is Lord', including their minds and their wills. Why should these be exempt from His otherwise universal dominion? No-one is truly converted who is not intellectually and morally converted. No-one is intellectually converted if he has not submitted his mind to the mind of the Lord Christ, nor morally converted if he has not

[9] Reported in *The Guardian*, 19 October 1967.

submitted his will to the will of the Lord Christ.

Further, such submission is not bondage but freedom. Or rather, it is that kind of willing Christian bondage which is perfect Christian freedom – freedom from the vagaries of self and from the fashions of the world (and of the church), freedom from the shifting sands of subjectivity, freedom to exercise our minds and our wills as God intended them to be exercised, not in rebellion against Him but in submission to Him.

I do not hesitate to say that Jesus Christ is looking for men and women in the church of this kind and calibre today, who will take Him seriously as their Teacher and Lord, not paying lip-service to these titles ('Why do you call me "Lord, Lord", and not do what I tell you?'), but actually taking His yoke upon them, in order to learn from Him and to 'take every thought captive to obey Christ'.[1]

This will involve for us, first, a greater diligence in study. We can neither believe nor obey Jesus Christ if we do not know what He taught. One of the most urgent needs of the contemporary church is a far closer acquaintance with Scripture among ordinary church members. How lovingly the pupil should cherish the teaching of such a Master!

It will also involve a greater humility in subordination. By nature we hate authority and love independence. We think it a great thing to have an independent judgment and manifest an independent spirit. And so it is if by this we mean that we do not wish to be sheep who follow the crowd, or reeds shaken by the winds of public opinion. But independence of Jesus Christ is not a virtue; it is a sin, and indeed a grievous sin in one who professes to be a Christian. The Christian is not at liberty to disagree with Christ or to disobey Christ. On the contrary, his great concern is to conform both his mind and his life to Christ's teaching.

And the reasonableness of this Christian subordination lies in the identity of the Teacher. If Jesus of Nazareth were a mere man, it would be ludicrous thus to submit our minds and our wills to Him. But because He is the Son of God, it is ludicrous not to do so. Rather is submission to Him just plain Christian common sense and duty.

I believe that Jesus Christ is addressing the church of our day

[1] Lk. 6:46; Mt. 11:29, 30; 2 Cor. 10:5.

with the same words: 'You call me Teacher and Lord; and you are right, for so I am.' My prayer is that, having listened to His words, we shall not be content with the use of these courtesy titles, but give Him due honour by our humble belief and whole-hearted obedience.